Memories

FRANCES PARTRIDGE

PHŒNIX

To my grand-daughter Sophie

A Phoenix paperback
First published in Great Britain by Victor Gollancz Ltd in 1981
This paperback edition published in 1996 by Phoenix,
a division of Orion Books Ltd,
Orion House, 5 Upper St Martin's Lane, London WC2H 9EA

Reissued 1999

A CIP catalogue record for this book is available
from the British Library.

ISBN: 0 75380 775 0

Printed and bound in Great Britain by
The Guernsey Press Co. Ltd, Guernsey, Channel Islands.

CONTENTS

ILLUSTRATIONS

Γ

Part One

CHAPTER ONE

Childhood in London

LOOKING BACK INTO childhood is like turning a telescope the wrong way round. Everything appears in miniature, but with a clarity it probably does not deserve; moreover it has become concentrated and stylised, taking shape in symbolism. Thus it is that I sometimes see my infant self as having been set down before a blank slate on which to construct a map or schema of the external world, and as hesitantly beginning to sketch in, with many false starts and much rubbing-out, the anatomy of my universe. Happiness and sorrow, love and friendship, hostility, a sense of guilt and more abstract concepts still, must all find a place somewhere, much as an architect lays out the plan of a house he is designing—hall, dining-room and bedrooms—but must not forget the bathroom. In a child's map, too, some of the rooms are connected by a serving-hatch, while others are sealed off behind baize doors. How can the fragments possibly be combined to make sense? Yet this map or finished diagram, constructed in the course of ten or twelve years' puzzling, refuses to be ignored, and for some time to come will make itself felt as bones do through flesh, to emerge as the complex organism which adults think of as their philosophy of life. Presumably it has its origins in both heredity and environment. So with heredity I shall begin.

My father was over fifty in 1900, when I was born—the last of his family of six. His head was already a pink polished dome surrounded by a fringe of white hair, and his high forehead and neatly trimmed beard gave him a little the look of Shakespeare's bust. He was tall and broad-shouldered, and dressed himself with old-fashioned elegance—his tie, for instance, being a wide strip of brocaded silk passed through an opal ring. In his youth he was a distinguished athlete, runner-up in the first Wimbledon lawn-tennis meeting, amateur figure-skating champion and a good 'real tennis' player, but none of his children inherited either these gifts or his fair complexion and blue eyes. He was above all a product of Lake District culture.

Though as an individual my mother figured much more importantly in her children's lives, what my father and his family stood for made a backdrop of as dominating a pattern as the Morris papers which covered our walls with their eternal screwdriver twists connected by tulips. The Marshall family stood for love of Nature particularly in its wildest and most romantic form; for long walks (my father and several uncles took part in Sir Leslie Stephen's famous 'Sunday Tramps'); for Wordsworthian poetry and its pantheistic outlook; for eugenics, agnosticism and the march of science; for class distinctions courteously observed. They stood also for hatred of bad craftsmanship, spots on furniture or linen, and chips on china, and in this connection but no others they waged guerilla warfare against servants and children, as the natural enemies of these sacred objects. I am reminded of my father's look of shattered despair when, at the age of about five, I took down an oriental dish which was suspended by invisible wires to the wall, in order to find out how this miracle was contrived, dropped and broke it. It was my first experience of committing the unforgiveable, and all other crimes I have committed since pale beside it.

My father and his three brothers and one sister had spent their youth in the Lake District, and there my surviving Uncle Frank and the widows of the other two (confusingly called Aunt Annie and Aunt Ernie) still lived when I paid my first visit to Derwentwater as a child. All the brothers had been fond of tramping the mountains in hob-nailed boots, of skating on the frozen lake in winter, sketching in summer, and reading poetry which they liked quoting at all seasons. When I think of these mythical uncles, all but one dead before I was born, I often remember a story my father liked to tell of an excursion they made one day to the waterfall of Lodore at the far end of the lake. He was standing on a boulder absorbed in watching the tumbling water, when he 'came to' to find himself reciting aloud from Southey's poem:

> How does the water come down at Lodore?
> Flying and flinging
> Writhing and ringing
> Eddying and whisking
> Spouting and frisking.

What was his amazement when he looked along the bank of the waterfall to see both his brothers similarly stationed, and to hear amid the rattle and roar of water on stones, two other voices chanting in the stentorian tones they reserved for poetry:

> And thumping and plumping and bumping and jumping
> And dashing and flashing and splashing and clashing
> ... *This* way the water comes down at Lodore.

When I was first taken to see Lodore I was naturally very much disappointed to see only a slender thread of water descending between the rocks.

Personal noise was a Marshall characteristic. Their voices were resonant and deep, their sneezes unbridled and catastrophic, and they particularly enjoyed letting them off in the underground passages of railway stations. Though my father set great store by good manners ("so-and-so was uncommonly civil" was a high expression of his praise), and seldom used bad language, his rare, violent and solitary DAMNs produced instant silence, shocked white faces and a sense that the outer trappings of civilisation had been roughly torn away. To reveal what? The Id, the psycho-analysts would perhaps say, but to me as a child it was as if a bull had charged, or a wild boar run grunting out of the undergrowth.

It was during my earliest visits to Marshall relatives in the Lake District that I first discovered the intense pleasure which could be got from the natural world, and which is still one of my strongest emotions; it had its origins for me in that clean chilly light, the all-pervading greyish-greenery, the steel surface of the lake, the hollow wooden sound of oars in rowlocks, and the pebbles seen through the clear water as I dangled my hand over the side of the boat. As a child of six, with my eyes and nose so fortunately close to the ground, I rapturously responded to the look of smooth grey rocks emerging from close-cropped turf, or springs threading between mossy stones, the smell of earth and wet bracken, and the intricate details of ferns and fronds, while with no conscious effort I imagined myself a midget to whom each weed was a palm tree, each pebble a cliff. I remember too the pleasure of drinking stream water from my collapsible picnic-cup tasting thinly of metal—a dearest possession—while the fells rolled away upwards into the mist, tinkling faintly with sheep bells.

Of course we used to visit the houses of all my Marshall uncles and aunts. Uncle Frank lived just beneath Catbells, the smallest and most domestic of the Cumberland hills, whose green slope started at his very back door. He was the kindest of men, a supporter of many high-minded causes like Women's Suffrage and Conscientious Objection, and his blue eyes looked mildly out from either side of an extremely crooked nose, twisted—we were warningly told—from sleeping on his face in bed. My Aunt had a passion for taming the red squirrels which lived in the woods along the lake's edge. She used to sit motionless in her bedroom, holding nuts in her hands and lips, whilst I and my brothers and sisters watched breathlessly for the squirrels to appear on the window-sill, and after many panic retreats venture across the floor. But the most romantic of the family houses was that of spherical old Aunt Ernie on Derwent Island. How wonderful to live on an island, with its garden stretching to the very water's edge instead of to a wall or road, and to have to take a rowing-boat to go shopping in Keswick! The eldest son of the house, Cousin Bob, was a very strange figure. He had been dropped by his nurse, so it was said, with the result that he had a short little pair of arms barely reaching to his waist, and identifying him in my mind with Edward Lear's character who 'perceived a large bird in a bush'. Short as his arms were, he used his hands with consummate skill making model boats of all sizes and colours, and was exceedingly kind to us children. Some of my most magic possessions belonged to those lakeland days. On a picnic by a waterfall a glamorous grown-up cousin had whittled and carved a stick to make me a little bearded man three inches high, who looked out at the world with folded arms. I called him Old Man Waterfall. His end was disastrous. Going south by train, I wanted him to have a good view of the passing landscape and balanced him on the ledge of the door. Alas, he fell down the crack and no amount of pulling on the strap controlling the window would bring him back. I was inconsolable. Other companions and friends were a collection of about thirty stones, carefully selected for their colour and shape from the bottom of streams, and ruled over by an ugly grey one, whose name—I can't think why—was Mrs Johnstone. Feeling it was too unkind to leave them out in the cold when I went to bed, I once put them all under my pillow. I have never spent a more uncomfortable night; I stuck it out obstinately, but next day I basely discarded them.

I was always inquisitive about my father's only sister, Aunt Theodosia, who had died young, long before I was born. A mysterious, romantically named young woman, whose brilliance and charm were sometimes hinted at, she had left nothing of herself behind except a faded silvery photograph, and a twist of light brown hair in which some insect had laid its eggs. Why did we hear so little about her, and that in discreet and lowered tones? It was not until I was about twenty-two and earning my living at Birrell and Garnett's bookshop, that I learnt some of the truth about Aunt Theodosia. I had developed a liking for whisky at that time, and one Christmas I brought home a bottle of Johnny Walker, a present from Francis Birrell, to my mother's house where I still lived. My mother very seldom interfered in my private life, but on this occasion she told me she was beginning to be alarmed by my addiction to drink, and was afraid I might take after Aunt Theodosia, who (perhaps I didn't know?) had actually died of it! Surely this must have been quite a feat for an unmarried girl of the mid-Victorian era, who spent most of her life in the wilds of Cumberland?

My father's heroes were Darwin, Ruskin, Lord Tennyson and

Leslie Stephen, all of whom he had personally known. Art, as
he introduced it into our lives, was typified by his books from
the Kelmscott Press, the Morris wallpapers and his own architectural drawings which hung on the walls. As for the wallpapers, there was no end to the pleasure to be got from them,
not from the designs themselves but because of the myriads of
gnomes and fabulous creatures, princes and ballet-dancers,
which could be—or rather which refused not to be—extracted
from their convolutions, and occupied many idle moments as I
lay awake in bed. Nor must I forget the early rapture of looking
at picture-books. The voluptuous excitement produced in me,
for instance, by the illustration of a pair of blue knickers with
crimson buttons in *Little Black Sambo* was in its way aesthetic;
certainly it was not literary—though that might be said of the
Gollywog books. Those with pictures by Caldecott or Walter
Crane introduced a lot of fresh elements such as technical skill
and the power of association, which are to be found in all works
of art admired by adults except perhaps pure abstracts. As for
Old Masters, when I was about six my next oldest sister Eleanor
and I were taken round many of London's galleries by a spinster
friend of the family. I was not at all bored by this, and the
picture that most impressed me was *The Fighting Téméraire*,
oddly enough. I soon got to love drawing and painting as a
pastime, and even acquired an uninspired facility which later
won praise from school art-masters. As for a real interest in the
visual arts, and speculation as to what they were 'about' or
'after', that was to be stimulated in my teens by fascinating
conversations with my second sister Ray, who was an artist by
profession; whereas the problem of the difference between my
visual pleasures in nature and in art has always interested me
deeply, and I have not solved it yet.

So that we should get a taste for good books, my sister
Eleanor and I used to go every evening into my father's study to
be read aloud to. He was a practising architect, and it was full of
such voluptuous objects as creamy tracing-paper, coloured inks
and fine pens. The monotony of Scott or Dickens was relieved
by each of us being given a fat six-sided pencil, one red, one blue,

and paper to draw on, and my father used suddenly to inter-
rupt his reading and yell out, "Change!" when red must be at
once swapped for blue. This odd sort of musical chairs and
typically Victorian compromise tended to blot out the book
itself, and only now and again did scenes from *Ivanhoe* or
Vanity Fair float into consciousness, what followed being
usually lost in the effort of illustrating them in red or blue.
Sometimes my ear would be caught by a love passage, which
embarrassed me greatly. I didn't much mind them myself, but
I felt my father ought to.

Music was my mother's department. She played the piano
quite well, and taught us all to sing in parts; it was not long
before the painful sound of practising on violins, 'cellos and
piano began to pervade the house. If my father could be
described as a finger-post or obelisk directing our lives, my
mother was a friend in need, a support, someone to be greatly
admired without qualification. I thought her beautiful, amusing
and interesting, and she was scarcely ever severe; and when—as
often happened—I was unable to get to sleep for hours, she
would come and gently stroke my forehead, talking softly at the
same time, until preliminary relaxation took the place of over-
stimulation. She had been one of the ten children of an Irish
clergyman, who took his whole family to New Zealand in a
sailing-ship. Orphaned very young, they were heroically
adopted by their uncle, the Provost of Trinity College, Dublin,
and his formidable wife, Aunt Do, a cow being especially put
to graze on College Green to feed the young family. None of
them 'came to very much', and there was even something
rather absurd about some of them, but one of my Lloyd aunts
had a good deal of glamour for me. After measles or 'flu we were
generally sent to stay with Aunt Alice at Playden Cottage, Rye
(a house that was at least once rented by Virginia Stephen).
Aunt Alice Dew-Smith was a dapper little figure, whose bright
brown eyes looked out from a face smothered in dead white
powder. She had published several books and was a close friend
of Henry James. The literary society that met around the tea-
tables of Rye included my two god-mothers, Lady Prothero and

Lady Pollock, and at the age of six I dimly remember being taken to call on the Master himself at Lamb House. But alas, all I can recall was being confronted by what seemed a bulky figure looking much like a butler, neatly dressed in sombre black, surmounted by a high white collar and smooth pink face. Henry James picked me up in his arms, where I remained for what seemed a very long time with legs dangling, while he kissed me and gave me his blessing as it were in a long speech beginning, "My dear child . . ." How sad for me that the rest has vanished!

My childish picture of the Pollocks converts my god-mother into one of those musical doorbells that play a tune when you press the button, for she greeted any remark I made to her with a prolonged trill of silvery laughter; whereas I see the eminent jurist, Sir Frederick, advancing into a Rye drawing-room behind her like a dancing bear that keeps on its hind legs with great effort (his were clad in long plus-fours and spats), holding its front paws helplessly drooping before it.

Aunt Ethel was pretty and had great sweetness of character. I saw more of her in later life, when she and I both took up skating and used to go to the Park Lane Ice Club together. I once took Arthur Waley with me; he was an ardent but extremely bad performer. "He's the Chinese poet, you know, Aunt Ethel," I whispered to her. "Oh dear," she replied, "do you think he'll be able to drink the Club tea?"

As I've said already, our mother was infinitely kind and under-standing, and a cross word from her was so rare that it had a devastating effect if it came, but painful points of contact between parents and children were at this time well padded by the changing armies of governesses, and above all the Norn-like nurses who presided over waxen-faced nursemaids and dispensed unquestioned justice in the nursery. Our family had only one faithful Nan, who came to us after the birth of my eldest brother Horace in 1888 and stayed until old age and infirmity took her to a 'home'. Lizzie Croucher was her extraordinary name. I was the youngest of our well-spaced-out family of six, so there was no one to supplant me in the honour and pleasure of sharing her bedroom. In the mornings I lay snug and warm in bed, watching the fascinating ritual of her getting dressed. There was never a flash of nudity, but like a skilled conjuror she inserted herself into bodice and stays and long frilled drawers, and then put over them two flannel petticoats, one red and one royal blue. After that she brushed out her long, straight, mouse-coloured hair, plaited it tightly and fastened it in a small knot behind her head. (It was so fine and silky that she once made substitute paintbrushes out of it when nursery supplies had run out.) What reassurance her whole appearance gave me! She was tiny, and therefore seemed halfway between a child and an adult; her face was pale and her small round head was like the top of a ninepin. Spiritually she was a natural object, a tree in the garden, something taken for granted and always relied upon to be *there*, sitting in the nursery mending stockings—someone who had a purely instinctive but effective manner of dealing with bawls, bangs or knots in crochet. She was aware of our failings but accepted them as we accepted her, so that there was no danger of disappointing her and letting her down, as there was with our parents. I wish I could remember all her runic sayings, like "If you want your hair to curl you must eat fried bread behind the door". (I did and it did.) And when later on I shared a bedroom with Eleanor, she used to call us with the mysterious formula: "Look at the moon! And the *stars*! And Eleanor's NOSE and Frances's WHISKERS!", pouncing on us with the last two, so as to rouse us thoroughly and send us into fits of giggles. She led a rich religious life centring round the picture of Gentle Jesus knocking on the door by Holman Hunt in her bedroom, and I am sure he was more real to her than any friend. "I dreamed of JE-sus last night," she told us once in the high sing-song voice she reserved for other-worldly things. "He came to me carrying a beautiful blue vase, and he said, 'Nan', he said, 'please clean this for HEA-ven.'" On her days off Nan went to visit her brother Bill, who lived in the East End and drank too much, so we gathered. She would dress up in a coat with a cape, while a pointed bonnet like a gnome's hat, trimmed with jet and artificial flowers, was tied under her chin with black velvet ribbon. A new bonnet for Nan was a great event and we couldn't bear the slightest deviation from type. She wore elastic-sided boots.

While this benevolent and reassuring little being stayed with us faithfully and ruled the nursery, one governess followed another, each more hysterical than the last. They had favourites among us, their surfaces bubbled and steamed with hidden emotional turmoil, their tempers and tantrums burst over us like tornadoes; I cannot think they taught us anything except that life has its seamy side. Worst of them all was Miss Wells, a tall, handsome young woman, whose hair and blouse were both puffed out, as I suspected, by artificial means. "She wears *pads* in her hair," we hissed to each other; it was the unforgiveable crime. One day she proved her wickedness by telling us in viperish tones that she had gone to the Boat Race and (being a strong supporter of Oxford) had forced the Cambridge boat to sink just by willing it. Of course she said this because we were all passionately Cambridge, and in the same spirit she used to tell us how frightfully ugly and stupid we were, strike out at us for some trifling reason and then try and stifle our sobs with her dirty handkerchief. Children are mostly fatalists at heart, and I don't think it occurred to us to split on her to our mother, but the end of Miss Wells was quite dramatic. I remember how my father told us all at lunch one day that some of my mother's jewellery and clothes, and a ring of his own, had apparently been stolen. I can see Miss Wells leaning forward to listen with polite interest, a slight flush on her cheeks. But she it was who turned out to be the thief, and she left that very afternoon. To the police station? There was a nursery rumour that it was to the lunatic asylum. My sister Ray had been her favourite and was genuinely upset at her going. She sat weeping on the stairs, which impressed me greatly although I could not understand it. It was the first time I had seen anyone cry for more than a scraped knee or hurt feelings. It was in fact my first glimpse of unhappy love, and I realised that enviable and exciting as well as tragic possibilities were involved. I couldn't bear to be shut out of this unknown world. 'I *must* cry', I remember thinking.

'I *must*—I *do* feel sad. *Poor* Miss Wells, we shall never see her again.' I sat down on the step beside Ray and tried as best I could to sob too, but all in vain.

Miss Wells had good taste. My sister Ray was my favourite too. Her hazel-brown eyes, set very wide apart beneath a broad and misleadingly tranquil brow, seemed to gaze out at the world with an expression suggesting that it was very different from what she would have liked it to be, but that she had her private consolations. When I was in favour she talked to me as an equal, although I was about eight years younger, and would draw back the curtain of her reserve to reveal such intoxicating possibilities as that nearly all ideas that people took for granted could be questioned. She made the future seem much more uncertain, but also very much more interesting. Most of the family friends thought her painfully shy, because there were times when the effort to speak, especially to answer questions, seemed too much for her. Then my father had noticed her artistic talent and was anxious to encourage her and get her to talk about it, but when subjected to such pressure Ray's lips would frame words which were scarcely audible. When a visitor asked her some well-meant question she had been known to turn on her heel and walk swiftly away without uttering a word, but her few friendships were strong and came from various social classes. I remember a large, ungainly Russian girl with huge eyes and a mobile charming face, who invited her to stay with her family in the Caucasus. I wish I still had the long letters Ray wrote me on very thin paper with small exotic stamps, describing days and weeks peopled by Georgian princes, a dancing bear, riders galloping over the mountains on elaborate saddles, crowds singing to the balalaika and an audience shouting frenziedly for 'ChaliaPEEN!' She brought back gramophone records of Russian songs, and when she played them her usual self-contained manner would suddenly explode into wild excitement, dancing and singing. "Ray has gone mad," someone would say, but not unkindly.

Until I was eight years old, when my father retired, we spent the business part of life in London and the holidays in the country. Our London house was a fine, old, creaking building on the corner of Bedford Square, and it seemed to take an eternity for my stumpy legs to get from the front door—trimmed with a sort of stonework astrakhan which I always associated with my father's fur coat, and surmounted by a bearded head very like his own—right up to the top floor where I slept with my dear old Nan. Underneath us my elder sisters, Judy and Ray, thumped and thudded on their trapeze in the day nursery, from whose window all that went on in the Tottenham Court Road could be seen, and from which, too, one heard the heart-stopping clang of the fire-engine by night, or by day could watch the commotion when a bus-horse fell down. (It amazed me that the driver could always get it up by sitting on its head.) Below this was my parents' room, made dark and jungly by yet more Morris wallpapers and curtains everywhere—birds eating strawberries on my mother's curtains, parrots on the wall of my father's dressing-room where I would find him in bed in his frogged pyjamas. If my mother was going out to dinner I was sometimes allowed to watch her dress, and adored going through her jewel-box, opening and shutting all the little leather cases with a snap, while they winked out their dazzling contents. Then she would rustle away in pale green silk, smelling of eau-de-cologne, kid and fur, while (craning out of the window in the dark) I listened for the wild zoological whistle which summoned a cab—a hansom probably, as my father preferred them. He had got engaged to my mother in a hansom, and for a long while kept a private one of his own.

A small child generally accepts and ingests the stream of its experience as steadily as it gazes over the brim of its mug, gulping down the milk and making a detailed survey of its physical surroundings to the same rhythm. For it finds these inanimate objects as real, I might almost say as alive, as human beings, and their loss (like mine of Old Man Waterfall) can be a serious bereavement. 'Things' are not only real, they are endowed with magic, and this magic may be black or white. Much as I loved the familiar rooms at Bedford Square, they contained both black and white magic for me. There was black magic in the short, unlit passage that led from the landing to the day nursery with its big windows and friendly, well-worn rocking-horse. I used to nip through it full tilt, my heart in my mouth. The same menace hung about the great mahogany lid leaning against the wall above the bath; I was convinced it was capable of crashing down and shutting me in, when of course I would be swirled down the drain with the bath water. After tea, dressed in white silk smocked frocks, Eleanor and I used to go down to the beautiful L-shaped drawing-room with its Adam ceiling and swinging chandeliers, and join my mother in the little alcove hung with oriental silks (a fashion of the moment, I believe) for a game of spillikins or a card-game called Casino. This would have been a time of pure white magic, except for the sinister black carved ornament that looked down at us from the top of the tall Dutch cabinet, and was at the same time a face and yet not quite a face. And if only it hadn't been necessary first to descend so many stairs, past so many landings and bulky pieces of furniture, spectrally inhabited. For at this time the great shadow cast over my otherwise happy childhood was my fear of the dark. Even during the daytime I couldn't forget that the hateful blackness was preparing to slam behind me like a massive door, leaving me shut in with fantastic terrors, with foxes, steam-rollers, mocking faces without bodies, and a sinister black and hairy being called Aertex. All day long at intervals I used to dread the moment when my mother would sit at the piano and play 'Wee Willie Winkie', her signal that it was time to go to bed. And I often looked at grown-up people, wondering whether they were really quite different from me, or whether, as I suspected, they each and all went into their own private torture chambers every night. It was my fear of darkness, I dare say, which often made me fly into a passion of tears when Nan came to fetch me for bed. Somehow or other she managed to convince me that this was a dreadful bore for my mother, and to coach me how to behave.

"When I open the door," she said, "you must get up at once from whatever you're doing, and smile and say, 'Here I come, Nan', and come tripping along." So next evening to my mother's amazement I got up at once when Nan knocked, and skipped out of the room saying, "Here I come, Nan. Here I come smiling and tripping along."

Our daily lives followed the usual middle-class Edwardian pattern. Up and down the great flights of stairs maids toiled with coal-scuttles and hot-water jugs, and in the dining-room we were waited on by beautiful Irish Mary. My father took an improper delight in getting her to blush, and I used to watch the sunrise cross the delicate skin of her cheek, while the potatoes wobbled at his elbow. The kitchen was a fiery inferno to which we were seldom admitted, and where a rapidly changing series of fierce and often foreign cooks raged among the pots and pans. No wonder they were cross, for there were a great many dinner-parties, and as many as ten courses might have to be dished up for each. From the stairs we younger children stared down at the couples marching in arm-in-arm like animals into the ark, the heads of the men in their tall white collars stiffly inclined towards the curved and waisted forms of their companions. Who were they all? Sir Johnstone Forbes-Robertson and his wife, Gertrude Elliott, were special favourites (in fact I think my mother was a little in love with him, and I was taken to see him as Hamlet when I was nine). There were Asquiths and Ricardos—neighbours in Bedford Square—Mr Furse, who had painted my mother's portrait, the classical scholar Jane Harrison, whom my parents were trying to marry to D. S. MacColl, Protheros, Pollocks and Nettleships. But we children were mainly interested in the tit-bits we got from dishes on their way back to the kitchen.

My mother taught me to read at an early age from a book called *Reading without Tears*, and the process was so entertaining that I got from it a rosy picture of what my education would be like. Avid for knowledge of the world as well as of books, I begged and implored to be sent to school, and couldn't understand my mother's melancholy and cynical smile when she at last agreed.

I had defeated one small but annoying handicap—a lisp. "Say 'sixpence' and you shall have one," my parents went on patiently saying, and for some time I painfully replied, "Thay thickthpenth." But at last the unwanted fuzz removed itself, though even to this day I am occasionally aware of letting slip an S that is not entirely clear. I was a plain, bullet-headed little girl of five, with a short strained-back plait, when I set off for my first day at the Infants' department of Queen's College, Harley Street, excited, willing and in high hopes, dressed in a scarlet jersey and brown skirt. But all I remember of that day was the end of it. When it was time to go home a wickedly grinning group of children barred my way, snatched my satchel (valued emblem of my status as a schoolgirl), emptied its contents and waved it jeeringly in the air. I suspect I had given them cause by disgusting priggishness, but when they shouted mockingly, "You're a mutton chop with blood running out at the top" (referring to my clothes), my heart was ready to burst, and I ran past them in floods of tears, leaving my poor satchel at their mercy. It was several days before I unburdened myself to my mother of what seemed the most terrible words in the English language, and then to my astonishment she burst out laughing. I found it hard to forgive her, yet there was an element of relief in her finding my dreadful humiliation unimportant. I think this was the moment when room had to be found in my scheme of the universe for the hostility of the outside world. At home (though of course I was often in disgrace) I had been secure and accepted; the walls of 28 Bedford Square had given me their towering protection. But now, suddenly, and—bitter thought—at my own persistent request, I was cast out into a bleak and alien no-man's-land, smelling of disinfectant, lacking all beauty or comfort, where I had to sit at a gnarled, inky desk, surrounded by superior or completely indifferent little girls, and little boys lost in their own mooning thoughts, and whose noses always needed blowing. Self-consciousness painfully dawned and horrid self-questioning began. What in the world was I like?

I soon got one answer. A friend of the family called Ethel Nettleship, sister-in-law to Augustus John and a professional musician, came every week to give Eleanor 'cello lessons and teach me the rudiments of violin playing on a small bright yellow fiddle with a screaming tone. I liked and admired her enormously, so it was a shock when one day I overheard her say to my mother: "Oh yes, one can do anything with Eleanor, but Frances is just *spoiled blackberry jam.*" More terrible words! I even made a few desperate efforts to reform. Very necessary, too: I must have been bad-tempered as well as spoiled, since I distinctly remember the look of my tooth-marks in Eleanor's arm.

But I wonder if adults always realise how their sayings are taken to heart by children. Another, just as effective but I think less justified, stands out in my memory. A year or two later my mother dropped the bombshell: "You should never cheapen your feelings for people by letting them be seen." What had called out this prohibition I can't now be sure, but I suppose I had been showing all too plainly how desperately attractive and dashing I found some of my elder brothers' and sisters' lively and amusing friends, and no doubt she merely wanted to stop my being a nuisance to them. But her shattering remark ate into me like rust, and I brooded for a long time over the possibility of accepting it as a formula for behaviour. It was so unexpected too, for clearly the feelings that made me bite Eleanor couldn't be 'cheapened'; it was love and admiration that were in question. I don't know how long it took me to come to a conclusion as nearly as possible opposite to hers. However, long before this happened, I had begun to hang a whole wardrobe of painful contortions and disguises from the clothes-peg of my mother's warning. And here I should say that though I believe she was a warm and emotional character (in an unguarded moment in her old age she declared she had never been out of love in her life, which I'm sure was true), she was rigorously undemonstrative. The delightful hugs and snugglings on her lap of early child-hood came to a sudden stop, and not even a peck on the cheek greeted return from boarding-school for any of us. I believe this was the result of the stern discipline imposed on an unruly family of Irish orphans by that old tyrant, the wife of the Provost of Trinity College, Dublin, and I bear a grudge against the old lady whose iron hand, reaching through the person of my mother, laid its grip on my own emotional life.

In our free time from school we usually went out to play in Bedford Square Gardens, and though the tree-trunks were black with soot and the leaves of the laurels had to be cleaned with spit before their interesting yellow spots were visible, the shabby old summer-house was an excellent centre for games with our friends, chief among whom were two of the Forbes-Robertson girls—Blossom and Jean.* Blossom was a great beauty, and it was bewildering to be told that one of her lovely blue eyes was made of glass. Jean was imaginative and lively and very good at inventing things to do.

London walks had of course sometimes to be taken, rather unwillingly. When possible I liked to go past the chocolate shop, in whose window a continuous sticky brown stream poured over rollers, its appetising smell reaching as far as the street. Another sight I loved was the water-cart that sometimes passed round the Square, sending out a wide spray of *pink* water; what was more, little red fragments could be picked up after its passage and carried home to make tumblers-full of the same beautiful colour. London policemen, I was often told, were friends to all children, and would take me home if I should ever get lost; but I felt differently towards them after once seeing two of them 'frog-marching' a wretched evil-doer through the streets. The drivers of horse-buses, on the other hand, were invariably amiable, and one of my greatest treats was to be allowed to sit on the front seat beside one of them, with the whip gently playing over the horses' backs, and my legs tucked under his macintosh cover.

* Later the well-known actress.

CHAPTER TWO

Childhood in the Country

IN THE SPRING and Christmas holidays we moved en bloc, with Nan and maids, dogs, cats, white mice and canaries, 'cellos and violins, to our country house at Hindhead, which my father had designed himself and enlarged as his family grew. There was no question in my mind that the country was much pleasanter than London, and although our Surreyfied domain with its bracken-filled corners, its sloping lawns and conifers could not compete with the ghostly northern beauty of the Lakes, I greatly preferred it to Bedford Square garden. Besides there was much more white magic in the country than in London: everything to do with Christmas for instance—glistening holly berries, the crackle of tissue paper inside a stocking at the end of my bed, the smell of candles beginning to singe the Christmas tree. At other seasons of the year there were countless magical delights—the hot smell of ponies, or of being in the middle of a head-high forest of bracken. A whole magic day could be devoted to creating a miniature village between the roots of a tree in the garden, building walls out of tiny pebbles and fences of broken twigs, bringing velvet moss for lawns, yellow sand for paths, and dark moist earth for flower-beds in which broken-off shoots of chickweed or speedwell sprouted like exotic blooms.

It seems that Hindhead had been a wild and desolate moor, until at the end of the last century it was discovered by a small group of people of 'advanced ideas', including my father. They started to build a colony of gabled, roughcast houses, and it spread rapidly. The first colonists were considered very eccentric. As the eminent scientist, Professor Tyndall, wrote to Professor Huxley: "Wicked people have spread the report that a colony of heathens is being established at Hindhead. *Your* presence here, even for a little while, would complete the evidence."

Tyndall's house was one of the first to be built. He had a morbid dread of the sound or even sight of other people. So when the houses of later arrivals approached too near, he had a huge protective screen constructed from tall larch-poles thatched with heather, looking like something built by savage tribes in central Africa. Brown and withered, this screen lasted much longer than the professor himself, and we used to gaze at it with awe when we were sent with polished triangular notes to invite Mrs Tyndall to tea. Part of this awe was attached to Mrs Tyndall herself—a tiny old lady always dressed in full widow's weeds—for the hair-raising truth was that she had actually *killed* her husband. The Professor, like Darwin and other eminent Victorians, was a life-long hypochondriac, and couldn't sleep, eat or work without loving attention and care from his wife. One night, in the dim light of his bedroom, she poured out and gave her husband an enormous dose of chloral by mistake for his milk of magnesia. She herself reported the conversation that followed:

"John," she said, "I have given you chloral."

"Yes, my poor darling," he replied, "you have killed your John." And so she had.

Professor Nettleship, whom we also used to visit, was making genetical experiments into the inheritance of albinoism, and kept large numbers of pekinese dogs, who rushed out yapping at the sound of the door-bell, hardly able to see through their bulging pink eyes. Then there was William Beveridge,* whose terrifying old mother used to point a large ear-trumpet at her visitors, or—that failing—push them a pad and pencil. Sir Arthur Conan Doyle, tall and moon-faced, sometimes came to dinner. The only odd thing we knew about him was that he was in the habit of photographing fairies. However, by the time I was old enough to take much interest in them, our neighbours were fast losing their distinguished eccentricity, and taking instead to golf, delphiniums and plus-fours.

Nearly every year we took our summer holiday far afield

---

* Later author of the Beveridge Report, and Lord Beveridge.

from Hindhead, in the Lake District, Cornwall, Wales, or—best of all—Ireland. For my father was nearly as Irish as my mother, and there were various O'Brien and Spring Rice relations to visit. If I felt patriotism towards any country it was to Ireland: I loved its soft sweet air, its greenness, the enormous blackberries that cluttered the hedges, the informality and *laissez-faire*, and the original replies that would be given to the simplest question. The answer to 'How do I get to X, please?' would never be 'First right, second left,' but an imaginative and probably unhelpful piece of creative prose. When I was about eight, Eleanor and I went with our parents to stay with Dermod O'Brien and his family in County Limerick. He was a painter, a sort of Irish Augustus John, large, virile and formidable; both he and his wife were our cousins. Their great grey house, Cahirmoyle by name, stood in vast untidy grounds through which long-legged Irish wolfhounds lolloped gracefully. No place could have impressed me as more romantic. In the evenings rustic characters, who might have been outdoor staff or members of the village, came up to entertain us with Irish songs and dances. Here I learned to dance the Irish jig (including the 'shuffle'); here, too, I passed the most recklessly tomboy days of my life with the two sons of the house, Brendan and David O'Brien, climbing into the 'tree house', at the top of a tall conifer, or onto the slate roof of the house itself, whence we used to throw pieces of wood through a skylight into the kitchen far below, and then slide down the roof, trusting that the rickety gutter at its edge would save us from what I imagine would have been certain death. I remember with shame my mother's anguished white face below, begging us to stop, and the fiendish way we refused to. But Cousin Dermod intervened, and Brendan and David got a sound thrashing with a stout leather strap, while their father eyed me covetously, saying, "If you were my child you'd get the same."

It was typical of life at Cahirmoyle too that though we were forced to go to church on Sundays, all our prayer-books had their insides removed and pages from boys' books inserted in their place.

When I was nine my father bought a brown saloon motor-car, which was supposed to travel at the amazing speed of thirty miles an hour! I think it actually did, but its performance up hills was a good deal more dubious, and there was always the fear that it would start to glide backwards, and we should all have to jump out in a hurry. There was also a strange terror of the dust that would be sent up by our headlong career, so that when Eleanor and I were taken by our parents on a short tour of the cathedrals of southern England—Winchester, Salisbury, Wells and Exeter—we were fitted out with thin white 'dust-coats', and hats known as 'motor-bonnets', with veils entirely covering our faces. I particularly loved Salisbury cathedral, and when visiting it again (a week ago as I write) I looked with delight at the slim green columns in the interior, and wondered whether pleasure in an early experience for ever enriches its repetition. I think it does. As none of the family could drive, a chauffeur in a brown uniform joined the Hindhead staff, and since he was young and pretty, with a mop of 'Bubbles' curls, his presence at mealtimes in the servants' hall gave rise to piercing squeals and cackles.

When we spent the holidays at Hindhead, as we often did, I found the weekend visitors from London or elsewhere a good deal more interesting than our neighbours.

My brother Tom played the violin well and sometimes brought musical friends home from Cambridge. Among these were Howard and Kennard* Bliss (brothers of Sir Arthur), two amusing, sophisticated young men with long pale faces, and features so marked that a clarinet hardly seemed a surprising prolongation of one of them. Though chamber music took up a lot of their time (I particularly remember their playing of the Brahms Clarinet Trio), they were good at acting and charades, and I was both flattered and mortified when Howard tied a stocking round his neck to represent my hair, clapped a straw hat on his head, and gave a brilliant imitation of my half-witted style of delivering telephone messages, to roars of laughter from the company. I envied Eleanor for being allowed to join in

---

* A member of the Cambridge Apostles, he was killed in the First War.

occasionally on her 'cello, but these frequent performances gave a fillip to my developing pleasure in listening to music, an emotion which seems to me to have quite a lot in common with human love. There is love at first hearing, love dawning slowly after several encounters, the 'honeymoon period' of intimate knowledge plus ecstasy—and sometimes a listless drop into over-familiarity, usually to be cured by a rest from the work in question. Musical masterpieces that have eaten their way into the soul at a tender age bite very deep, and retain their magnetism, and I was very lucky in being taken to hear a good many from the age of nine or so. First-rate concerts were organised at Haslemere, a few miles away, by Frances Dakyns, who secured such outstanding performers as the Aranyi sisters, the Casals-Thibaud-Cortot trio, Leonard Borwick, Fanny Davies and many others. Of course there was an element of boredom in sitting still so long, but somehow or other this did not diminish —it almost added to—the dense absorption of being subjected to this high-powered experience. My greatest love was Casals, with his winning personality, bold attack, marvellous phrasing and even his gentle snoring, as he played the Bach Unaccompanied 'Cello Suite in C, for instance; but Jelly d'Aranyi was also a great favourite, as much for her oriental beauty as for her dramatic performance of the Bach Double Concerto with her sister Adila.

It was because my mother was a keen Suffragist that an important stage of my education was reached—I got my first sight of Stracheys. Three of Lytton Strachey's sisters—Pippa, Marjorie and Mrs Rendel (with her daughters Ellie and Betty) —all visited us. Though the Rendels' cousins, the Ricardos, had long been close friends, this was something quite new in family flavours. "I don't believe a SINGLE word you say," I heard Mrs Rendel say, and to my father, of all people. Nor did he seem to mind. I was astonished that adults could talk to each other in this way.

One Strachey led to another. On a memorable Sunday afternoon, as Eleanor and I sat playing chess in the drawing-room, the door opened and there glided in unannounced two dashing young men, bedizened in polished leather and khaki, monocled, booted, even spurred. They were the Rendel brothers, Dick and Andrew. Dick was the taller and more elegant, with an indescribably stylish way of collapsing at the joints like a Dutch doll. I was bowled over; he became my idol from that moment, and for at least four years no-one replaced him. I remained in fact faithfully in love with him.

From now on our house was filled on every suitable occasion with lively young, for my brothers and elder sisters had reached an age to enjoy dancing and the company of the opposite sex. We gave small dances; cavalcades of horses arrived in the drive and I enviously watched the riders set off to gallop over the moors; there were tennis parties with everyone dressed in snowy white from head to foot. Up till now I had enjoyed being the youngest of a large family, and therefore included in some outing, or getting a chance to taste my father's claret, before my time. But now, in this scintillating atmosphere of gaiety and romance I was definitely out of things; looks were exchanged and words flew well over my head, while in a fever of communicated agitation, like a dog leaping up to catch a ball that is thrown out of reach, I tried in vain to intercept the current of excitement. But just as my rôle on the tennis-court, accepted *faute-de-mieux*, was to field the balls that went over the wire netting, and with luck creep along behind the base line and hand them to some Adonis in white flannels, so I had to make the best of what crumbs I could pick up from the feast of sociable delights. Meanwhile my curiosity about the geography of adult love, with all its mountains, rivers and promontories, grew ever more insistent. True, I was in love myself, but that seemed a natural phenomenon about which I was not inquisitive at all. It never occurred to me that there was any satisfaction to be got from my own emotion except that of being in the presence of the object of my adoration, so that when Dick Rendel married my eldest sister Judy I was enraptured that there would now be more opportunities for my doting contemplation.

With the first pangs of love, I come naturally to my first researches into sex.

Though my parents believed themselves to be enlightened, and certainly wished their children to know the facts of life, they shied away from actually imparting them, to us two 'little ones' at least. Perhaps they hoped we would absorb them from our elder sisters, or maybe it was that the attitude 'the thing must be done of course, and properly too, but at the latest possible moment' merged imperceptibly with the belief that it *had* been done. Jokes and speculations about puppies and kittens had been lightly shrugged off in our early years, and there followed a 'latency period' in which our lack of interest in the subject may now seem as incredible as the fact that by the time I went up to Newnham in 1918 quite a few girls were still absolutely ignorant. Anyway, at the time I'm writing about I was fully aware of my mother's dislike of the subject, and I wouldn't have dreamt of asking her to solve any of the problems that bothered me. Old Nan had been more likely to get my questions at first, but she probably didn't know the answers.

However, things looked up when at last I made my first real friend and co-research worker.

When my father retired in 1908, Bedford Square was given up and we lived entirely in the country. A new school had to be found for Eleanor and me, and we rattled to it every morning in the pony trap. It was kept by Miss Grüner and Miss Gibbings. Miss Grüner was a little old German lady, guttural of speech and fiery-tempered. Her eyes were bottled away behind the thickest spectacles I ever saw, and she could only read by moving her book rapidly to and fro an inch in front of them. But any child who went off happily wool-gathering instead of doing her sums might suddenly find a pair of grey eyes boring into her, and a ruler brought smartly down on her knuckles. When in a good temper she told us thrilling stories about being chased by wolves when travelling in a sledge through the snow in east Germany. Miss Gibbings was lame, sentimental, and one of the best teachers I ever came across. They had about twenty children under their care, including a giggling Hindu girl, a sister of Aldous Huxley's who was always in tears, and the chemist's son and daughter, who were persecuted by the rest of us for purely snobbish reasons. But news soon arrived that a little Strachey, about my own age, was to come there as a boarder. This was Julia. In view of my mother's friendship with her aunts and step-mother she was at once invited to spend every Sunday with me.

I greatly looked forward to my days with Julia. It was a new experience to have a boon companion so imaginative and amusing, and with whom I could talk about anything at all. If the weather was too bad for climbing trees we could always spend the whole day in the hayloft over the stables immersed in the strong effluvium of horses and harness. Here at last was someone with whom I could thrash out all sorts of problems, such as what happened after death, the existence of God, suicide and even Free Will, but first and foremost about the arch-mystery of sex. We were almost as interested in the psychological as in the physical aspect, and one thing I remember puzzling about was in what framework of words a proposal of marriage really took place. As for the physical facts, we ploughed with unflagging eagerness through dictionaries and medical books, and the pages of trashy novels such as were read in the kitchen and kept in a drawer with the dishcloths and wooden spoons. All in vain. There was on my mother's bookshelf, very likely left there on purpose, a small green book called *How we are Born*, and this we read from cover to cover, discussion and textual criticism following. It was as good as its word, and the function of child-bearing did begin to take grisly shape in our understandings—but strange to say, this unhelpful little manual gave no clue at all to the masculine part in the business.

As we clambered among the logs in the woodshed Julia and I used to speculate as to what it could possibly be that married people did together in order to produce a child. We had no glimmering that there could be any other purpose or pleasure involved, nor yet that it was ever performed by people who were not married.

"Now let's both think of all the possible things they might do," said Julia, "and decide which of them seems the most likely."

"Perhaps it would help," I suggested, "if we thought of some of the actual married couples we know, and then tried to imagine them doing it. Captain and Mrs Buzzard, for instance."

The Buzzards were an unfortunate choice as it happened. They were a middle-aged pair who had come to live in our village recently, and who generally trailed up to tea on Sundays, when my mother kept open house to her friends. The Captain was a jolly man with a polished, red, knobbly face, and a repertoire of stories, trotted out diffidently and followed by a prolonged wheeze. If encouraged by laughter the stories usually began to get shadier, and the wheeze louder and longer to cover his confusion. Mrs Buzzard had frizzy hair and was as thin and blanched as a stick of celery. Sometimes we went to tea with them in their small dark sitting-room festooned with paper snakes and other souvenirs from abroad, and here Captain Buzzard's wheezing was re-inforced by comic songs on an old phonograph. If there were any sexual allusions in these we failed to spot them, yet we had a curious feeling we were 'getting warm'. Then one day, sitting unnoticed with a book in the window-seat of my mother's writing-room, I overheard an emotional outburst from Mrs Buzzard to my mother, as she confided in hysterical tears that the Captain had for years been a practising exhibitionist, and was now in serious trouble with the police for exposing himself out of his bedroom window to the servant girls opposite. In fact he seemed doomed to go to prison. Soon afterwards the Buzzards faded from the scene, and though I faithfully reported this extraordinary conversation to Julia, they left the sex mystery as clueless as before.

It was Julia who found the solution, I don't remember how. But one holiday I got a letter from her containing the epoch-making words: "I've found out how ladies are fertilised for babies. You simply won't believe me when I tell you." When next term came, she did tell me, and indeed I hardly could.

A long time later, when further research had filled in nearly the whole picture, my mother unluckily found this letter of Julia's lying about, and not realising that it was now ancient history, felt in duty bound to enlighten me before some garbled account reached my ears. I was too embarrassed to stop her, and she did her best, but it was a miserable ten minutes for us both.

I often went to stay with Julia at Ford Place, the home of Logan Pearsall Smith and Alys Russell,* or Uncle Logan and Auntie Loo as we called them. I always enjoyed my visits there, and in her slightly elephantine way Aunty Loo was very kind to us and let us do almost anything we liked, for instance dress up in her best clothes, hats, gloves, coats and all (they must have been far too large) and trail along the road to Littlehampton, where it was our fond belief that everyone took us for 'grown-up ladies'—we were about eight and nine—and we shopped and ate tea in cafés, relishing this fantasy. The Pearsall Smiths had both been brought up as Quakers, but only Aunty Loo retained the characteristic 'thee', and its possessive case 'thy'. Among other visitors to the house I met there the children of Desmond and Molly MacCarthy, Rachel and Dermod. Dermod was then a little boy of about five, who was generally known as 'Bumpy' because he fell down so often. Molly told me later that he had been very much puzzled by the Quaker form of address. "What do you mean, Dermod? Tell me how Aunty Loo talks to you." "Well," said Dermod, "she might say to me, 'Dermod, when thee leaves the room, don't forget to take thy hippopotamus with thee.'"

It was while staying at Ford Place that I first met Roger Fry, who took Julia and me and his two children for a day's outing to Littlehampton. I remember how in the train he explained to us in his beautiful deep voice why it was wicked to like peacock blue; and that—once on the beach—he constructed a marvellous sand-castle with a complicated network of descending pathways down which we rolled marbles, guessing at the route each would take. I thought him one of the most fascinating men I had met, and was flattered and stimulated by his way of talking seriously to children, and listening to their opinions as if they were worth hearing.

Not everyone thinks arguing fun, as I only fully realised much

* The first Mrs Bertrand Russell.

later, when I started asking my friends whether they liked it. "No. I like telling," said one, and another, "I like being told." So it was lucky for Julia and me that we both enjoyed it. Sometimes of course we got cross with each other, but not nearly so often as happened in my conversations with Eleanor, for instance. (She and I would arrive back from school to be greeted by Nan with "You've been quarrelling again. I can tell it from the way you draw your eyebrows together.") At Ford there was a perfect place for confabulation, known (we believed) to no-one but ourselves—a secret attic, close beneath the roof of the old house, and only reachable through a box-room filled with furniture that creaked, and jugs and basins that rattled whenever one moved, making an orchestral accompaniment that suited our eerier topics—ghosts and the next world for instance. Here we spent wet days covering the walls with frescoes (which we heard were taken quite seriously by later occupants as the work of Sunday painters), or arguing as to whether we both really saw the same colour when we talked about 'blue', or working ourselves into a masochistic state of agitation about possible spooky manifestations. We both liked reading such stories as those of M. R. James, but I was less imaginative and more sceptical than Julia, and in a rather plodding way rejected most of the evidence for the supernatural. My father had once been mixed up in Psychical Research, with his cousin F. W. H. Myers, the Sidgwicks, Edmund Gurney and others, and I remember him tentatively setting before me an explanation for ghosts as we strolled in the garden one day. He suggested that they might be imprints left on the scene of some tragic event or deep emotion, somewhat in the manner of photographs or gramophone records. It is a fairly common view, but I remember being impressed by it, as well as flattered at being let into his thoughts on the subject. But no—the more I thought about it, the more clearly I seemed to see it wouldn't do. And if there were no ghosts, no angels and no Holy Ghost, then there could surely be no God either?

God finally dropped out of my universe as a result of a rather ribald breakfast-time conversation between Adrian and Karin

Stephen, who were staying at Ford Place at the time. They discussed his character and appearance just as if he was a human being; but it was something about the tone rather than the content of what they said that flashed its message into my mind like the beam of a lighthouse. *They* obviously didn't believe in him, yet faith was supposed to be the *evidence* for his existence. Why then should I? I had only to ask myself the question to realise that I no longer did, and I was conscious of an immense sense of liberation which was purely pleasant, nor did I ever feel the least temptation to believe in God again. I didn't mention my conversion to my family for some time, although I thought about it a great deal. I realise now that my father had for long been an agnostic, but my mother and all my brothers and sisters were believers and had been 'confirmed'. A year or two later, while sharing a bedroom with Eleanor one holiday in the Isle of Wight, a sudden compulsion came over me to reveal my dark secret. So as I turned down the oil lamp and hopped into bed, I daringly exclaimed: "Eleanor, you know *I don't believe in God!*" I created even more of a sensation that I had hoped.

This, then, is how the first twelve years of my life look to me now: how the various categories—love, friendship, hostility and the rest—seem to have taken shape in my mind. But I wonder how much the element of fantasy that exists in memory has moulded the clay of reality. Our Hindhead house was not given up until my father died when I was twenty-one, so of course I have always carried about with me a vivid picture of house, garden and surroundings. However, some fifteen years later I found myself driving down the very hill on which I had fallen off so often when learning to ride my bicycle, past the familiar white gate. I boldly went in and asked if I might look around, and since it was no longer a private house but a convalescent home, the gardener willingly agreed. But what a nightmare! It was all subtly different from my mental picture; it wasn't only a question of such superficial things as the absence or presence of trees. The very slope of the lawn was less dramatic, a distant hill was in the wrong place, all was somehow radically, crucially different. I hurried round, feeling like Alice after she had climbed through the looking-glass, and was soon glad to go away. For a week afterwards I remained uneasy and rattled, while the old picture obstinately warred with the new. Then this uncomfortable state of double vision faded, and peace returned. It wasn't my recent impression, however, but the old distorted picture that won, and it has been there ever since. The moral of which I hesitate to draw.

CHAPTER THREE

School and the First World War

THE TRANSITION FROM childhood to adolescence is not a gradual climb up a slope, but a progress by fits and starts. As in a game of Grandmother's Steps, one takes two strides forwards, stops still, and then breaks into a hasty run. Vaguely looked forward to as a time of greater freedom, a meeting-place of many exciting roads, adolescence in fact turns out to be a period of uneasy adjustment, of boredom and anxiety, when one is neither fish, flesh nor fowl, when everything has to be questioned, every bed has to be looked under, and every happiness is contingent, if only on a fine day.

I had been in that uncertain state for a couple of years when I began to take an interest in the discussions going on around me among my elders about the possibility of war with Germany. They seemed to be mainly concerned with the race to build battleships.

When he retired, my father had enlarged our Hindhead house by the addition of several bedrooms (but astoundingly enough no second bathroom), and a very long drawing-room, papered with dull gold wallpaper, intended to set off the pastel portraits of his six children, as well as 'good pieces' of highly polished furniture and a few better pictures, while one whole end of the room was filled by a huge open fireplace over which stretched a scene from *As You Like It* illustrated in low relief and conventional colours. He was pleased with this creation and many visitors went into raptures over it, but when one of them (I think it was his cousin Bernard Darwin*) said roundly, "I can't *abide* it!" I was filled with amazement and a sort of protective embarrassment on my father's behalf, but realised that I secretly agreed.

* A journalist, writing for *The Times* for many years.

Imagine the whole family, then, except for my two brothers, gathered in this room after dinner one night. I would probably be perched on the wood-basket engaged in the endlessly enjoyable occupation of tinkering with the fire, or trying to save the lives of the enormous hairy spiders—too large to go under a tumbler—that raced frantically among the burning logs. Ray might be drawing, Judy sewing and Eleanor turning over a bound volume of *Punch*, while my mother lay with her feet up on the sofa reading something out of the newspaper aloud to my father, who sat at the baize-topped table in front of one of his interminable Miss Milligan patiences, muttering from time to time: "The cards are very disobliging tonight."

Red six on black seven: German destroyer on English cruiser. I thought of them piled up like my father's cards. I knew what battleships were like very well, having recently been invited to a Christmas party on board one, where the young guests were pushed down a chute by the muscular arms of bluejackets, or taken on a conducted tour of the ship's mysterious iron entrails. It had been too huge and frighteningly solid to help me imagine the 'battleship race' between the nations, much less war at sea, and as for the nations themselves, I pictured them as they appeared in the cartoons in old copies of *Punch*—France with her great thrusting bosom and tricolour cockade, the Russian bear, the unspeakable John Bull.

My parents were patriotic but not belligerent. They cannot have thought the danger of war imminent, however, because in the spring of 1914 my brother Tom, a charming and clever nineteen-year-old, my mother's favourite child and destined for the Foreign Service, was sent to Weimar to learn German.

In the summer of 1914 Eleanor and I were staying with cousins in their Sussex farm. Uncle Charlie had been a regular soldier, and was comically like the White Knight to look at, though inwardly conventional; but we adored the company of his lively twins, Winnie and Maurice, and I had tacitly decided that I should marry Maurice one day, as such an attractive near-brother would provide a good solution to that difficult problem.

But it so happened that he was killed at Zeebrugge while still a midshipman, and his twin sister, who bitterly resented not being a boy, did her best to behave like one. She began her career by taking charge of prize bulls, combing them and currying them, travelling with them to agricultural shows and sleeping in their stalls. (Much later, during the Second World War, as a result of a love affair—she was fascinatingly pretty—she joined the crew of one of the last windjammers as sail-maker. What wartime function these ships carried out I do not know, but hers went down with all hands as the result of enemy action, and Winnie drowned with them.)

We spent the first days after the cataclysm of August 1914 in a state of bewilderment mixed with sheer excitement inspired by the drama about to engulf us like a great arching wave, shot with flashes of wild hope and black fear. My uncle and aunt were staunchly patriotic. "It can't possibly last more than three months," they repeated (Three months? An age!). Or, "Why don't they come IN," meaning the United States. Maurice was recalled to his ship, and I felt almost shocked—probably quite unfairly—by my aunt's apparent eagerness to send her adored only son to war. My own dazed mood is encapsulated for me in a clear image of a walk I took with Winnie across the fields one beautiful evening, when the silhouettes of the Sussex sheep stood out black against a red-gold sky, their little wooden legs disappearing into swathes of diaphanous mist, and the picture they made was so arresting that Winnie and I stopped talking about the war and began discussing how much we should like to be painters (something neither of us had the least gift for). The baleful colour of the sky tinged the fields, and aroused a feeling of sudden dread. What was to be the real nature of this unknown experience we were advancing into so confidently, even with a sense of adventure? I walked back deeply disturbed to Battle Farm, as it was appropriately called, and spent most of that night tossing on my lumpy flock mattress, anxious and awake, or dreaming fitfully of seeing news placards bearing sinister announcements in coarse black letters on a red-gold background.

Returning home to Hindhead we found my parents in the greatest possible agitation, and pulling every string they could to try and get Tom out of Germany; but in spite of all their desperate efforts he was trapped by the thoroughness and efficiency of the German machine and interned in Ruhleben Camp with thousands of other civilians for the entire duration of the war.

My own first patriotic reaction was given a jolt by finding some of the neighbours at home wearing red, white and blue ribbons in their button-holes and hanging Union Jacks from their windows. What were they trying to say by means of these pathetic gestures, and to whom were they directed?

I don't intend to recapitulate those unhappy years of wild rumours (Russians with snow on their boots, handless Belgian children and crucified Canadians), of white feathers, and bleakly unreal 'field postcards' that contrived to make contradictory statements at one and the same time ('Everything is perfectly all right.' 'This is absolute Hell.') We carried on our normal existence among cross-currents of violently repressed emotions, but there was an almost complete failure to communicate between the young men returning on 'week-end leave' from the unspeakable horror of the trenches, and those who remained undislodged from their comfortable peacetime furrows, and lacked the imagination to bridge the gap; nor was this entirely their fault. My brother-in-law, Dick Rendel, told me long afterwards that he had been physically incapable of even trying to give my serenely pregnant sister the slightest idea of the nightmare he was living through and had only briefly left behind. What must he have felt when, as I clearly remember, a brisk little bridge-playing spinster said perkily to him: "I suppose you're *longing* to get back to the front, like all the rest of them!" I remember too the expression that crossed his face unnoticed by her—an expression of agony, hastily twisting itself into a mask representing the reaction she expected. I often wonder how so many people managed to suppress their curiosity, or whether they longed to ask but thought it would be bad manners. (Nor, in parenthesis, was the silence broken when the

war came to an end. For it is surely highly significant that over
ten years passed after the first war was over before two notable
books about it were published—*All Quiet on the Western Front*
and *Goodbye to All That*, both in 1929. How different from the
spate of literature that began to appear while the second war was
still in progress.)

But I will turn from this vast and horrific scene to the pleasanter one of friendship. If not sooner, I certainly became aware
of its key importance in the scheme of things when Julia left
Miss Grüner and Miss Gibbings's school to go as a boarder to
Bedales. I pined for her; I mooned about; my mother laughed at
me a little and tried to rally my spirits. I put up with her absence
for a term or two and then asked if I might join her there. My
parents hadn't intended any of their four daughters to go to
boarding-school, but reluctantly went to look at it and
consented.

I was already fifteen and the war a year old when I and my
school trunk arrived and were handed over to the Head of the
girls' house, a lady whose smile seemed barely to conceal her
instant dislike of me. A more congenial figure, Matron, who
wore her hair in two smooth dark wings like Mrs Bones the
Butcher s wife, fitted me with my green gym-tunic, red tie and
white shirt ('the Italian colours, the colours of liberty' I was told)
and showed me how to loop my hair at the sides round a velvet
head-band called a 'snood', and plait the rest. It was thought very
'un-Bedalian' to have one's snood too wide—I do not know
whether this was anything to do with the fact that the word is
defined in my dictionary as 'once a badge of virginity'. Matron
then took me up to my dormitory. Its note was artiness and
discomfort. Decorated in sickly greens and yellows, its windows
had leaded panes and were open in all weathers even when snow
was blown in onto our pillows. It contained almost nothing
beside six narrow beds, furnished with wooden laths where the
springs should have been. These squeaked whenever one
turned over and were hideously uncomfortable. My first
'dormitory boss' was a kind and intelligent girl whom I admired
and liked. (She afterwards became a notable benefactor of

children as Lady Allen of Hurtwood.) Every morning she would stand at the door and call our names, whereupon we had to leap out of bed, strip naked except for a very small towel round our shoulders, race along the passage and jump into a cold bath.

Next morning, after the obligatory pre-breakfast run, I was initiated into the Co-ed part of the school—a set of what seemed to me like ugly prison buildings arranged round 'the Quad', an immense area of staring white light sandwiched between a concrete floor and a glass roof, where a great many boys who looked to me like full-grown men were lurching and banging about in loutish horse-play. They even called each other 'louts'—'you great lout' was a Bedalian boy's term of affection. My heart sank. So boarding-school was this bleak place of cold baths, unpleasant smells, and above all no privacy, and I spent most of my first week in floods of tears in the Staff lavatory. (It was the only one I could bear to visit. Members of the school were expected to use long, stinking communal ones known as 'sets', into which we were quite fruitlessly herded each morning. We held our noses and got out as soon as possible.) Oh for the warmth, the Morris wallpapers, chocolate cake for tea, and scrupulously suppressed signs of parental love which I nevertheless knew to be there!

But adolescents are on the whole adaptable creatures, and long before my first term was over a transformation had taken place in my feelings for my surroundings. Many of the 'louts' had turned into amusing human beings, or handsome athletes all in white performing dazzling and graceful feats over a vaulting-horse, and the Quad was revealed as the evening meeting-place of pairs of self-conscious and somewhat inarticulate lovers. These 'affairs' were certainly a civilising influence and atoned for the more barbarous aspects of Bedalianism, such as ganging up against any girl who committed the unforgivable sin of 'trying to look nice' ('being silly' in Bedalianese), or against children of either sex who enjoyed work and were therefore approved of by the Staff. I had some narrow escapes on this score, for Miss Gibbings had left her mark, but luckily I made a new friend, a clever, lively girl called Margaret Leathes,* as well as several other boon companions, for Julia turned out to be physically separated from me by the year's difference in our ages and her dislike of lessons. She spent most of her time wrapped in coats, rugs and scarves in one of the practising-rooms, bouncing up and down on her chair and shadow-boxing over the piano keys, as she miraculously poured forth a stream of improvised jazz. No-one could have been a less conformist Bedalian; but her originality and imagination were a constant delight, and she, Margaret and I had a great deal of sheer fun together, exhausting ourselves with laughter. Margaret was half Russian, which gave her a special glamour for me as I was under the spell of the Russian novelists at the time. Bedales girls were an interesting collection on the whole, coming from *avant-garde*, artistic or often Quaker families; but in those remote days it was thought more questionable to send a son there, so that quite a few of the boys were physically delicate or unable to stand the stress of public school. Some were neurotic or even a little mad, like poor Jack W., who was unmercifully ragged by the other boys, and egged on to perform various antics, such as rushing into the girls' lavatory to relieve himself. Nor did those Bedalians who distinguished themselves later often show premonitory symptoms. Malcolm MacDonald was a great wag, very popular and obviously clever, though he appeared to despise anyone who took work seriously. John Rothenstein was chiefly notable for a flourishing and precocious moustache; while among the girls, Joan Malleson, afterwards a doctor of some eminence, spent most of her time in the sixth form enveloped in a nest of rugs on the library floor, fast asleep.

Teaching was patchy, and the Staff were a mixed lot. The Headmaster, always called 'the Chief' (or less amiably, 'the Chump') was not an accessible man. His well-trimmed beard, and his rather eerie method of progress, walking stiffly erect

* Daughter of an F.R.S. (Fellow of the Royal Society), she afterwards married in turn two extremely clever men, Lionel Penrose, F.R.S., and Max Newman, F.R.S. One of her sons is also an F.R.S.

through classrooms and corridors in soundless sandshoes, looking neither to right nor left, led to his being identified with Jesus Christ. I think he was painfully shy. However, he was an excellent, if alarming, teacher of the Classics. "Get it right, man! Get it right!" he would explode to girl and boy alike, tapping his rubber-soled shoe impatiently on the floor. Yet he conveyed to us his own genuine enthusiasm, for Greek in particular, and it was rumoured that his favourite girl of the moment used to be summoned to private Greek tuition, and have her hand squeezed under a rug. The whole school knew who was the Chief's reigning sultana at any one time. He had a connoisseur's eye for a flawless complexion and lovely, expressive eyes. I would hardly have dared to sum him up then, as I do now, as an old hypocrite and a far from admirable character. But during my last year, naked (but not mixed) bathing was instituted in the swimming-pool, the only exception being that something had to be donned when diving off the top board, since it was twelve feet high and its occupant visible for miles. Diving (plain and fancy), swimming and plunging ranked high among Summer pleasures, but this new decree was not popular with all the girls by any means, particularly the fat ones. What was more the Chief took it upon himself to come and coach us for our Silver and Bronze Life-saving Medal tests, and criticise our diving in preparation for the swimming sports, thus being the only man ever allowed to be present among this naked bevy. ("Hands not high enough! Legs should be closer together! Get it right, man!") It was really going a bit far, and there were cynical comments at his expense, but I had no idea then—nor have I now—what he believed his motives to be.

There *was* a Mrs Badley, though she was liable to be forgotten, and I don't remember her husband ever speaking to her or even looking at her. Small, with her fluffy grey hair bound in a snood and a crunched-up face that seemed too scared to smile, she dressed in pre-Raphaelite style and spoke in a pleading drawl. In our last term girls who were leaving were summoned to 'Ma B's' drawing-room, where we sat 'informally' (but in acute embarrassment), most of us on the floor, and listened to the do's and don'ts that constituted the rubber-stamp of Bedalian-ism she fondly hoped we would carry out into the great world. I can only remember one, but I believe she felt it was the most important: "and never, never wear corsets!"

I was neither a favourite of the Chief's nor one of the un-happy few he chose to practise subtle forms of mental sadism upon; the master I got on best with was Mr Heath,* a clever dwarf with a basso profundo voice and a furious temper when roused. I resisted the temptation to provoke it, but few of the boys could. And I was grateful to him because when I decided to go to Cambridge he coached me in Logic, which at that time was the only alternative to Paley's *Evidences of Christianity* as a subject in Little-Go, and succeeded in giving me some taste for abstract ideas.

It should be clear from what I have written that after the first few weeks I was very happy at Bedales. There was considerable freedom; on Sundays we took long bicycle-rides into the beautiful Hampshire country, with sandwiches and fizzy lemonade in our pockets. In Winter whole days off would be granted us to skate, or toboggan down Butser Hill; there was endless talk, profane, serious and frivolous; and reading and music happened to be so much the fashion at the time that it was the 'done thing' to walk to your classroom with your nose in a book. Games gave way to swimming in summer, unless one was good at cricket, and though I was quite hopeless at it I enjoyed lying on a grassy bank with Julia or Margaret to watch the boys' matches, admire the stylish, speeding figures, listen to the click of bat on ball and thank my stars I wasn't out there braced in agony at point, the position sadistically chosen for duffers. However, I only once watched the Bedales boys' boxing matches and nothing in the world would have induced me to go to another. I shall never forget the scene in a great dark barn, where two rather small boys had been attacking each other like tigers, and now sat slumped against opposite walls with thick

* Afterwards Professor of Philosophy at Swansea University.

blood pouring from their noses. It was not the blood so much as the looks of naked, murderous hatred that blazed from their eyes that so horrified me as to contribute to my growing conviction that physical violence was indefensible—and indirectly that war was never justifiable.

But there were other things to look forward to, like the weekly dance. I had always loved dancing, and by my last terms was taking part in the exciting ritual of 'kitchen lancers', where the girls whirled round with bodies and legs parallel to the ground, supported on the interlocked arms of their partners. Then of course there was love. My own schooldays—and I'm sure those of many others—were irradiated by its golden glow. How ludicrously inhibited those amours would seem to modern adolescents! For I think very little passed between the couples who met and strolled in the corridor round the Quad after high tea, and further afield as well. My own score in two years was exactly one kiss, yet I don't think I lacked my share of admirers nor certainly of admired. I doubt if the first two or three objects of my admiration ever suspected its existence, though my last school 'affair', which was mutual, caused me intense happiness and some misery. Our tentativeness may now be seen as a waste of time, but I don't believe the muffled state of our passions made them less important to us; and I can't help feeling there was some charm in that slow-motion approach of girl and boy, if only that every step was thought about beforehand, savoured to the full and dreamed about afterwards. One doesn't get the highest possible satisfaction out of a landscape by driving through it at a hundred miles an hour.

What the Staff thought about sex still perplexes me. I sometimes think they were pretending it didn't exist. We addressed masters and mistresses alike as 'Sir'; the Chief, as I have said, called us all 'man' when he was angry, and there was a small but ultra-Bedalian contingent in the school who made a show of thinking all awareness of sex 'silly'. We were 'all good friends', they would say, 'and really didn't notice whether someone was a girl or a boy'. Presumably this was fostered by the Staff, yet at least one of the masters made serious advances to girls. Homosexuality appeared to be very rare, but sympathetically accepted when recognised.

During my two years at Bedales the war ran its relentless course, and by the time I was in the sixth form I had become friends with boys whose military career stood in front of them like some pitiless guillotine waiting to fall. News came of those who had left being killed or wounded. Their names were added to the school Roll of Honour in gold letters on shiny brown wood. Oh when would it stop? Would it last until Shawcross or Harrison had to go? Selfishly, we thought of the war for the most part as a dark, threatening cloud overhanging the otherwise enchanted landscape of youth, and fervently longed for it to be over.

In the holidays it was even less possible to ignore it. Hindhead was surrounded by camps, and at weekends the army invaded our house on my mother's invitation. Rooms were set apart for them to read, write letters or play cards in, but what they liked best was singing songs to her piano accompaniment. The Cameron Highlanders were her favourites; with swinging kilts and stately tread they would advance to the piano, and 'My Bonnie is over the Ocean' or 'Will ye no' come back again?', sung in a heartfelt baritone, often brought tears to our eyes and always to theirs. When they left for the front their Pipe Major gave us an earsplitting concert on the bagpipes, marching round and round our long drawing-room, as a gesture of farewell. Then there were the food-parcels and letters to be sent to Tom in Ruhleben, the uncertainty and agitation caused by his rare replies, and by inarticulate ones from Dick Rendel at Ypres. Ray had a horrifying time in the glass-roofed hall of her Art school during a Zeppelin raid.

A more frivolous aspect of the war was manifested in the dances given by local ladies for the officers at the camps; and any girl over sixteen, and dancing-mad as I was, had what is called 'a good time'. Our escorts were mainly Canadians, and considerably less backward than the Bedales boys. Hating the idea of a 'flapper's' bow, and still more of hairpins and 'buns', I was an early convert to bobbed hair in the style of Mrs Vernon

Castle,* and I'm sure this gave me an air of more sophistication than I really possessed, so that I had quite a success, including a serious suitor who pursued me with appallingly dull letters and suggestions of visits when I went back to school. My mother strongly disapproved of the Canadians; they were so unlike her dear Cameronians, and I gathered from a conversation I was not intended to hear that our family doctor had been asked to perform abortions on some of their wives (a subject viewed very differently then and now). They even had several murders to their credit, and she discouraged me from walking through the woods in the dark to visit a girl friend. She noticed my stalwart Captain's attentions and was appalled, and believing—quite erroneously—that my head would be turned by his admiration, she intercepted his letters and sent him packing. I regret to say that I took an inquisitive but completely detached interest in the business of being courted, while not caring a pin for the Captain himself. In fact—though unaware of it at the time—I must have behaved like a cold-hearted flirt.

During one of my last holidays from Bedales I experienced a 'moment of truth' which was the closest I believe I have ever come to the 'mystical experience' so many of my friends describe. I was walking alone along a broad macadamised highroad bordered by a cluster of ugly shops, a famous old inn and a post office, on my way to carry out some errand and ruminating as I walked, when suddenly, as if a flash of lightning had penetrated my brain (though really, no doubt, thrown up by the tide of my thoughts) came the blinding conviction that my ideas and beliefs were *my own* and would always be so, that though I might be forced to go where I had no desire to go and do things I hated doing, no-one and nothing could make me *think* against my own grain, or divert my beliefs from their chosen channel. This experience was far from that sense of being 'one with the Universe' which so many describe; on the contrary I was elated, intoxicated by the feeling that I was

---

* An exponent of ballroom dancing, who enjoyed great popularity at the time.

FREE, my own mistress, in the middle of a vast expanse made up of possible adventure, discovery and independence—even though at the moment it was merely represented by a grey macadam road bordered by Scotch firs and little shops advertising Mazawattee tea. For quite a while this revelation guided my reflections. Nor, may I say, has its effect ever quite left me.

CHAPTER FOUR

Landwork at Castle Howard

IN THE SPRING of 1918 the end of the war still looked as far away as ever; but, having left Bedales and passed into Newnham College, Cambridge, I still had the summer months to kill before going up in October. It was decided that it would be good for our bodies and our souls if Eleanor and I did some work on the land. I for one had so vague an idea of what this would be like, and that rather romantic, that I raised no objection. Among our Hindhead friends were Winifred* and Christina Roberts, children of Lady Cecilia Roberts of Castle Howard. The Howard family needed help on their farms to do the work of men gone to the war. We took the train northwards therefore to Malton in Yorkshire, and were lodged with a young farmer and his wife who fed us superbly on Yorkshire puddings and pies, but never spoke to us at all. Meals were consumed in *total* silence except for the repetitive babblings of their small boy, and I got the impression it would have been the same in our absence. It was now that I first began keeping a diary, but as I didn't want anyone—even Eleanor—to read it, I hid it in a hatbox under our four-poster bed. Unfortunately this turned out to be where the farmer's wife kept her best hat; she found my diary and handed it to me with a reproachful look and in *total* silence. I was deeply ashamed, and wrote no more.

After breakfast, out we went every morning to the intolerable boredom of land work, for such it proved to be. Boredom can be active or passive—this was ferociously active. For hour after hour, with aching arms we had to progress across a gigantic field, hoeing turnips, our faces dripping with sweat and coated with buzzing black flies. (It was useless to brush them off, yet

* Later Nicholson, the distinguished painter.

sometimes sheer disgust forced one to make the effort.) Or—
even worse—we would creep on all fours along a row of mangel-
wurzels, singling them. I loathed the very name of those
vegetables. We were supported by a boy and two men—the
Waggoner (generally known as 'Wog', a large robust fellow
with arms like the Village Blacksmith's), and 'Old Etty' who
spent as much time as possible over the fence, on the pretext of
having to make water. Eleanor and I were too hot and miserable
to talk much, but we sang a little—such songs as 'Ich grolle
nicht' and 'Es war ein König in Thule' for some reason—whose
dark refrains and to me incomprehensible words relieved my
feelings a little, but must have made a strange accompaniment
to the scene.

There were less onerous tasks, however. When it rained we
sat in a shed brushing the mould off cow-cake; then there was
hay-making, when I rode aloft on the seat of a spidery metal
horse-rake, above the splendid round and gleaming hind-
quarters of an animal which responded most gratifyingly to my
voice alone. I only remember one word of horse-language:
'Arve!' but it gave me joy and a sense of power to pronounce
it in a loud gruff voice, when the horse would stop or turn as the
case might be. As I have always been visually orientated, it
surprises me that I remember more smells (hot horse, musty
cow-cake) than sights from those arduous days, but I can still
see our harvesting interludes in vivid colour and movement.
The sky is royal blue with great white, flat-bottomed clouds
sailing by, and we hustle along, snatching up two heavy-
headed sheaves of corn, one under each arm, and propping
them into rows of card castles that wend their way over the
rolling biscuit-coloured stubble fields. Later came the strenuous
business of carting and stacking, when we used often to work
late into the dusk, and then fling ourselves down, exhausted, to
drink the strong Indian tea in thick mugs brought us by a procession of wives and children.

Our free moments were spent in a stuffy unused parlour,
playing and singing over and over again the only piece of music
that lay on top of the tinny piano—the 'Flower Song' from

Faust—'Gentle flowers lie ye there, and tell her from me . . .'
ad lib. But best of all, and looked forward to all day, were our
evening visits to Castle Howard lake, where we would meet the
Roberts girls, tear the clothes off our aching limbs and plunge
into the tepid dark green water. Even so, I had only to close my
eyes for the first blissful dive, and a row of turnips or mangel-
wurzels would shine on the curtain of my lids, like a slide in a
magic lantern.

Every weekend we went up to the Castle, climbed the marble
staircase between handsome statues to the bathroom allotted to
us, and often descended, much refreshed, for a meal and the
company of the Howard family for the rest of the evening.
Castle Howard was ruled over by Rosalind, Countess of
Carlisle. Though she had only a few years more to live she was
still a formidable character, best known for the story—whether
apocryphal or not—that on her honeymoon she descended to
the cellar and poured all the valuable wines it contained down
the drain. In any case she was an active campaigner for teetotal-
ism, and highly suspicious of 'loose behaviour' and sex in
general (though the mother of eleven children), and at the same
time a staunch liberal, free-thinker and supporter of higher
education for women—a curious combination. Her relation,
Bertrand Russell, noting that she had 'an eye like Mars, to
threaten and command', added that 'this eye was hereditary on
both sides'. She was in fact a tyrant and a bully. She was short
and very fat, and usually wore her hair scraped back into a tiny
knob, and a plain high-necked dress with a little apron. She was
unpopular with her tenants and fierce to her children, especially
her youngest, Lady Aurea, whom she had reduced to a state of
near-childishness though she must have been in her thirties
when we were at the Castle—a gentle creature, whom I remember proudly showing us the Canalettos, garbed in a long flounced
high-necked dress of white flannel dotted with rosebuds and
fastened with a pink sash. Her mother liked her to dress as she
did herself when young. She "didn't think much of modern
clothes".

All the family were not so meek, however. Eleanor heard the

sole surviving son of the house say to his mother, "My dear Mother, you're a perfect fool!", whereupon Lady Carlisle angrily hurled her slice of bread into her soup-plate. They often argued ferociously.

Of the other members of the family who came and went, Lady Cecilia Roberts was a jolly version of her mother and looked rather like a good-natured cook; Lady Dorothy Henley was handsome in a brassy way and with a brassy voice—I see her in a gold evening-dress, her tawny hair crowned with metal leaves. Gilbert Murray and his wife, Lady Mary, seemed a pleasant civilised pair, who made less impression than the rest, except when the Professor gave one of his astonishing thought-reading performances. He would go to a room at the far end of the passage, while the rest of us sat silently thinking of a chosen sentence, with the utmost concentration. On his return he very often got it nearly word-perfect and almost always captured its drift. Sometimes he would reverse the process and will those in the drawing-room to perform some action or repeat a sentence, but his successes here were less striking.

It was the Howards' passion for parlour games that gave me the chance to see Lady Carlisle in one of her famous rages. We were playing charades, and the subject chosen for one was Maud Allen dancing as Salome. It was all too topical a choice, for in the summer of 1918 the notorious Pemberton-Billing libel case had revealed Maud Allen to be 'a lewd, unchaste and immoral woman, whose performance was obscene and designed to encourage unnatural vice'. Lord Alfred Douglas had even been called as a witness! Lady Carlisle was outraged; she exploded like a bomb, and her wrath fell upon her son-in-law, Charles Roberts, M.P., whom she held responsible for this shocking display. For the moment she was insane.

Small wonder that Eleanor and I found these evening diversions frightening.

CHAPTER FIVE

Cambridge

W͏ʜᴇɴ I ᴡᴇɴᴛ up to Newnham at eighteen my father settled £2,000 on me, invested it, gave me a cheque-book and told me I must pay for my college fees, clothes and all expenses out of the proceeds. I have never ceased to be grateful to him, for it taught me—albeit painfully—how to manage money. Though I felt as rich as Croesus I soon found I was not, and that things like a pair of shoes might cost as much as *forty-five shillings!*—so that I could only afford one pair a year at most. Then there was the terrible expense of train fares, and one vacation I had the bitter humiliation of having to decline an invitation to go to London and lunch at the Ritz (which seemed to me then the summit of glamour) because I had not got the return fare—ten shillings. Did I never think of borrowing it? I suppose not.

My arrival at Peile Hall, Newnham, was almost as disappointing as my first days at Bedales; indeed it seemed still more like a school because we were all females. The hierarchy between 'years' was rigid, and until any of my seniors uttered the mystic formula "May I prop?" she had to address me as "Miss Marshall". The first 'freshers' who came my way looked like dowdy frightened mice, and I experienced all over again the unpleasant sense of lost identity. I soon afterwards discovered that many of my fellow-students were charming, intelligent and even eccentric; however, after a few days there arrived someone I took an instant fancy to—a very pretty Scottish girl called Dot Mackay, with rosy cheeks, bright blue eyes, a vivacious manner and infectious laugh. She remained my best girl friend for the whole time we were up.

My memories of those three exciting years shift and change pattern like the pieces in a kaleidoscope whose colours clash at one moment and are in ravishing harmony the next. What more perfect setting for the euphoria of youth could there be than Cambridge, with its idyllic beauty, surprising inhabitants, and a mental climate in which ideas sprouted, grew and changed shape? The place itself has not altered much since then, except that there are now, alas, no shiny brown hansom-cabs, nor ancient, learned-looking individuals traversing the streets on tricycles. Newnham College was never beautiful, its austere cream-washed corridors and common-room had a conventual air, yet, spinning downhill to lectures on our bicycles we felt we were members of the University, as we were sure the Girton girls—coming in by 'bus from their gloomy fastness—could not. Moreover, we had a charming garden where lilac and roses bloomed in profusion, and nightingales sang all night. So greatly did their exotic music thrill me that one fine summer I rigged up an uncomfortable species of chair-bed, on which it was impossible to do more than half lie, half sit, on a tiny balcony overlooking the garden, and slept there every night.

At weekends we often walked across the fens, past the sliding river, or down the footpath to Grantchester to pick bunches of red berries and leaves to decorate our rooms—that path, too, seems still unchanged except that it is no longer haunted by the disquieting presence of the village idiot. In Spring there were the famous displays of crocuses on the Backs, and soon afterwards the cherry trees spread their flowery arms over long grass full of scarlet tulips and martagon lilies, in faithful imitation of an Impressionist painting. And there was the Cam itself. Narrow and often muddy though it might be, there were many ways of possessing it. One could swim in it; take a canoe up to Byron's Pool and beyond, join a punt party with a picnic, or moor oneself alone in a secluded backwater with a book, enjoying the calm that comes from that perfect horizontality which is the keynote of the Cambridge landscape.

Did we discuss the good, the true and the beautiful, as undergraduates are supposed to do? Yes, certainly, but a great many much more frivolous subjects as well; and a new set of rather naïve political or moral topics swam into our ken—egalitarianism versus individualism, for instance; free love versus marriage; whether there should be inherited wealth (this worried me a good deal), and even whether it was right to breed and kill animals for our food. For a short while Dot and I were registered as vegetarians, but our resolve soon crumbled before the starvation diet the college chef allowed us—one stuffed tomato does not make a dinner.

The Principal of Peile Hall was Pernel Strachey, sister of Lytton. In my clearly remembered portrait of her she has the engaging appearance of a shy, faintly amused giraffe, and advances into the room with her arms folded round her tall, slender body, while her small intelligent face—tilted back (as if in reluctance) on her long neck—is almost obscured by the large round lenses of her spectacles, brilliant with reflected light. From this face emerged a small, precise voice which manifested the peculiar dynamics of her family in miniature. I feel sure that she was deeply absorbed in French literature and other erudite subjects, and therefore found the business of administration a fearful bore—though not so distressing as the occasions when students knocked on her door and came to lay their religious or amorous problems hopefully before her. She guarded her privacy jealously; she was aloof, and so far as I know had no intimates.

A very different sort of character, and far the most distinguished among the other dons, was Jane Ellen Harrison. An eminent Classical scholar, she had decided to spend her old age at Peile Hall, which she graced with her noble presence: she had a fine head crowned with wiry grey hair, and her grey-blue eyes shone with curiosity as well as intelligence, for she wanted to know about everything and everybody, and treated the young absolutely as equals. I had never before met a much older person who had this gift and I found it irresistible. As she had been a friend of my parents she sometimes asked me to tea in her rooms. She no longer lectured on Greek art and literature, but her passion for languages had led her on to Russian, and her love for the Russian language and literature somehow embraced bears. Her room was full of them—pictures of bears, wooden bears, silver bears. "I *love* bears," I hear her say in her deep voice. Her statuesque appearance concealed a warm character, and she enjoyed a close friendship with the writer Hope Mirrlees, whom I often met with her—a much younger woman, beautiful in a dreamy way, romantically dressed and wearing long swinging earrings. Hope must have been infected by Jane Harrison's two latter-day enthusiasms, for in 1926 the Nonesuch Press published a delightful little book of stories and poems translated from the Russian by the two of them—and all about bears. The illustrations were done by my sister Ray Garnett. It is a scarce book and I was very happy to receive a copy from a kind American friend, only a few days ago as I write.

In October 1918 the propriety of the women's colleges and the virtue of their inmates were protected by a system of regulations as prehistoric as the walls topped with broken glass which used to enclose great estates. And, of course, for four years there had been few marauders. But in my very first term the War ended and young men flooded back, many of whom had been in the forces and were anxious to make up for lost time, and more interested in dancing and taking girls out than in swotting for their degrees. Amongst those who appeared were some ex-Bedales boys, my brother Tom and a lot of naval officers on a course. What was to be done about the antiquated rules which decreed that no female undergraduate could visit a male one in his room, or entertain him in hers, unless a married lady was present as chaperone? It seems quite incredible now, but so it was. For my part I was reduced to inventing an imaginary duenna called Mrs Kenyon, whose services I called on quite often. Of course Pernel Strachey didn't believe in her; she must have been well acquainted with all the Cambridge ladies, so I think it was mainly to tease me that she suddenly said to me one day, when I was lunching at the high table: "And what is this Mrs Kenyon like? Do you find her charming?" Goodness knows what nonsense I mumbled.

But there was gunpowder in the air, and it finally exploded at a meeting between students and dons, convened to consider the question of chaperonage, when a brave girl stood up and asked why it was that an exception was made for those girls rich enough to have a sitting-room as well as a bedroom. In a dead silence she enquired: "Is this because it is thought that the sight of the beds in our bed-sitting-rooms would be too much of a temptation?" This occasion, if not this actual remark, sounded the death-knell of chaperones. After this we met the men freely, played tennis with them, went punting and on picnics, and above all danced with them. All England had gone dancing mad and so had Cambridge. A University dance club called the Quinquaginta was formed, meeting weekly and admirably supplied with music by a jazz band of undergraduates. Dot and I were original members, and immodesty compels me to admit that we were among the stars, and our programmes filled up a week ahead. Lord Louis Mountbatten was one of the early members and I used to have a dance with him every week, though too shy to make much headway into friendship. But money for clothes was hard to come by. I had only one evening dress (an old one of Ray's), and Dot not very many more, yet we were so ashamed of always looking exactly the same that we bought or begged lengths of stuff to make one or two variations on our monotonous themes. I had neither skill nor knowledge of dressmaking, and being impatient by nature I cut and stitched away at random, adding a bit of ribbon for a belt, elastic in the hem to give the fashionable 'Turkish trouser' look and heaven knows what beside. I must have looked a perfect fright and was lucky not to come to pieces in mid-tango, yet no-one seemed surprised. Finally I got so sick of Ray's old dress that I dyed it black (an 'unsuitable' colour for girls at the time), and removed most of the front and all the back down to the waist, so as to give a startling décolletage which I vaguely shrouded in some pieces of gauze rather like wings. In this get-up I was reported to look very 'fast' indeed—and that I certainly was not.

The difficulty about this obsessional dancing life was that all we cared about in our partners was their technical ability—they must be first-rate performers—and such young men were often great bores to talk to. We finally got paired off with two good dancers with whom we invariably went to May Week Balls. We always behaved with impeccable decorum and chastity and our conversations were of the most superficial sort, but I believe my partner must have had a great deal more in him than I credited him with, as he ended up Lord Chief Justice, and Lord Parker of Waddington.

Of course a good many other young men from the dancing world asked us out to picnics and entertainments as well as dances, and made advances which were neither chaste nor decorous. Looking back, I think that both sexes were in a far more confusing position than are the permissive generation of undergraduates of today. We were ludicrously inexperienced. I have been told that some male undergraduates suffered painfully from sexual frustration, and as for us girls—it was delightful being made up to, but surely B. was an awful ass? And how did the pleasure got from these attentions connect with love or lust, and how did one know if and when one was what was called with such delusive neatness 'being in love' (as if slipping into a garment)? We spent a lot of time when we should have been reading Chaucer or Malory thrashing out such problems as these.

The confusion only became greater, and the colours in the kaleidoscope began to clash, when we started to make friends with much more interesting and less amorous males. Music was one means to this. Bravely deciding to have an audition for the Newnham Musical Society, I was accepted, considerably to my surprise, and soon found myself swept into Boris Ord's group of madrigal singers, and the Bach Choir. (I was even called upon to sing solos in concerts—anything from Dowland to Duparc—a process so agonising that I vowed each time I would never do it again. I was petrified with terror, and had absolutely no platform sense. My friends declared that I marched onto the stage with an expression of stony despair on my face, which never left it until I had made my escape.) I was much more at home in play-reading meetings, when we generally chose Elizabethan or Restoration works; here I got to know such intelligent young men as Patrick Blackett,* Lionel and Alec

* Later Lord Blackett and a Nobel Prize winner.

Penrose, the Davidson brothers (Angus and Douglas) and Dadie Rylands. Through my brother Tom, who shone as an actor in the Marlowe Society, I met older men like Dennis Arundel, Donald Beves, J. T. Sheppard and Professor Adrian. But the dichotomy between dancing and intellectual interests produced a form of schizophrenia, one of the unpleasant symptoms of which was blind panic when members of different worlds happened to be present at the same time. I was like a jelly that had only partly set. I took over the mode of behaviour and language of whomever I was with at the time; how was it possible to speak at all when two sets of idioms were current at once?

I have written a surprising amount about Cambridge without mentioning the work we had gone up on purpose to do. My reason for choosing the English Tripos was the very bad, or perhaps lazy one that I liked reading and had done a good deal of browsing in the bookshelves at home, guided by my father towards the Lake Poets, Thackeray, Scott, and R. L. Stevenson. I had also been drawn to *Tom Jones* and *Tristram Shandy* by his evident doubt whether they were 'suitable', and to Henry James and Virginia Woolf because of the discussion they aroused at the luncheon table. (Someone mentioned that Virginia compared taxi-cabs to 'spiders in the moon', and this took my fancy greatly.) Among other modern writers I was stimulated by Dorothy Richardson, dutifully read the Georgian Poets, and Rupert Brooke with pleasure. My appetite was often sharpened by the sight of a long row of volumes seeming to invite me to munch my way through them, but only sometimes did I put this into practice, as when I read the whole of Spenser's *Faerie Queene*, given me for my thirteenth birthday by my kind Uncle Frank of Derwentwater—an imaginative present; it is the right age to read it. Later I developed a passion for Shakespeare and the other Elizabethans, and at Cambridge I discovered the Metaphysical and Carolean poets and the erotic poems of Marvell and Carew.

Amongst the dons who taught me English, the outstanding stimulus came from I. A. Richards, who not only had a lot that was interesting to say but gave the impression of thinking as he talked, which added greatly to the freshness of his ideas and compared favourably with the obviously oft-repeated dronings, delivered with glazed eyes, of some of the lecturers. Richards would stand in front of a blackboard on which he made cabalistic marks with immense delicacy and dedication, thus elucidating some subtle complex of ideas both to himself and us. There was a strong vein of abstract thinking in his talk which appealed to some interest first set going in me by little Mr Heath at Bedales, and which diverted my mind from English literature towards more speculative subjects. It is impossible to overestimate the effect of one good teacher on the direction taken by his pupils' minds. I had spent two years studying for and passing Mays and Part I of the English Tripos (which I took in a shockingly frivolous spirit, going out of one paper at half time in order to watch a tennis match). I should by rights have spent my last year with Beowulf and Anglo-Saxon, but the prospect bored and depressed me so much that instead I took advantage of the excellent Cambridge arrangement allowing one to combine two disparate subjects in one degree. I. A. Richards' collaborator, C. K. Ogden, inventor of Basic English and editor of the *Cambridge Magazine*, took some kind of interest in me, and helped me decide that my new subject should be Moral Sciences. The only trouble was that I should have to squeeze a two-year course into one year, but I determined to try.

Moral Sciences is a dodo among triposes—it no longer exists, anyway in its original form. In 1920 it consisted of four subjects: Philosophy, Psychology, Logic and Ethics. All four held exciting promise, and there was the charm of the unknown in most of them, for I had read nothing but a little rudimentary Logic and Bertrand Russell's *Problems of Philosophy* in the admirable Home University Library.

I had bicycled to my English lectures with Dot, but she was now reading German and my present companion was an old Bedalian, Lettice Baker, who afterwards married the most brilliant of young Cambridge philosophers, Frank Ramsey. We Moral Science students were a small group. Select? I'm not sure.

Beside some dedicated swots sat the unexpected figure of Claude Hulbert, later a well-known comedian, who couldn't help looking funny even during a lecture on Hegel, and also a young man in whom I noticed, without being able to diagnose them, some symptoms with which I was later to become very familiar. That voice? It reminded me of all the Stracheys I had ever known; it had a life of its own, starting low and soft, rising to a faint scream, stopping altogether, swallowing itself, and then sinking to the depths again. Then there was a vocabulary full of such words as 'superb', 'grim' and 'sublime'; the elegant, precise walk, very different from the usual undergraduate slouch; the interesting cameo ring; the cloak, sometimes worn instead of a coat. This was Sebastian (W. J. H. or Jack) Sprott,* who, though I doubt if we exchanged a single word at the time, afterwards became one of my dearest friends. The disease he was suffering from was, of course, incipient Bloomsbury. He had not caught his symptoms from Lytton, but by way of Maynard Keynes, with whom he was closely involved. It is my belief that the Bloomsbury voice was a product of the Strachey family and the Cambridge intellectuals combined, although the Cambridge strain had a special quality, being softer, more monotonous and less violently emphatic than the original virus—whose powers of resistance must indeed have been great for it to persist from 1903 (when Lytton went down) at least until 1921 (when I did). For all I know some mutation may still exist there.

The Moral Science dons of my last year make a more impressive portrait gallery than those of the English faculty. G. E. Moore was still in residence but no longer lecturing, so that I was not subjected to the enormous influence his originality and personal charm had exerted on a previous generation; but the Bloomsbury bible, *Principia Ethica*, was still obligatory reading for Moral Science students. I duly read it and was impressed but not bowled over: J. S. Mill and Bentham were among my heroes and I didn't find his attempt to demolish their theories

* Later Professor at Nottingham University, and author of several books on Sociology and Psychology.

convincing. Greatly daring, I sometimes attended the Moral Sciences Club, an informal evening gathering in one of the men's rooms, where undergraduates and their betters argued in blue clouds of pipe smoke. Only once do I remember seeing Moore there—a middle-aged, middle-sized, greyish man, who sat on the hearthrug holding his ankles in both hands and tying himself in knots, while he endeavoured to pinpoint "what one *exactly* meant when one said one was going to Madingley that afternoon". It was amazing the way these great men could make such apparently trifling issues so important, but that they were important and led to profitable molelike tunnelling in all directions I never doubted. (" 'All Cretans are liars,' said the Cretan"; "the present King of France is bald", or "the case of the child who says, 'Shan't say thank you'!" were other such.) Behind Moore stood a tall, cadaverous man, with a noble forehead, goggle glasses and an inconspicuous nose, who was the only one really brave enough to challenge the Master—and he spoke in 'the voice'. This was H. T. J. (Harry) Norton, a mathematician whose brilliant promise foundered under successive nervous breakdowns, and who had financed Lytton Strachey while he wrote *Eminent Victorians*.

Among those whose lectures I attended were two outstanding thinkers: first J. R. McTaggart, who expounded Hegel to us without, I fear, very much success. He certainly didn't talk down to us, but I got the impression he didn't greatly care whether he enlightened our incomprehensible ignorance or not. Sebastian Sprott was the sole exception, and with him McTaggart would hold a spirited dialogue at times. But he was, I'm sure, a kindly and certainly an engaging man. His tall, portly form used to float into the lecture-room like a barrage-balloon, and he held his big, round baby's head with its benign expression and spectacles so much on one side that he generally drifted after it. This one-sided trend kept him walking along close to any wall that he encountered as he crossed the quads or even a room, and I can quite believe the story that he once floated up to the fountain in Trinity Great Court, and continued circling round it deep in thought until some kind passer-by detached him. He had many interests and achieved the feat of believing in immortality but not in God; incidentally he was a great friend of Roger Fry's.

Professor W. E. (or Willy) Johnson was the chief lecturer in Logic; he had a brilliantly lucid mind that is said to have influenced Maynard Keynes. To my eyes immensely old and frail, he was a very shy but affectionate man and a born teacher. He invited all his students to tea during their first term with him, and finding that I loved music and could be induced to sing he asked me to all his musical evenings, for his two passions were Mozart and playing accompaniments. In my mental picture of Willy Johnson he is enthusiastically performing a Mozart piano sonata, his white head bent forward and peering at the music. Then, suddenly leaning back, he raises his right hand high in the air and brings the little finger down with a triumphant *ping* on the highest note. I am turning over for him, and wondering which are the yellower—the piano keys or his false teeth, and his tall gaunt sister Fanny stands listening with a plate of cucumber sandwiches in her hand. I really loved Willy Johnson, and he was the only Moral Sciences don who offered to give me tutorials, and asked me if I had any special problems he could help me with. Why, yes, of course I had! Free Will and Determinism. All my instincts, my belief in Causality inclined me towards Determinism, but how to explain the inexplicable sense that I was free, the very emotion that I have described in my account of my 'mystical experience' at Hindhead? "But you see," said Willy (and naturally I am paraphrasing), "the feeling of freedom is not only consistent with Determinism, it depends upon it. When you exercise your will—make a choice—the *you* that makes it is the product of a long causal chain forged from heredity and environment. Naturally therefore you feel *you* are responsible for your choice, and so you are. But the Indeterminist, who holds to the theory of Free Will, believes that his choice may be partly at least controlled by something *outside the causal chain*—chance, an accident in fact. What is there free about that?"

I'm not quite sure when I first got to know Frank Ramsey,

who afterwards married Lettice Baker and became a close friend. By common consent he was a philosopher of genius, and his death at the age of twenty-six a disaster. But he really belongs to a later period of my story, and I shall have more to say about him during the last few years of his life; also about another genius whom I got to know later with the Ramseys—Wittgenstein.

I had perforce to work a good deal harder for the Moral Science finals than I had for English, but all was well, and so my last year came to an end with what in those pre-Women's Lib days was known as 'the equivalent of a degree', in a flurry of dances, flirtations, concerts, and plans for holidays abroad.

All the same, leaving Cambridge was like taking an awkwardly long step at full stretch over a deep ravine, looking neither behind nor below but only ahead where everything was veiled in uncertainty. Constitutionally an optimist, I viewed the future with happy confidence at first, but a few weeks after going down from Newnham I lived through a strange episode in which this euphoria was connected with gloom as surely as a lamp is with its shadow. The realisation of the passing of time, tick by tick, moved suddenly into the foreground of my consciousness and remained as a horrible obsession for several days. True, twenty-one was not a great age, but *I would never be twenty again*. You can't 'bid time return'. I was staying with older friends at the time, but I never mentioned my preoccupation to anyone. If they had asked, "What are you worrying about?" I should have had to answer, "Growing old," and they would probably not have believed me. Yet it was the truth. I went for walks alone, trying to shift the incubus from my back by thinking and thinking. And gradually it disappeared, was soaked up like ink by blotting-paper, until in the end I had completely accepted the flight of time as part of the cosmos, and growing old has given me very little anguish since. I have often wondered if other people have had similar experiences. The fact that the years, days and minutes gather speed as one gets older is evident to everyone, and there seems a good reason for it: a purely mathematical one. At all ages one's life appears to have gone on 'for ever'. At the age of one, a single year is therefore eternal, but when seventy of them go to make up that same eternity, each year seems vastly diminished in extent, and flashes past more rapidly. This, at least, is the only way I can understand that terrifying word.

CHAPTER SIX

London and Bloomsbury

DURING MY LAST year at Cambridge the very long illness my father had been suffering from came to an end. His decline towards death had been so gradual, sweeping the whole house along with it into an all-pervading current of enforced silences and doctors' visits, of 'good days' and 'bad days', and peopling it with nurses who were likewise 'good' and 'bad', that when the news came I must confess it didn't move me very deeply, although it made the first breach in our family circle. I see now that after a space of great sadness it was a liberation to my mother. A long marriage to a dominating though much-loved man fifteen years older than herself had been a considerable restraint on her, and her courageous, naturally independent personality began to fight its way to the surface. The Hindhead house was sold and she moved to London and started to take up new interests, such as politics, and devote herself more to music: always a Women's Suffragist, she now became openly left-wing and joined the Labour Party. She brought her Steinway grand piano to Brunswick Square, Bloomsbury (where it was the centre of many musical parties), as well as a lot of all-too-familiar objects, which I sometimes caught myself eyeing with claustrophobic distaste. She also brought old Nan of course; and an ex-steward from a Channel packet acted as our house-parlourman.

At this time people were beginning to discover that the large old London houses, designed to be looked after by servants toiling up from the basement, were too inconvenient, and the 'communal house' was finding favour with some, especially professional and business people living alone. My mother tried to make 27 Brunswick Square into a communal house, by allotting separate bed-sitting-rooms to Eleanor and myself, to be decorated as we chose. With a pathetic attempt at getting as far away as possible from *As You Like It* and old-gold wallpaper, I had mine painted a hideous emerald green, and hung the walls with framed illustrations from a book Ray had brought me from Russia.

I knew it was time to launch from the nest, but had little idea how to set about it.

Meanwhile Ray had taken a room in another communal house just off Gordon Square, where she met David Garnett whom she later married. I met Bunny Garnett for the first time before the family move, when I called to see if Ray could give me a bed for the night while I went job-hunting. He came to the door when I rang, fixed me with a searching blue gaze directed by a sideways swivelling movement of the neck, and told me in a very soft version of 'the voice' that Ray's room was occupied at the moment but he would be pleased to let me have his on the ground floor for a night or two. He was then a well-built, fair and ruddy-complexioned man of about thirty, and I liked him immediately. I accepted his room thankfully and spent the night there, but its lack of furniture amazed me. There was a bed, it's true, a wooden sailor's chest containing clothes, an early Duncan Grant of a nude sponging herself in the bath, and one nail hammered into the wall from which a large bunch of ties was suspended. I felt I was glimpsing a new, strange world.

My first attempts to find a job were frustrating. I went to see the arch-feminist Pippa Strachey in her employment exchange for women, feeling reasonably confident, but my degree didn't impress her in the least.

"What did you think of doing?" she asked. I suggested some form of applied psychology, but this was still an infant science and she knew nothing about it.

"Or perhaps a librarian?" I said hopefully. She rustled the pages of several fat reference books.

"Well, you would have to take a librarian's degree first—is it four years or only three? I forget." Then, seeing my dismay, "Even if you wanted to be a *cook* you'd have to go through a period of training." I got the impression that her chief object was to show me how impossible it was to get jobs. I didn't want to be a cook in the least, and came away mortified, as well as surprised that someone so prominent in furthering women's rights should so unhelpfully denigrate the value of higher education for females.

Next I went to see Professor Cyril Burt, a power in the world of Educational and Industrial Psychology at that time, though the subject of more recent criticism. Yes indeed, he would be delighted to give me research work to do but unfortunately there were as yet hardly any paid jobs. For a while I carried out intelligence tests for him on nine-year-old children in some of the state schools. I enjoyed this very much, though it was soon borne in on me that the tests were extremely limited in their value, and made too little allowance for such qualities as imagination and inventiveness, while concentrating entirely on the power to perceive and apply 'relations'.

"You must pretend you've lost your ball in this field," was one of the things I had to say to my victims, pointing to an outline on the paper before us. "Take your pencil and show me how you would walk in at this gate and look for your ball, so as to be sure to find it." A bright-eyed little boy with well-sharpened pencil at the ready set about his task systematically, and scored good marks, but my heart went out to the dreamy imaginative child, who was clearly picturing some tall thistles and wondering whether the ball might be lurking behind them, while his pencil wandered after his projected ego. Many years later I was appalled to discover that virtually the same I.Q. tests were still being done on schoolchildren, though well-known to the teachers who coached them. Burt at least recognised the large genetic component in intelligence, but no-one, so far as I know, has been able to invent tests that isolate that component from the influence of the environment.

Dr Burt then offered me a job in what was called Industrial Psychology; I was to invent and carry out tests on Lyons' waitresses to find out why they broke so much china. I was wobbling furiously over this, when salvation came out of a blue sky. Bunny Garnett and his great friend Francis Birrell had started a bookshop on the ground floor of the communal house in Taviton Street, Bloomsbury; they invited me to be assistant and accountant at the princely salary of three pounds a week, temporarily at first, but later as a permanency.

From the first I was happy at Birrell and Garnett's. It occupied the large ground-floor front, and the books made a pleasing, natural covering to the walls like lichen on a rock face; they looked at home there, if not very well organised. There were sets from the libraries of the fathers of the two partners— Augustine Birrell and Edward Garnett; Constance Garnett's translations from the Russian and all the publications of the Hogarth Press; modern French novels settling on their haunches as French books will; seventeenth- and eighteenth-century books in warm brown contemporary bindings. We did a profitable trade in Henry James—having discovered that the first editions of several of his books were still in print at Macmillans, we issued a catalogue including for instance: 'Spoils of Poynton. First Edition; mint condition, as new', and as orders came pouring in, especially from America, one of us would hurry round to the publishers' trade door, buy copies and despatch them. Then E. M. Forster put us in touch with one of his Indian potentate friends, who commissioned us to select books for Hyderabad State, and send them out in tin-lined boxes. By means of devices like these, and considerable, if sometimes misplaced, energy, Birrell and Garnett was kept afloat, for all our lack of expertise in shop-keeping. My job was to run errands to publishers, do up and post parcels, and keep the accounts—which, as we had no proper till at the time and anyone was likely to abstract their taxi fare from the box that did duty for it, was well nigh impossible. I also helped prepare and send out our catalogues, some with special messages of love and admiration to heroes not personally known to any of us, like Charlie Chaplin. Then came the excitement of waiting for orders to arrive. We rushed to look at the post each morning like fishermen hurrying to see if their bait has been taken, and when far too many orders came for one item we knew we had priced it too low. When left in sole command I naturally committed some howlers, as when I tried to 'sell' Proust—whom I was in process of excitedly discovering myself—to Beryl de Zoete, Arthur Waley's consort, and her ironical smile made it plain that she knew all the hitherto published volumes backwards.

To get into the bookshop one had to ring the bell and then walk along the corridor, to be very probably greeted by Francis Birrell, standing in the centre of the room like a small fierce Aberdeen terrier, with an abrupt bark of "Yes? What d'you want?" He was in fact one of the sweetest-natured men I ever met and the friendliest, but manners were not his forte, and he may well have been annoyed at being interrupted in a fascinating conversation—as likely to be concerned with the gossip of the days of Madame de Sévigné or Dr Johnson as with that of the present. The result was that any casual customer attracted by the window display was quickly frightened away. Frankie was also a very 'unsoigné' dresser, usually wearing a good suit well-covered in spots and drips, and a very wide black hat with the bow worn in front, but underneath which was a wide, irresistible grin. Partners and assistant all spent our spare time reading the stock; Frankie was an untidy reader, and buyers were not always best pleased to find their 'new' copies covered in fingerprints and tobacco ash, or with badly cut pages. Our clientèle was therefore limited almost entirely to friends, and friends of friends, and were for the most part denizens of Bloomsbury, both physically and spiritually.

Thus it was that I first got to know these remarkable people—for such I'm convinced they were, however much attitudes to them may change. They all bought their books from us—the 'Woolves', the Bells, Duncan Grant, Maynard Keynes, the Desmond MacCarthys, the Adrian Stephenses, the Stracheys, Anreps and Saxon Sydney-Turner. These, I reflected, were the sort of people I would like to know and have friends among, more than any others I had yet come across. I was instantly captivated and thrilled by them. It was as if a lot of doors had suddenly opened out of a stuffy room which I had been sitting in far too long.

The bookshop was a centre for friendliness and conversation, and I soon began to be invited to dine with Clive Bell or Leonard and Virginia Woolf, and to spend weekends at Charleston or Lytton Strachey's house at Tidmarsh, to both of which I went in some trepidation. I asked Bunny for advice.

"You'll find they all spend a lot of time—anyway the mornings—shut away in their studios or libraries, engaged on their own activities," he said. "So take something of your own to do—something to write, one of your patchwork quilts, perhaps. They'll go for walks and talk, but they won't 'entertain' you otherwise." It was good advice.

So much has been written about Bloomsbury—far too much, say some—that I propose only to select from the *personal* impressions I received at the time, to which I have added some later comments and analytical notes aimed at giving an idea how *Then* appears to me *Now*.

To begin with, they were not a group, but a number of very different individuals, who shared certain attitudes to life, and happened to be friends or lovers. To say they were 'unconventional' suggests deliberate flouting of rules; it was rather that they were quite uninterested in conventions, but passionately in ideas. Generally speaking they were left-wing, atheists, pacifists in the First War (but few of them also in the Second), lovers of the arts and travel, avid readers, Francophiles. Apart from the various occupations such as writing, painting, economics, which they pursued with dedication, what they enjoyed most was talk—talk of every description, from the most abstract to the most hilariously ribald and profane. I had never, even at Cambridge, come across people who set such a high value on rationalism (a word that now raises many eyebrows), integrity and originality. Their standards were as high as their spirits. In my home circle even the more civilised had shied away from words like 'good' and 'beautiful' and would veil their appreciation of works of art in phrases such as 'That's rather a jolly bit,' or 'Isn't this amusing?' But the Bloomsburies called spades spades and said what they thought; they didn't keep afloat in a social atmosphere by the wing-flapping of small talk—if they were bored by the conversation they showed it. This disconcerted the unconfident and gave them a justified reputation for rudeness, nor do I think it any more admirable now than I found it then; but they could nearly all of them be extraordinarily kind at times, if they liked you—even the alarming Virginia, who was full of curiosity about other people's lives and liked to question 'the young', partly perhaps motivated by an unconscious desire to make fools of them.

Comfort didn't rank high in Bloomsbury houses (though beauty did), but there would be good French cooking, and wine at most meals (often imported in the cask and bottled at home), homemade bread and jams (Virginia was good at making both). In winter you might suffer seriously from the cold, and the bathroom pipes might be clad in old newspapers, but you would find a superb library, as good talk as I've heard anywhere, and a great deal of laughter. They valued friendship extremely highly, but saw no reason why it should annihilate their critical faculties. Very far from it. So they laughed at one another often, but on the whole affectionately, and told stories about their friends that may seem (and sometimes certainly were) malicious. And since they believed marriage to be a convention and convenience and never celebrated it in church, love, whether heterosexual or homosexual, took precedence over it and its precepts. They were serious but never solemn, and nothing was sacrosanct or immune from mockery and fun, certainly not themselves. Nor were they 'indoor' people, as has sometimes been supposed. Clive Bell was a good rider and shot, Arthur Waley an expert skier, and Ralph Partridge was chosen to row for Oxford. Even Lytton Strachey played badminton in a style all his own on the Ham Spray lawn, where Lydia Lopokova distinguished herself by never getting the shuttlecock over the net once. Lawn bowls was popular both at Rodmell* and Ham Spray.

What then were these 'individuals' like? Lytton Strachey was by no means ugly, as some have implied. Tall, willowy, and with very long and beautiful hands, he displayed a peculiar

* House of Virginia and Leonard Woolf.

elegance in the way he used to walk, or rather stalk, across the lawn under a white sunshade lined with green, and fold his long legs away into a deck chair. His velvety brown eyes were full of expression. He spent most of his mornings reading or writing in his library, which was lined with a fine collection of French and English books.

"How many of them have you read?" I once boldly asked him. "All," was his reply. He told Ralph Partridge that when writing a book he would pace up and down the room thinking out a whole paragraph in his head, and not put pen to paper until it was complete. This, he felt, was conducive to the *enchaînement* as he always called it—to him a vital ingredient in good writing. In the afternoons he usually went for a walk with his devoted companion Carrington; more reading or writing followed tea, and in the evening—when poker or piquet were not being played—he sometimes read aloud in a surprisingly deep and emotional voice, emphasising the crucial phrases with movements of his long hands. Shakespeare, Donne, Sterne, Racine—the range was wide. Lytton was alarming to be with because he was shy as well as somewhat arrogant, but if asked for guidance in reading no-one could be more helpful, and he had a brand of comedy all his own, expressed by fantastic gestures, a few arpeggios sketched on the dinner-table before leaving it, and a characteristic vocabulary, including such words as 'macabre', 'funeste' and 'abject'. Children in general were given the dismissive title of 'petit peuple'. His literary references could be surprising. Once when Carrington offered me a choice of puddings I said they both looked delicious and it was 'all one to me'. Lytton laughed and said, "I see you're like Hippocleides —at his betrothal feast he stood on his head and waved his legs in the air, and when told this had lost him his wife he said, 'It's all one to Hippocleides!' " Perhaps this character from Herodotus was a special favourite in Bloomsbury, for I later heard Leonard Woolf declare, "I'm like Hippocleides, who stood on his head and said, 'Hippocleides doesn't care!' " I preferred Lytton's translation and said so, but Leonard was obstinate. "You see, I had a Classical education," he told me.

Lytton's brother James, and Alix his wife, were both practising psycho-analysts. James loved music and had a scholarly knowledge of it; later on he sometimes wrote the programme notes for Glyndebourne. The first time they performed *Idomeneo* there, we found him walking in the grounds with the assumed gait of a sheepish centenarian. "*What* do you think has happened to me?" he said. "It's TOO awful! I've fallen madly in love, and with a prima donna!" It was Sena Jurinac, who was singing Ilia, and I don't think he missed a performance. His three heroes were Mozart, Freud and Lytton, with Fritz Busch not far behind. Once when a visitor to Ham Spray suddenly stood up in front of the fireplace and testified to his belief in God, James silently rose and left the room. We found him reading a book in the dining-room later. "I make it a point never to stay in the room with a Christian," he said. This wasn't as pompous as it sounds—he was really laughing at himself as well as the visitor.

His wife Alix's Red Indian profile, thick dark hair and level grey eyes gave her a striking appearance; her brain was like a first-rate machine which she sometimes appeared to have fed with material showing unexpected innocence of the world, yet she was inquisitive about almost everything. She adored an argument, and a premise had only to be thrown down for her to pick it up and toss it about. She also loved a joke, and her sudden wild laugh was a delight; everything she did she did wholeheartedly. So it was that in her late thirties she developed an exorbitant passion for jazz and dancing. She was the only one of the many who worked at the Hogarth Press who stayed exactly one day. "Leonard and Virginia were very kind," she told me. "They said they would leave me to get used to the press while they went for a walk. It was quite *incredibly* boring. I said to myself, 'I can't possibly spend the rest of my life doing this,' and when they came back I told them so. They took it very well, I must say."

I do not feel I can add anything to all that has been written about the Woolves. Brilliant as she was, I found Virginia less lovable than her sister Vanessa, whose passion for colour she emulated in words. I think perhaps she was really a little jealous of Vanessa for actually having the power to squeeze her colours from a tube on to the canvas. Both the sisters were apparently unself-conscious about their remarkable beauty, but their two faces reflected an essential difference of character. Virginia's bore the stigmata that are to be seen in many who have been gravely mad—a subtly agonised tautness, something twisted; the way she held herself, turned her head or smoked a cigarette struck one as awkward even while it charmed and interested one. As Julia Strachey said of her, she 'was not at home in her body'. The lines of Vanessa's beautiful face had been graven by human emotions, and responses to other people, with the traces also of her unexpected bursts of hilarity and recklessness. She was famous for her mixed metaphors (like 'the longest worm has its turning' and 'in that house one meets a dark horse in every cupboard') and she could be delightfully witty too. As she got old and moved more slowly, it was as if one of the statues from the Acropolis had stepped down from her pedestal and was taking a stately walk.

In Virginia's house there was always electricity in the air, and though enthralled by the display of lightning, few people were entirely at their ease there, or could fail to wonder where the next flash would strike. She seemed at her best with Clive Bell, of whom she was genuinely fond, and who would act as mid-wife to her verbal fantasies with a gentle "Ye-e-*e*-*es*, Virginia?" But then Clive was a born host, with the rare gift of wanting his guests to shine rather than trying to do so himself. He was in some ways an eighteenth-century character, part country squire and part man of unusually wide reading, particularly in French history and memoirs. I always envied him his amazing memory for what he read, and until the day of his death (when I visited him in hospital) his mind remained perfectly clear and he never lost his consideration for others. He was a staunch friend, and above all a great *enjoyer*, whose enjoyment was as infectious as his laughter. Even his more comic habits were endearing, though we might laugh at them—the French phrases that larded his conversation ('entre la poire et le café' was a favourite, which sometimes emerged as 'entre le café et la poire') or his gestures to emphasise a point, such as a hand sweeping towards far horizons, the compulsive pulling-up of his sock-suspenders as if his life depended on them, and anxious rearrangement of the thick carroty hair that grew on only part of his cranium, and had a way of getting out of place, much to his agitation.

Since Leonard Woolf outlived many of his friends, his fine Rabbinical appearance in old age, with his bright eyes, melodious but slightly tremulous voice and even more tremulous hands, became familiar to many. He had roots in both animal and vegetable worlds, as he showed by his pleasure in his splendid flower-garden and in the smelly old dogs which he treated to occasional kindly kicks.

Anyone who heard Roger Fry lecture on art must owe him an immense debt of pure pleasure, for he had the rare gift of conveying his own love for paintings, even when their attractions were not obvious, even when the slides were put in upside down. But his admiration had limits. When I went to India a few years ago I saw exactly what he meant by "the nerveless and unctuous sinuosity of the rhythms" of Indian sculpture. I don't think he was ever reconciled to it. Yet his mind was much more 'open' than most, and among his wilder beliefs were that Shakespeare's Sonnets were just as good in French as in English, and that if a doctor was going to do something particularly unpleasant to him a brick under the bed would absorb the pain. He was a keen chess-player, and sometimes got me to play with him. He liked to win, and generally did, but if the issue was in doubt he would say, "Oh, I don't think it was wise to move your *bishop*. Better go there with your knight", and that would do the trick. He was charming to children, enjoying talking to them and always taking their remarks seriously and laughing at their jokes. For instance he was much amused by a record owned by the Anrep children* called *The Song of the Prune*, especially by the lines "We have wrinkles on our face. Prunes have them every place."

* Baba and Igor, children of Boris and Helen.

There was something avian about both Desmond and Molly MacCarthy: they reminded me of a pair of china birds on the chimney-piece, partly because they were more complementary than alike, and both sharply observant as all birds are. Molly's varnish of conformity concealed an original and unexpected response that was close to genius. Desmond's feathers were often somewhat ruffled, though he spent much more time than any other Bloomsbury in the houses of the rich and great. He was a first-rate conversationalist, who used his voice like a musician, with rubato, pause and diminuendo as an essential part of his talk. No wonder that the typist, hidden in a corner on a famous occasion to record his words, failed to convey their quality. He also had an exceptional gift for sympathetic understanding— something which is often attributed to women, though its most sensitive exponents may be men. Molly's deafness interfered greatly with her happiness and sometimes with other people's. At one time she had a deaf-aid in the form of a small box, which she would push eagerly towards her neighbour at the dinner-table. Then, after listening for a few moments, she would sigh deeply and switch off. The effect was both amusing and crushing, but she had a brilliant talent for extracting the humour from people and situations, which would turn her face scarlet, with tears running down her cheeks. She was the creator of the term "Bloomsberries", and also the Memoir Club, where a few of us met and read papers supposed to reveal the whole truth about some part of our lives.

Duncan Grant's charm was legendary. He never stopped painting, even during those years when his work was out of favour and his name unknown to the young; nor did it seem to affect him when fame returned to him. And he loved music. When he was well over eighty I invited him to the opera. Undeterred by having spent five mortal hours that day carefully studying an exhibition at the Tate, he arrived by Underground and on foot (not dreaming of taking a taxi), looking as usual remarkably like a tramp, with hair that seemed never to have known a brush, sat through the opera with unfaltering attention, and came back to supper afterwards with two much younger guests whom he easily outdid in animation.

E. M. Forster appeared to dress himself carefully to look like 'the man in the street', in impossibly dull grey suits, a woolly waistcoat perhaps and a cloth cap, yet there was no mistaking him for one of his similarly-attired fellows. Was it the curious shape of his head—large at the top and tapering to neck and chin—or the disconcerting gaze of his light blue eyes? I have run into him in unexpected places, like the quay at Dover or emerging from the caves at Lascaux, and recognised him instantly from afar. The sentimentality which is sometimes distressing in his books never appeared in his conversation or his letters—even the wording of a postcard announcing the time of his train had originality, as did his handwriting. He accompanied his most amusing remarks with a look of anguish and a high explosion something like a sneeze, which seemed to express amusement and self-depreciation at one and the same time. He was more musical than most Bloomsburies, with the possible exception of Saxon Sydney-Turner, a ghostly figure who hardly ever spoke (though he often nodded emphatically), but if he did could tell you at the drop of a hat who sang Brünnhilde or Don Giovanni in any year or opera house during the past century.

All these people bought their books from Birrell and Garnett.

I have as yet barely mentioned someone who was visiting us at the time as traveller for the Hogarth Press—Ralph Partridge. If anyone had told me then that I was to spend over thirty years of extremely happy married life with him I should not have believed them. I saw him as a tall, good-looking and very broad-shouldered man ('an ox's shoulders and a healthy brain' was Virginia's early impression of him, and both were true— later she became more censorious). His remarkably blue eyes never seemed quite still, conveyed an impression of great vitality held in check with difficulty, and often flashed in my direction, as I couldn't help observing. Strangely enough this was not our first meeting. During my Newnham days I had been invited to join a house party for the Henley Races, and had seen Ralph stroke the Christchurch boat to win the Ladies' Cup.

I had even joined in shouts of "House! House! House!", egged on by some friends of his in our party, and later looked on speechlessly and quite unnoticed when the winning hero was congratulated and welcomed with strawberries and cream by our hosts. However, I took no particular interest in him during my early days at Taviton Street. I was otherwise engaged. My pocket diary for 1922 has miraculously survived the passage of years and gives a faithful but summary record of how I filled my spare time. I spent at least one evening a week with each of two suitors, both of whom I liked and found attractive though uncertain which I preferred, for I was in the grip of my old schizophrenia. Keith belonged to my dancing Cambridge past, to punts in the moonlight at May Week balls; he was an extrovert, fond of tennis and other out-of-door occupations, affectionate, sweet-natured and on the whole philistine. We had little in common, but I was very fond of him, eager (I suppose) to be in love, and ignorant of the emotion in its mature form. Lawrence, on the other hand, had links with some of my exciting new friends, and shared many of their intellectual and artistic interests; he was more likely to take me to the Wallace Collection than to a dance. Indeed I owe to him the stimulation of a dawning pleasure in looking seriously at pictures.

Besides these two I spent my spare time with other friends both male and female, much of it in dancing, but also in going to theatres, concerts, ballet and opera, while my new life was represented by Roger Fry's lectures, play-reading meetings at Brunswick Square, 'tea with Lady Strachey' and my first Bloomsbury party in Duncan's studio that November. The diary ends with some rather pathetic accounts, including bus-fares at 2*d* to 6*d* daily, and an odd library list: Fry, *Vision and Design*; Betrand Russell, *The Analysis of Mind*; Fulke Greville's Works; Baudouin, *Suggestion and Auto-Suggestion*.

Up to what age, I wonder, is it possible to go on making drastic changes in one's way of life, taste in people, books, places and ideas? There seems no reason why everyone should follow the same graph, though it is common enough to see people past middle-age make a U-turn in the direction of right-wing views and conventions, and desperately try to prevent their children from plunging into a current they eagerly entered at the same age themselves—a good deal more common anyway than the reverse process. Others have had the seal of their up-bringing, their parents' values or those of Winchester or Eton, so firmly impressed into the wax of their personalities that they scarcely deviate throughout their lives. In my own case a fairly dramatic change took place in my twenties, accompanied by the temporary schizoid symptoms I have described. But no such transformation can take place either quickly or painlessly. In 1922, then, at the age of twenty-two, I had hardly begun to chart my preferred course among the manifold attitudes and values that I saw spread out before me like a varied landscape seen from the top of the downs, with its hedged fields, rivers and tall trees. Perhaps I felt strongly attracted by some path winding among shrubs below, but I also saw sizeable bogs of humility among disconnected reedy tufts of self-confidence. And pre-ference is a long way from attainment. Socially, I could never count on being at my ease with strangers, or indeed anyone except close friends; the business of keeping my end up in conversation often seemed to be beyond my control—an almost physical issue. As I sat in a taxi in my best dress on my way to a dance or a dinner-party I would be seized with panic, and go through a series of auto-suggestive incantations which I thought of as winding myself up like an old-fashioned gramophone, and which usually ended by my muttering unconvincingly, "What do I care about these people?"

CHAPTER SEVEN

The Definitive Years

NOT EVERYONE WOULD agree that Freud's brilliantly original theories are effective therapeutically in the form of psycho-analysis, but it surely cannot be denied that they have silently invaded many departments of modern life—family, work and finance for instance (who can forget his famous equation 'baby = faeces = money'?)—and been unconsciously absorbed by nearly everyone from schoolmasters to stockbrokers, even coming to the surface in rather ludicrous forms such as the remarks of nannies when telling their charges to love their new sibling, or putting them on their pots. It isn't necessary to have read Wordsworth to realise that childhood experiences are never left entirely behind.

Between the ages of twenty and thirty most young adults feel a need to put down roots, decide on a way and a place to live, and perhaps even make a nest, in all of which activities they are moved by the same constructive impulse as the child building castles out of bricks. And when their social instincts come into play and they begin juggling with human relationships, they may be repeating their experiments with their dolls, teddy bears or toy theatre. If they had one of the last, and it was anything like mine, it had charming cardboard scenery representing moonlit forests deep in snow, or palace halls decorated with red swags, gold tassels and stags' horns, while a boxful of little people—likewise made of cardboard—could be pushed on to the stage on stands made of tin, singly or in groups, advancing and retreating (often hastily and backwards).

Places and houses exercise a powerful attraction for most people, and they have the advantage of being possible to modify or adjust to some extent by means of decoration, furnishing and garden-making; they are in fact more adaptable than human beings, whose identity cries out to be respected. At the age of twenty-two, however, I was under the sway of my toy theatre rather than my box of bricks. I was passionately interested in other people, and much less moved by such questions as where and how to live, or even what profession to follow, than by my choice of friends and ultimately of someone to share my life with. So that some of the cardboard characters who used to advance and retreat on my toy stage were now replaced by young men who did likewise. I have mentioned two of them, Keith and Lawrence. Under a certain amount of pressure I hesitantly and provisionally agreed that my friend from the Cambridge years (Keith) and I should one day get married, other things being equal. And after a time this led to the final retreat of my more highbrow admirer, Lawrence. It was not long before I realised that Keith and I would never be happy together, but I was unskilled at the art of saying 'No' gracefully, or putting into practice the adage that there are times when it is kinder to be cruel. So I havered and bungled, like some clumsy village matador who is unable to dispatch the bull. I finally arrived at what I thought was a brilliant solution—I would *bore* poor Keith till he longed to be rid of me. It seemed a fool-proof method, but I cannot recommend it; it didn't really work and I bored myself instead. Of course I know what appalling selfishness, what smug desire to be always in the right, what craving to be liked, what hypocrisy can be concealed by aversion to causing pain, but I have never been able to grow out of it. Anyway I have remained a Yes-person right into my old age, and still always find it hard to say 'No' even to such questions as 'Would you like to come to Egypt (Turkey, India, Russia, or Mexico) next month?'

But in the early Twenties, I was above all a working girl, who had to earn her living. In 1923, aided by capital from a new partner, Ralph Wright, Birrell and Garnett's bookshop moved to new and much more professional quarters in Gerrard Street. Brushing past the prostitutes who haunted that street, one entered two rooms lined with handsome polished wood shelves and a much larger stock of old, new and foreign books than we

could house at Taviton Street. We even employed a delivery
boy on a bicycle propelling a scarlet box painted with the firm's
name, and relieving Frankie and me of much toiling round to
publishers by bus or tube. Reggie was an amusing cockney
character, who soon made himself at home with us and the
books. "Six Seducers!" he would shout into the basement of the
Hogarth Press (Vita Sackville-West having just published
Seducers in Ecuador) and Frankie believed that he had caught
Reggie having a squint at the 'Curious' section of our stock, but
that I doubt. The accounts, which were part of my province,
had now to be made more efficient, and that involved a process
called 'double entry', which was as alarming to me as the clutch
to a learner-driver. Two professional accountants, known to me
privately as 'the foxes' came to teach me how to handle it and
check results. I don't think I really understood what I was doing,
but at least they taught me to add up quickly. As for our handsome new till, with its revolving strip of paper, a large element
of fiction had to be involved in transcribing from it, since
Frankie still took his taxi-money out of it and usually forgot to
enter it up.

Altogether I worked for nearly six years in the bookshop;
they were years of hard work and hard play, both of which I
enjoyed, though the two combined on occasion to produce
strain and lack of sleep. However, I cannot really understand
some people's dislike of work; it has served me well as compass
and lifebelt, and I have more sympathy for those who have too
little to do than for those who complain of having too much.
Towards Christmas we were always frantically busy.

We work all day like niggers, [I wrote to Ralph Partridge in
December 1923], and have to lay in a special stock of whisky
to take before we go home, else we are too exhausted to face
the horrors of the tube.

[And later, on the 27th]: We had a rather gay Christmas
eve in the shop, giving each other presents and doing no
work. Bunny gave Frankie a pair of jazzy silk pyjamas; he was
absolutely delighted with them and insisted on putting them

on and holding court in them for the rest of the day. He gave me a bottle of whisky, the first I've ever had of my own. We finished the day having drinks at the Criterion, and went home cheerful and tipsy.

Frankie's normally unself-conscious attitude to his appearance and dress was very engaging. During a slack moment at the shop (others were spent in backing horses) we once or twice played a game in which we marked each other and ourselves between 0 and 10 for such qualities as intelligence, beauty, etcetera. Frankie's highest rating for 'elegance' was 2, and this upset him so much that for several days he arrived at the shop having made an obvious attempt at neatness, with his buttons properly done up and the bow on his hatband in the right place.

It was a relief to be quit of all those last-minute Christmas orders, which had to be fetched from publishers, wrapped up and posted, for we prided ourselves on fulfilling them in time. There was also the mental effort of helping customers choose their presents, at which Frankie unexpectedly shone. He could polish off a whole family—including a sporting uncle who had never read a book in his life, a senile grandmother and children of all ages—with the greatest aplomb.

But the business side of our daily life was seldom boring, and our new central position had enlarged our clientèle. We received periodic visits from Osbert and Sachie Sitwell, for instance. Impeccably dressed in dark blue overcoats, and carrying black hats, they made an impressive entry, bought a book or two, stood side by side in the middle of the shop retailing the gossip of the town and making us all laugh with their amusing stories, then left as elegantly as they had come. Two others who generally arrived in a pair were the Gathorne Hardys, Eddie and Bob, at that time employed in Elkin Matthews' bookshop. They had a high and deserved reputation as experts on seventeenth- and eighteenth-century English books; both wearing monocles, they glided round our shelves, carried off some under-valued item, and vanished again. There was little trace as yet of Eddie's infectious ribaldry or Bob's bubbling loquacity, which enlivened many years of friendship during later years. There was the local office-cleaner who couldn't resist buying a French book about Rudolph Valentino (of which she couldn't understand a word) because she adored him and he had just died. And there was a variety of book thieves—the most convincing being the so-called gardener of a lately-deceased Devon clergyman, who produced from his pocket a crumpled list of the books his master had left him. Almost every desirable eighteenth- and nineteenth-century rarity figured on it, and "could we help him dispose of them?" he wanted to know. "Yes," said Ralph Wright, "I'll certainly come down to Devon and look them over for you." The gardener seemed very grateful; then he brought out something else which aroused Ralph's suspicions— it appeared to be a contemporary map of the Battle of Bunker's Hill. We didn't buy it, but many other London booksellers gave him five or ten pounds apiece for the dozen or so identical copies he had in his pocket. Of course the Devon clergyman and his books didn't exist.

Nor did our Bloomsbury friends desert us; the shop was often the scene of animated talk and laughter, so that some intending customers imagined there must be a party going on and hurried away.

So much for hard work. As for playing hard, the Twenties were the dancing years and also the era of Bloomsbury parties. The original 'members' were still far from old, and around them a host of quite young fringe-Bloomsburies had collected— some from Oxford, like Raymond Mortimer, Eddy Sackville-West, Bob and Eddie Gathorne-Hardy; some from Cambridge, like the Davidson brothers and Dadie Rylands; musicians like Constant Lambert; Arthur Waley; the sculptor Stephen Tomlin (always known as Tommy), young Bells, young Stracheys, young MacCarthys, Slade students and many, many more. I have sometimes wondered what a sociologist would make of these parties. They were not in the least like that dreary cere- mony, the modern drinks party, which is so often fired by guilt or at least social conscience. There was an element of orgy about them; most people got rather drunk and some very drunk indeed, and I hazard a guess that this was partly because they drank much less in the ordinary course of their lives than people do today. I never knew of anyone taking drugs. There was of course a great deal of talk which seemed at the time profound and illuminating, but got less and less memorable as the hours passed. There was a certain amount of casual lovemaking, and above all there was continuous passionate dancing, dancing of a high standard, whether Blues, Charleston or Black Bottom, which went on until three or four in the morning, when everyone reeled home to bed, some alone, some with a new temporary companion, some having fallen seriously in love. Parties were places to let off steam, sexual and otherwise, to relax from work, and sometimes to pursue the quest for a mate. On the whole they bred amiability and fostered friendship; those who got quarrelsome when drunk were very few and not asked again.

Far the most congenial setting for them was Duncan's studio in Charlotte Street, a vast, mysteriously shadowy apartment, reached by a metal staircase and corridor apparently suspended in space, which clanked under our footsteps, and on which one or two amorous couples would be standing enlaced. Inside the studio, Chinese or Spanish pottery, draped stuffs and dusty still-lives stood about on tables, leaving a large central space for dancing and performances. Much later I heard Duncan describe the trouble he had had clearing the studio of cockroaches when he first took it over—from Sickert, I believe. His chemist had provided "some form of stink-bomb that finished them all off".

"Do you know what it was?" asked Desmond MacCarthy's son Dermod, who was a doctor.

"Yes, it was called Such-and-Such," said Duncan, blinking nervously.

"Good HEAVENS! I hope there was no-one in the building?"

"Well yes, there *had* been an Italian family on the ground floor. I never saw them again. I hope it wasn't dangerous?"

"Highly, I should say."

"Oh dear . . . Now I come to think of it, I did meet some men carrying a large box downstairs later on."*

The parties I have been describing were made up, I imagine, to the same recipe as those of today; youth, high spirits, alcohol and gregariousness being the chief ingredients. In one respect they may have differed: they frequently centred round some quite elaborate entertainment, written, rehearsed and produced with considerable care. Virginia Woolf's play *Freshwater* was first performed at a Bloomsbury party. The occasion for another was that someone found a whole sturgeon at his fishmongers and got a Soho restaurant to cook it for us. Lydia Lopokova danced and sang Victorian songs afterwards. Yet another, at the Keynes's house in Gordon Square, put on a revue based on the topical and notorious Hayley Morriss case, in which Irish wolfhounds and beautiful kennelmaids figured sensationally. It had an elaborate script written by a Cambridge don, Denis Robertson, which could be read in two ways, satirising Bloomsbury itself as well as Morriss. Duncan Grant took the part of chief wolfhound, Tommy was Morriss, and there was a chorus of tall, handsome young men dressed as kennelmaids in full evening dress with pearl 'chokers', and rather small girls (including myself) in white tie and tails. Finally, Maynard and Lydia brought the house down with a can-can, listed on the programme as the Keynes-Keynes.

It was at a party in the late summer of 1923 that I first really got to know Ralph Partridge. We danced, talked and spent most of the evening together. I found him attractive, disturbing and puzzling, and this made me fall silent. Next day I got a letter from him:

Have I committed an atrocity? I can't go to sleep without some sort of apology. You became so aloof. I'm unhappy about you, not that it matters to you. I don't want you to dislike me if you can help it. You were absolutely charming

* Not to be taken too seriously, but in part at least as a product of Duncan's fantastic imagination.

to me, and I have doubts what I was to you. It was your party for me.

That was the beginning of a long, high-powered and concentrated courtship such as I had never been subjected to before. I don't propose to follow it stage by stage, nor quote from more than a few of Ralph's almost daily letters. Yet I feel I must try in some hopelessly inadequate way to give an account of what was by far the most decisive period of my life, in spite of the difficulty of presenting something so vitally important to me, in a manner that is neither falsified nor tasteless.

Ralph was at this time studying book-binding at the Polytechnic, and this brought him to London from Tidmarsh several times a week. We lunched, dined and danced together, and whenever it was impossible to meet I got a letter. These letters amazed me; they were so closely analytic, so intent on the business of communication, of filling in the gaps between mind and mind with the mortar of words. I was moved by their trustful outspokenness, something I had not encountered before, but was immediately drawn to. I wrote back trying to express my astonishment:

It's obvious that your and my standards of intimacy are very different. I don't believe I've ever been so intimate with anyone in my life as you want to be with me. And as I want to be with you, only don't you see *you've* got to take me in hand and not the other way round.

Though the story has been told many times, I must here go back several years and briefly explain on what terms Ralph had come to be living with Lytton Strachey and Dora Carrington, or 'Carrington' as she was always called. At the end of the First War he had returned to finish his education at Oxford, devoted himself chiefly to rowing, and made friends with Noel Carrington, who had very naturally taken him over to the nearby village of Tidmarsh, where his sister was living, in the Mill House—a house shared by several friends at weekends, but basically the home of Lytton and Carrington. As is now very well known, Lytton was a homosexual, in spite of which he was the great love of Carrington's life and had developed a close and happy friendship with her. Into this household Ralph was introduced, as a good-looking, healthy and lively-witted ex-Major of twenty-five. It did not take long for Lytton to fall in love with Ralph and Ralph with Carrington. Lytton soon realised that Ralph was hopelessly heterosexual, but they became lifelong friends—each, I would say, was 'the best friend' of the other.

As for Carrington, the view of her as a wildly promiscuous *femme fatale* is, I am sure, quite incorrect. Her love for Lytton was the focus of her adult life, but she was by no means indifferent to the charms of young men, or of young women either for that matter; she was full of life and loved fun, but nothing must interfere with her all-important relation to Lytton. So, though she responded to Ralph's adoration, she at first did her best to divert him from his desire to marry her. When in the end she agreed, it was partly because he was so unhappy, and partly because she saw that the great friendship between Ralph and Lytton might actually consolidate her own position. As she wrote in one of the most moving of her letters to Lytton, on the eve of her marriage in 1921:

> So now I shall never tell *you* I do care again. It goes after today somewhere deep down inside me, and I'll not resurrect it to hurt either you or Ralph. Never again. He knows I'm not in love with him ... I cried last night to think of a savage cynical fate which had made it impossible for my love ever to be used by you. You never knew, or never will know the very big and devastating love I had for you ... I shall be with you in two weeks, how lovely that will be. And this summer we shall all be very happy together.*

'That summer'—it was 1921—just three months after the

---

* *Carrington, Letters and Extracts from her Diaries*, chosen and with an introduction by David Garnett.

marriage of Ralph and Carrington, the trio (Lytton included) spent a few weeks at Watendlath in Cumberland. Here they were visited by Gerald Brenan, a great friend of Ralph's from the war, and here it was that Gerald and Carrington—who had met before, and indulged in a light flirtation—finally fell in love. The feeling was deep on Gerald's side, and they had a good deal in common; but Ralph was quite unsuspicious, merely delighted that they were getting on so well together, and unaware of their secret meetings and love-making, so that when later on the truth came out, the wound he suffered was intensified by the fact that trust and candour were as necessary to him as secrecy was to Gerald and Carrington. He had lashed about like an animal in pain and behaved irrationally. Very largely thanks to Lytton's affection and patience the trio gradually came to terms with the situation, and (what was more) realistically, but the process took two years. On the surface everything would now go on as before, but there were vital changes. The marriage between Ralph and Carrington was never the same again, and each considered themselves free to choose their own lovers and friends, though this unusual trio were still bound by ties of devoted affection to each other and to their shared life at Tidmarsh Mill House.

This, then, was the state of affairs when I began seeing a great deal of Ralph in the autumn of 1923. Among other things, he told me that he and Carrington planned to visit Gerald in Spain that winter—an important event, marking the fact that the scars left on them all three by what was always referred to as 'the great row' had at last healed. (The reconciliation between Ralph and Gerald was completely successful and only a few months later they had reached a state of equilibrium in which he acted as confidant and adviser to *both* Gerald and Carrington in their somewhat stormy relationship.)

Before they left for Spain I was invited to spend a weekend at Tidmarsh, where I was alarmed by Lytton, charmed by Carrington, amazed that we ate stewed plums and milk pudding at every meal (the latter was apparently a necessity to all Stracheys), and thankful to find Raymond Mortimer as my co-guest, and be taken for a walk by him away from what at that time I found almost too rarefied an atmosphere. Carrington loved the country and came rather seldom to London, so that I had seen little of her hitherto. Her unique personal flavour makes her extraordinarily difficult to describe, but fortunately she has painted her own portrait much better than anyone else could in her letters and diaries,* which no-one can read without recognising her originality, fantastic imagination and humour. Her poetic response to nature shines from her paintings, and from letters whose handwriting was in itself a form of drawing. Lastly, her craving for independence and privacy made it no accident that she concentrated her intensest love on someone who made no emotional demands on her, and was thus in a sense unattainable—Lytton. Physically, her most remarkable features were her large, deepset blue eyes and her mop of thick straight hair, the colour of ripe corn. Her movements were sometimes almost awkward, like those of a little girl, and she would stand with head hanging and toes turned in; while her very soft voice was also somewhat childish and made a first impression of affectation. Her laugh was delightfully infectious.

Incidentally my warm friendship with Raymond started on this occasion, and continued without a break until his death. He must have been just under thirty at the time of our meeting, lively and intelligent, darting after pleasure and intellectual stimulation like a dragon-fly, always eager to explore new areas in literature or the visual arts. Travel was almost his greatest joy and he was especially at home in Paris, where he had many friends. But his intense curiosity took him everywhere, and though he was something of a sybarite, hating discomfort and probably quite unable to boil an egg, he would put up with really tough conditions in order to see some remote place that had aroused his interest. Ralph and I later made many happy journeys with him abroad.

At this stage my emotions were a good deal less engaged than Ralph's, and his letters from Spain complain that I am a poor

---

* *Carrington, Letters and Extracts from her Diaries, op. cit.*

Frances, aged about 10

The author's father,
William C. Marshall

The author's mother, 'M.A.M.'

Drawing-room at Hindhead

Frances at Cambridge, 1920

Julia at about 10

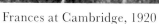

The Marshall family at Hindhead, about 1906
from left: Ray, Judy, Tom, Eleanor, Frances, Horace

David Garnett and Ralph

Ralph

Clive Bell and Francis Birrell at Charleston

Right: Lytton Strachey and
Carrington at Ham Spray

Below: Ham Spray

Lytton, Ralph and Frances at Ham Spray tea

Breakfast on the Verandah
from left: Julia and Stephen Tomlin, Lytton and Frances

Picnic in Savernake Forest:
from left: Frances, Ralph, Bernard Penrose and Rachel MacCarthy

Ralph with Eddie Gathorne Hardy and Raymond Mortimer

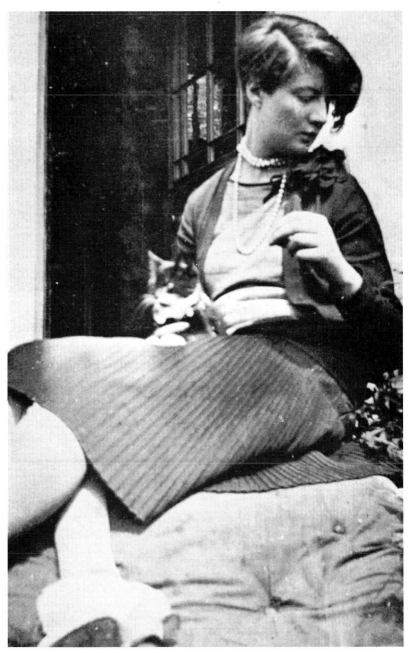

Julia with cat

correspondent: "Your letter is so thumbed by now that the writing is almost obliterated." His to me contained long fascinating accounts of life in the remote mountain village of Yegen, mixed with flirtatious teasing, and serious declarations of love.

Meanwhile, I had received a brotherly warning from Bunny, which amused but did not offend me. It amounted to the fact that Ralph had a roving eye, and wasn't a man to be trusted. This in fact was exactly what he was. I had never then, nor have ever since met anyone so realistic and dedicated to the truth, who was so deeply interested in what other people thought and why they thought it, and who always said exactly what he meant himself. Naturally this last trait was not popular with everyone.

Then in January 1924, after the Christmas rush at the bookshop was over and its aftermath of bills dealt with, I took a week off to meet Ralph and Carrington in Paris on their way back from Spain. I arrived first at the Hôtel des Saints Pères, to be joined next day by the Spanish travellers, bringing me a beautiful old shawl of crimson silk embroidered in pale yellow, which I still possess. They had also bought a great many old Spanish plates, but were in despair because many of them had been broken by savage treatment from a porter at the Gare du Nord. We stayed in Paris for a week, during three "pleasant but exhausting" days of which Lytton was with us. Hitherto, all my holidays abroad had been taken with girl friends, and generally walking in the mountains with rucksacks on our backs. Paris restaurants were a new delight; so was the Louvre, Mistinguett and the Comédie Française mouthing Racine. I noticed with surprise that Lytton never committed himself to speaking a word of French. He left all such practical matters to Ralph.

After our return at the end of January, Ralph wrote:

How devilish it is having to make arrangements again days ahead, instead of for the next five minutes only. I hate it. I hate not seeing you every day, it makes each day like a visit to Spain. I'm restless and uneasy without you—I don't want to alarm you, but rather more uneasy than before Paris. You seem to have attached most of my interest in anything. I hesitate to go on with Proust—I waver over going into my money and my business—I feel silent before Lytton, and Carrington has an awful headache and stays in bed where I can only look after her and not talk to her. I wish I felt more certain about you. What did you wonder when you wondered what the change from Paris to London would bring about? Because I did some wondering too, but I've never yet wondered whether I'm going to stop caring for you, or care for you less, because these hypotheses are outside present possibility. All the curiosity generated by seeing you so much for a week is now bursting out in me. Immense areas in your character open up like a vista.

I did my best to reassure him that I too had become much fonder of him since Paris. Later he wrote:

That is the one thing I hanker after, to see you without fail every day of my life. You are my good angel who keeps me happy, and I don't want any more angels ever again. I think of turning over a new leaf and burning all my old letters except yours. *You are of the utmost importance to me.* I'm never satisfied with you—I never have enough.

Early in 1924 Lytton and Ralph jointly purchased Ham Spray House in the Wiltshire downs, registering it in Ralph's name, as he was considerably the younger. During that Spring electricity (self-generated) was installed, as well as a massive central heating system, whose large, formidable-looking radiators never managed to attain anything above mild tepidity, even when the boiler was constantly stoked with hods full of coke. No matter, the house was a dream, and the beauty of its position and its view—looking out towards downs that were neither too close nor too far away, but composed a perfect whole, set off by the beechwood hanger on their domed top— was a source of perpetual joy. Lytton wisely took himself off during the process of decoration, which was planned and carried out by Carrington aided by a squad of helpers—Tommy

[Tomlin], Barbara Bagenal, myself and a glamorous *femme fatale* called Henrietta Bingham, daughter of the American Ambassador, who had come to England with her friend Mina Kirstein to be psycho-analysed. Both these girls were beautiful in different ways. Mina was highly intelligent, something of a blue-stocking; Henrietta had nothing to say for herself, but managed by her meaning silences and her husky singing of negro spirituals to a guitar, to break many hearts belonging to both sexes. I'm not sure whether the fact that both Tommy and Carrington were obsessed by her at the time speeded up the painting of Ham Spray, but it went ahead with fervour. An enormous ladder was set up in the hall to reach the upper landing; it once collapsed when I was standing on an upper rung wielding a brush full of distemper, but I was none the worse.

The front hall is all yellow [wrote Ralph in July], the arches in the passage to the kitchen Giotto blue—but it's really more Fra Angelico. The fluster of moving has embarked on a crescendo—more and more tradesmen have to be dealt with every minute—change of address cards, new notepaper, and now there's a barrel containing 160 bottles of wine waiting at Hungerford Station. I'm to take over control of the electric light plant today, ducks and chickens have to be suppressed and turned into potted meat. [An eccentrically-spelled PS from Carrington, who often added them to Ralph's letters, said:] It's very charming of you, you know, to come and help us so much at Ham Spray, and you must forgive my crabidness, which is only the reaction to this comotion of a move.

On July 17th the move finally took place. Ralph's last letter from Tidmarsh was not very happy:

I feel further away from you than I did in Spain—I hardly feel in the world at all. I'm merely uprooted like a tree and waiting to grow more roots. Carrington has tears in her eyes very often but I'm not moved like that in the very least. I feel uneasy because I'm engaged on something that you can't

really share with me. I *shall* be glad when I get back into the
world again. I've so much to say to you.

Very quickly, it seems, looking back, normal life began again
and visitors who were not house-painters started flowing in.
There were Lytton's two new friends from Oxford: Philip
Ritchie, clever and amusing, a devotee of chamber music and
discussions on abstract subjects, whose character had as original
a twist in it as his far from handsome face. (I remember him
starting an argument as to how much money one would
require to change one's name by deed poll, and maintaining
that he would gladly become 'Sir Philip Filth' for a very small
sum.) And the extremely handsome and charming Roger
Senhouse, who was as uninterested in the truth as Philip was
addicted to it.

That September I took an Italian holiday with my brother
Tom and two friends, Jane Norton (our newest partner in the
bookshop) and Colin Mackenzie, going from Lucca to Pisa,
Florence and Siena and ending up at Venice, a journey that
inflamed my love of Italian painting. The Giotto chapel at
Padua struck me as one of the wonders of the world even
though I was so weak from dysentery that I had to lie on the
floor to see some of it. A recent visit has confirmed this impression. Ralph wrote to me almost every day describing the doings
at Ham Spray; often he would write about the books he was
binding. He had now become quite expert and acquired as
large a clientèle as he could want. He used various coloured
'niger' morocco and marbled or Italian papers, some of which I
had promised to bring from Varese. However, the chief
subject of the letters was Gerald, who had arrived from Spain
and settled in Fitzroy Street; but since his main object was to
see Carrington he was often at Ham Spray, or looking for
rooms in villages near Ham.

Conversation rages as you can imagine [Ralph wrote]. We
pace up and down the verandah and then round the ping-pong
table, and what's it all about? Gerald's character chiefly,

which I've been explaining to him amid continual protests. I've never seen anything like it—from room to room he wanders, from book to book; he will spend half an hour indoors describing the beauties of the English country-side, which he alone understands, and half an hour walking in the fields describing the beauties of Fitzroy Street and the advantage of a grimy environment for the literary temperament.

So the months passed, with Lytton arranging his books in his library, Carrington beautifying the house with charming tiles and painted papers, Ralph cutting down trees and binding books. The first Ham Spray Christmas was celebrated by a house party, and a play called *A Castle in Spain*, written by Lytton for the occasion and performed by himself, Carrington and Ralph, Roger Senhouse, Dadie and me. Beyond the fact that there was a good deal of transvestism involved I remember little about the script, which has probably vanished. Boris Anrep brought a magnificent Russian Easter cake stuck all over with almonds like a porcupine, and was offended because it was so rich that hardly anyone could eat it.

Meanwhile, my own life went on, superficially unchanged. I still worked from nine to six at the bookshop and lived at my mother's house in Brunswick Square. However, my hours of freedom had become increasingly congested. Friends have a way of multiplying if one lives in London and goes to parties. For nearly a year Ralph had been the focus of my emotional life—but during the summer of 1924 a new character, Hamish, had come onto the stage, and a mutual attraction developed between us strong enough to set up an uneasy balance in which my feelings for him and for Ralph were suspended. Hamish had great charm and many interests. A delightfully lively companion, he shared my passion for dancing and was a first-rate performer. Ralph was much too acute not to realise that here was a more serious rival than the others I went out with; he questioned me closely, and I couldn't conceal anything from him. But my letters of that autumn and winter show that I was even more shaken by the conflict in my feelings than I knew at the time. I began sleeping appallingly badly, often not until five in the morning, and then had to get up early to go to the shop. After a muddle in plans I wrote apologetically to Ralph, adding, "I'm so tired though, I simply want to collapse into bed—too tired to talk even to you, darling. But I don't don't don't want and can't bear you to be unhappy, and through my stupidity."

On December 7th Ralph wrote: "I'm so disturbed by your not sleeping. I keep recurring to your state of health. I can't discuss anything else with you until you're well," and Carrington added one of her postscripts: "I am buying you some Postum food for next weekend to cure your sleeplessness, so you must promise to take it."

Such is human perversity that when strong incompatible emotions are grinding away at one another like the bones in a broken limb, and the pain becomes unendurable, two contrary conclusions are apt to haunt one's mind. 'Something has *got* to be done to stop this'—and again, 'This impossible situation *could* linger on almost indefinitely'. I was sleepless by night, exhausted by day, torn between my feelings for Ralph and Hamish, both of which seemed to have become intensified, but the fact is that agitation, like toothache, has its intermissions of positive happiness. So it was during the first half of 1925. Among the people I saw a good deal of in London was Gerald, with whom I went to music-halls, the circus at Olympia or on the Giant Racer at Wembley. He was an amusing and altogether delightful companion, and our conversations ranged from Hume's philosophy to the difficulties of his love affair with Carrington. Gerald had his Machiavellian side, and I knew that some of his remarks about Carrington were made in the hope that they would eventually reach her ears, so that I felt rather like a loaded gun, which may do an equal amount of damage whether it goes off or not. Or there would be occasions such as "a very nice dinner-party at the Ivy—Molly [MacCarthy], Raymond, Roger and Philip, and Frankie. Everyone in high spirits, and delicious food and drink. Raymond said he was looking for an ideal wife, and there was a long general discussion as to whether I would do. As I had none of his three essential requirements—chic, money and docility—I resigned my claim. Janie [Bussy] and Julia [Strachey] were suggested but also rejected." Or the comic relief of my being taken by an elderly admirer whom Ralph always referred to as the 'Pont du Gard' (because he was 'an old ruin') to his *garçonnière* as he called it, which was ludicrously reminiscent of the last Act of *Rosenkavalier*. And the early months of 1925 were much occupied by plans and rehearsals for Lytton's play *The Son of Heaven* which was put on at the Scala that July.

Nevertheless, I look back on the following months with very little pleasure: my feelings were in too great a turmoil, and subject to violent ups and downs. I knew that if I were to agree to marry Hamish it would be an end of my relationship with Ralph, in anything like its present form. Ralph knew it too, and his letters make painful reading:

> I suppose I mind a great deal about Hamish. I minded the attraction going to a dance with him had for you ... I am desperately in love with you, more hopelessly embedded ... I had a bad night about you, and thought of so many possibilities that I couldn't go to sleep and became terrified whether the possibilities weren't probabilities ... You're having dinner with Hamish three times this week, I was so agitated on Sunday night that when I felt inclined to cry I gave way as I thought it would relieve the tension. ...

Naturally, I was profoundly upset by such letters. I knew that it was for me to make the decision, and although Ralph and I talked remarkably little about the long-term future, I must also have been aware of the strong obstacle to our happiness together represented by Lytton, Carrington and Ham Spray combined, whereas in the case of Hamish the way was clear and unobstructed. Ralph questioned me closely, and I would have felt it treachery to conceal anything from him, such as a visit to Hamish's family, or two walking weekends I spent alone with him, yet I detested causing him pain. And what of Hamish himself? I believe he was confident that all would turn out as he wanted, but his nature was entirely different from Ralph's, and this may have been partly because (being much less analytical and inquisitive) he was not really *au fait* with the true position.

Some time that summer Ralph suggested that he and I should go to Spain together for a month at the beginning of October. Purely tactically it was a brilliant move. I had never been to Spain, but he had whetted my appetite with his stories; it seemed at the time to be shelving the decision and I agreed with a feeling of relief. But I think I subconsciously knew that it was more than that—I was making it.

> I don't feel as if I shall be quite happy until we've started [Ralph wrote in September]. Lytton said to D.C.* the other day, 'It would be too appalling if Frances ever thought of giving Ralph up,' but he didn't realise how *absolutely* hopeless it would be.

I sometimes wonder how much any of us speculated as to what the future would be like if I made my choice for Ralph. For my part, it had been all I could do to survive the nerve-racking present. On September 29th I wrote to Ralph:

> I feel much happier somehow, partly because there seems to be only a limited quantity of agitation inside one and it gets used up. Last night I talked to Mother a good deal about Spain, never mentioning who my companion was, though we got out maps etcetera. She never asked me and I don't believe she will, unless at the very last moment. I must say I think it is remarkable of her.

A few days later Ralph and I left for Spain.

---

* Carrington.

CHAPTER EIGHT

Gordon Square

I HAVE SEVERAL times been asked, usually by girls, how they are to know for certain that they are 'in love', and not merely in the grip of a temporary and perhaps mainly physical obsession. "If you ask yourself the question 'Am I in love?' then you're not," was probably my reply. "Well, what exactly does the expression mean?" the same girl might persist. To my mind no-one has defined it more luminously than Stendhal, with his adoption of the word *cristallisation*. You are in love when every single thing experienced is related to the loved one in some way or another: 'If only he were beside me listening to this music— looking at what I am looking at! How I shall enjoy telling him about this,' etcetera. It is a form of obsession, though not purely physical. It doesn't preclude criticism, and with luck it will evolve into one of the gentler but no less warm forms of love.

This, at least, is how I am using the phrase when I say that on our return from Spain Ralph and I were both very much in love, and our one desire was to spend our lives together. In a different sense I had lost my heart to Spain itself, though I shall not write much about this first experience of it. I was knocked backwards by its potent atmosphere as soon as we got out of our luxurious train at Segovia. (We travelled on first-class kilometric tickets, which took us anywhere we liked, but put up at humble and very Spanish hotels, unfrequented by tourists, where the food and sanitation were sometimes disastrous.) It was dark and I was tired; a powerful waft of mixed smells enveloped us—aromatic plants, charcoal fires, hot dust, mysterious cookery—as we climbed into a rickety bus, which set off at a gallop, and astonished me by failing to slacken pace while it charged up quite a long flight of steps. From Segovia we went to Madrid, Toledo, Cordoba, Seville, Cadiz, and briefly to Tangier. Our luggage

included two important items—an eighteenth-century set of
Clarissa Harlowe in eight volumes, which we read aloud to each
other, and a mosquito-net from the Army and Navy Stores.
This could be suspended from the light-flex above the bed and
tucked in under the mattress, whereby it kept at bay bed-bugs
as well as mosquitoes. Spain in 1925 was very different from
Spain of today, yet something still remains of the thrilling,
noble, harsh and uncompromising quality I found there on first
acquaintance. I quote from a letter Ralph wrote me during the
dark weeks after our return:

> I thought of so many things that have made me happy—the
> beach and the sun at Tangier, our walk that first day through
> the market to the camels, the smiling Moor who wouldn't
> sell us shoes, the nights at the Kursaal in Seville with the
> flamenco dancing and that divine singing, the cathedral at
> Toledo and the nun's podgy hand thrusting you the white
> flower, the great eagles over the gate and you trying to take a
> photograph, and then the walk outside the walls with the
> little boy chanting on his donkey, the motor-bus at Segovia
> with you clinging tight to me . . . and I couldn't remember
> anything else but how all my happiness comes from you and
> without you I have nothing.

Ralph went back to Ham Spray, I to Brunswick Square and
the bookshop, where I found a crushing amount of paper-work
awaiting me (including all the accounts and bills), as my stand-in
for my holiday had failed. Our letters to each other after our
return give a very similar impression: it is as if we had each been
stunned by a blow on the head. I wrote: "The part of my head
that is able to realise that you were with me yesterday and might
be with me now has somehow gone into a kind of numbness,
become anaesthetised." And Ralph to me:

> I feel so completely stupid since I left you that I'm unfit for
> any society, and now Henry Lamb has come to tea and I can't
> talk to him or hear what he says. I got back to find every-

thing just the same—Lytton full of stories of Queen Elizabeth's wickednesses, which he's extracting from history books. My own mind is very numb—I have taken refuge in *Clarissa*, and as I couldn't go to sleep last night I read till 3 in the morning and finished it. Please, please write to me as often as you can, even just the shortest letter. My mind is perpetually dodging back to my feelings for you. I move about in a trance hardly knowing what to do.

Otherwise our positions were different. Ralph had come up against a strong wall of agitated and articulate opposition to our plans in Lytton and Carrington, who told him among other things that should we set up together, he and I would probably never be able to come to Ham Spray together, as we had so often done in the past ever since the beginning of our love affair. Ralph had suggested our moving into Alix and James Strachey's house in Gordon Square. "I told them about the basement at 41, but they burst out against basements, which they say make one utterly oppressed with the whole weight of a house on one's back." Meanwhile, Carrington had got in touch with my old friend Julia, to see whether she and I could not share a ménage, in which Ralph would be more or less a visitor, which neither he nor I wanted.

Two things in particular emerge when I ponder those painful and turgid weeks—one is how remarkably unprepared, considering all the circumstances, we all four were for this crisis; the other that, bad as it was for us all, it was certainly worst for Ralph, who was being torn in half between us. He came up to London to see me every few days, and showed his practical kindness by spending a lot of time at the bookshop helping me with the accounts; then he would return to a renewal of fruitless discussions.

I had another long conversation with Carrington [he wrote] and one with Lytton. Carrington was calmer but very sad. Lytton was unemotional—the upshot was that he's gone off to town today with the intention of an interview with you,

dearest, which I expect has already come off. I have no idea
what he'll say or what you'll feel about it, but he said he
hoped it might clear up his and the Ham Spray position.

I approached my meeting alone with Lytton much as a
schoolboy sets out for the headmaster's study door, but fired by
the determination to stand up for what I believed to be the right
Ralph and I possessed to our joint happiness. My object, I told
myself, must be to convince Lytton that I hadn't the least
desire to drive a wedge between Ralph and Ham Spray. He and
I were deeply in love, and surely it was not unreasonable for us
to want to live together? We were not suggesting anything so
drastic as divorce. Perhaps blindly, I couldn't see why they
should suppose I wanted to seduce him away from his dearest
friends (and I might perhaps add that I never did in fact try to
do so). Apart from everything else it would be against my own
interests even to attempt to persuade him to make such a
sacrifice; I knew much too well how deeply rooted were his
affections.

Surrounded by the portraits of empire builders, Lytton and I
sat opposite each other in two stuffed chairs in the only room in
the Oriental Club allowed to be sullied by the presence of
females. I have never felt more as if I were pleading my case in a
court of law. I think I stated it clearly, though it could not have
failed to seem egotistical. It was. Unless Lytton and Carrington
found it painful, I said, I hoped that I might go on visiting
Ham Spray with Ralph at weekends, as often as they liked.
Lytton heard me out with dignified courtesy, but now followed
the bombshell:

"You see," he said, "I rely very much on Ralph's practical
support, sound sense and strength of character. Fond as I am of
Carrington I fear she loses her head sometimes. So that I think
I ought to warn you that if you and Ralph set up house together
I can't promise to stay at Ham Spray with Carrington, and I
think you know what this would mean to her. What would
become of her?"

Indeed, there was almost nothing I didn't know about the past relations of the three of them, and I was well aware that Carrington's ruling passion was her single-minded devotion to Lytton. Stendhal's *cristallisation* applied perfectly to her feelings for him—every elaboration of inventive imagination with which she beautified Tidmarsh and Ham Spray, every curlicue she painted on a tile, every owl on a cornice, was for Lytton. He alone 'could do no wrong'. Ralph, Gerald and her other lovers must always take second place to Lytton's desires, and of course as soon as they fell in love with her they found this unbearable, so that their futile attempts to limit her freedom sometimes forced her into desperate measures. She was not in the least cruel; it was rather her dislike of causing pain that drove her into evasions. The usual Tidmarsh trio might well have survived the cataclysm of the 'great row' had not Ralph been a man of unusually strong feelings, which couldn't be permanently satisfied by light affairs.

I left the Oriental Club, therefore, pierced by a poisoned dart. So far I had not felt I was acting like a criminal. Ralph and Carrington's marriage had received a mortal blow four years earlier, and though superficially healed, their disagreements were frequent and distressing to witness. But as soon as I had digested Lytton's ultimatum I realised that he was saying in effect: "If you and Ralph take this step, Carrington may well lose *me*." It would be her death sentence. How could I possibly contribute to inflicting it upon her? This, it was clear, was the danger she had been so greatly fearing.*

Nor was this my only problem. Hamish, who had been Ralph's rival before we went to Spain but was no longer, had in his turn become desperate and subjected me to constant pressure. I felt that I should probably crack up myself if I didn't get away and try to think things out by myself. I decided not to see Ralph for a week. "Don't feel more resentful against me than you can help," I wrote. "You know the only reason I have done this is

---

* According to Michael Holroyd, Lytton later said that he would never have deserted Carrington.

that I couldn't bear going on being a nuisance to you, myself and everyone else. Dearie, it's hopeless to talk to me of my choosing courses. I didn't feel, don't you see, that any decision I make would be valid if I was to make it alone? I had an awful evening with Hamish. He wants to marry me *now*."

I spent my solitary week at Owley, the beautiful old house in Kent belonging to my eldest sister Judy Rendel and her family. It was bleak February weather. I discussed my problem with no-one; sometimes I even stopped thinking about it altogether, but got what balm I could from reading Jane Austen, walking in the woods and picking enormous primroses. Towards the end of the week I received a letter from Carrington, which magically changed the prospect. "We each know what we have all three been feeling these last months," she wrote. "Now it is more or less over. The Treaty has to be drawn up." She was obliged to accept the situation, she went on, although "the happiness of my relation with Lytton, ironically, is so bound up with Ralph, that that will be wrecked". And she asked me "to be generous" and let her keep some of her friendship with Ralph.

I was amazed, and also profoundly shocked, that she should still believe that I wanted to do otherwise, in face of all I had said to Ralph and Lytton. I at once wrote back an ill-expressed but desperately sincere reply:

I never never feel that if R. should live with me I should want him not to see you very often and go on being fond of you. My greatest hope, but I've feared an unreasonable one, was that living with me he should still be able to see you continually, and eventually even that we should all be able to meet together without any of our present awful feelings—but R. seemed afraid that you might feel you couldn't bear to see him at all. Do believe that that is the most awful thought imaginable to me as well as to him.*

* Carrington's letter to me and mine to her are printed in full in *Carrington*, edited by David Garnett. I cannot find mine to Ralph, whose papers were in great confusion at the time of his death.

Both Carrington and I declared our warm affection for each other. At the same time I wrote to Ralph, and these three letters together dispelled the cloud of misunderstanding and distrust which had thrown its dark malignant shadow over the scene for us all—unnecessarily as it now appears, for during the five and a half years' life together that remained to Lytton and Carrington not only did they keep Ralph's friendship and support in all its strength, but he and I very frequently visited them at Ham Spray together, while their own relationship became more and more like that of a long-standing married couple.

My letter to Ralph brought this reply:

The change in me since your letter this morning is so violent that I don't quite know what I'm saying—the weight lifted off me makes me feel light-headed. I think I must be happy— I actually want to see the end of the day and tomorrow and next week. My love, you tell me now to write to you and I shall. Darling love, I thought you'd given me up because you didn't care for me any more, as I only made you unhappy. O, I've been so wretched and miserable—day after day and night after night, and nothing to think of except that my love had gone and I couldn't go to her, and she was curing herself of being fond of me, while I couldn't cure myself of loving her so much I wanted to die. I was only broken to pieces and the pieces scraping together. And this morning after this hideous week it's such happiness that I'm stupid with relief and gratitude, because you'd got so far away from me that I couldn't reach you any more, and were trying to mend your heart while mine was breaking . . .

I wrote back to him: "The thing that made me happiest in your letter was Carrington seeming to think that if you lived with me she would still want to see you. Did I get that right? I hope I did; I want to believe it so much." It seems that I had got it right, and a turning-point had been reached: everyone concerned now accepted the new situation. Ralph and I started seriously searching for somewhere to live, and by March our prospects were transformed. On the 2nd Ralph wrote:

> I am writing to Alix, suggesting that we should have dinner
> with her on Thursday night to consider if she can't find a
> niche for us at 41. It seems promising. What do you say to
> spending either this weekend or next at Ham Spray, and the
> other with Lettice [Ramsey]? I feel so happy that I haven't any
> misgivings. [And on the 3rd:] When I remember my condi-
> tion a month ago I can hardly believe I'm the same person.
> I'm passionately fond of my Saint Simon, which tempts me
> away from everything. But I don't just sit in a chair and read
> all day as you may picture me. I have made great progress
> with putting the covers on five books. [And again, after the
> Ham Spray weekend:] I enjoyed my weekend so very much
> that I must write and tell you—you were such an angel to me
> and so nice to everyone else. Lytton seems very pleased that
> we are going to 41 and didn't say a crabbing word. He also
> thought the weekend had been one of the nicest. [I replied on
> the 9th:] I was so happy myself. It seemed too good to be true
> that we should be at Ham Spray together. I felt so grateful to
> Carrington for being so charming to me.

Alix now wanted to let her handsome L-shaped first floor,
looking out on the noble plane trees in the square garden, with
their scarred trunks and dangling bobbles. We liked the idea of
having for close neighbours Clive Bell, Maynard and Lydia
Keynes, Oliver and Julia Strachey, Dadie Rylands, Arthur
Waley and Beryl de Zoete, Lady Strachey, Pippa and Marjorie,
Adrian and Karin Stephen. Moreover we should have access to
the gardens and be able to play tennis there.

We went shopping at once for distemper and brushes, and
painted the walls of our large light rooms ourselves—one pink,
one green. Next we furnished them rather sparsely, with book-
cases, a solid oak table and a sofa all made to measure, as well as
a dresser covered in beautiful Spanish plates in the sitting-room,
and very little beside a large double bed, chosen after much
bouncing at Heal's, in the bedroom. Chairs, Kelim rugs,
pictures and ornaments followed in due course.

James and Alix occupied the top floors of No. 41 in Yonghy-Bonghy-Bo austerity, while their consulting-rooms were just above us. If we met patients on the stairs on their way to be psycho-analysed, we were told to ignore them, and more than once I came across one of them leaning against the rails outside the front door, ashen-white and obviously unable to face ringing the bell. There was a time when James asked Ralph if he would come to his aid at once if he knocked loudly on the floor above. He had a patient with a frightening habit of getting off the couch and stealing softly round behind him—he might be dangerous.

"I keep a heavy stick by my chair to thump with," he said. "That'll be the signal for you to rush upstairs and rescue me." All this gave 41 an interesting but somewhat psychopathic atmosphere.

We moved in on May 14th 1926, after profiting by the emptiness of the rooms to give a house-warming party. Just before the move, however, everything was blotted out by the excitement of the General Strike. The ferment of political emotion and furious partisanship that this aroused has now almost faded from memory, but though it only lasted a week it was a week during which many were forecasting revolution and even civil war. In the bookshop knots of customers gathered to argue and prognosticate, and no work was done. The air was dense with emergency. Our newest partner, Graham Pollard, was an ardent Communist; he was restless with excitement, and kept hurrying out to mysterious trysts, and returning to assure us that we were all in for serious trouble. There might well be bloodshed. "Your day is over," he said with relish, standing defiantly in front of the gas fire, hands in the pockets of his pink Oxford bags.

Ralph and I and most of our friends were left-wing, and felt that the strikers' case had much to be said for it; most of us supported the Archbishop of Canterbury's proposal to seek a compromise solution by what would now be called 'getting round the table'. Ralph was one of those who spent much of his time working hard to get signatures to the Archbishop's petition from prominent people, especially writers, and was joined in this by Gerald, Leonard and Virginia, Osbert Sitwell, Desmond MacCarthy and others. But of course we also had friends among those who were violently against the strikers, and among them were some young men who eagerly volunteered to drive buses and trains, which they did to the grave danger of the population, for quite a few bricks were thrown at the buses by the strikers, whereas amateur train-driving involved Ralph and me in the only railway-accident of our lives.

Returning from a weekend with the Garnetts on the Cambridge line, we stopped as usual at Audley End, where I noticed a vague young man with hair and tie flying, obviously an undergraduate, leaning well out of the signal-box and having an agreeable chat with the driver of our train. Suddenly there was a deafening crash and all the suit-cases fell off the racks among us. I was extremely frightened, particularly because for some unknown reason I imagined this was only a preliminary and the real crash was about to follow. 'We must get out,' I thought, with the panic reaction of a rat in a trap. As all those in our carriage jumped on to the platform, shouts of "Doctor!!" went up, and several old people turned faint and were helped to seats, while an extraordinary sight met our eyes. A second train, evidently ignored by the amateur signalman, had come charging into the station and clambered on top of ours, so that the two of them looked like animals copulating. In so doing it had knocked down the pretty Victorian canopy trimmed with wooden scallops that made a roof over the platform. Three people were killed, one being the driver of the second train and another someone who was waiting in the station. I was not at all proud of my lack of physical courage; had there been bleeding casualties—as fortunately there were not—I should have been of little use to them. Moreover, the moment in which I was beset with 'rat-in-the-trap' feelings had bitten deeply into my psyche, and left me for several years with claustrophobia, which I had had no trace of before. It was as if a demon had been let out of my unconscious; the underground, formerly my favourite method of travel, now became torture, and long tunnels on the railway almost worse.

Now that we were living in the geographical centre of Bloomsbury we naturally spent much of our free time among its denizens. It was a joy to have James and Alix under the same roof, and we very often ended the evening either in their room or ours, talking of everything from parties to psycho-analysis, or listening to some of their marvellous gramophone records. A new friend was Adrian Stephen, whose immensely tall lean figure was often to be seen loping round Gordon Square, sometimes accompanied by his clever, deaf wife, Karin. I was reminded of him as I wrote about our railway accident and the shouts of "Doctor!!", because he once told me that on the very day he had gained his medical degree (in order to practise psycho-analysis) he went to the cinema, and it so happened that an urgent voice from the door interrupted the film with a cry of, "Is there a doctor in the house?" "Like a fool I said 'yes', said Adrian. "However," and here he gave his characteristic laugh— long, melodious and ironical—"there wasn't much I could do. I was confronted by a man who had been run over—and his head cut off!" Adrian's striking face with its rather haunted expression might have been that of an eminent philosopher or scientist. In fact he liked girls, enjoyed parties, and had a very dry sense of humour.

My old ally Julia Strachey had also now come back into my life, and was never to leave it until her death. Certainly she was outwardly a very different Julia from the little girl of our confabulations in the hayloft at Hindhead, or the jazz-player at Bedales: slim as a sapling, with long elegant legs, an Eton crop and an eye to fashion (she had in fact worked for a while as model for a couturier in Paris), yet the outer gloss of sophistication did not disguise the originality and eccentricity that modulated her every word and action, the movements of her hands ('they seem to have a life of their own', her charwoman said to me) nor her absorption in details (she would watch a kitten's antics for hours with hoots of laughter and eyes narrowing to sea-blue slits, as intensely as if she was inwardly describing them in words—as no doubt she was). True, her fastidiousness made her a difficult guest. Nothing was ever quite right; she was always rather too hot or too cold, or wondering 'whether you happen to have such a thing as a pair of curling-tongs anywhere about'. She offended Ralph bitterly once by saying, 'If Ham Spray were mine I should sell it!' (It *was* a cold house in winter.) And reduced me to tears by telling me I ought to take much more trouble with my appearance. Nevertheless, she repaid our efforts to please her a thousandfold by her appreciation when we succeeded, and by the ever-surprising entertainment her company provided, whether we did or not. Moreover, I have realised, now that she is dead, that a very early friend is more than a mere influence; she is in a sense a part of one; she has provided some of the ingredients in the cake that has become one's self, for good or ill—in other words a self is not a discrete entity but has a permeable shell like that of an egg, and its very yolk and white are infiltrated by the personalities of early friends.

So Ralph and I settled into our life together, and for me it was also the change from a single to a double life, than which there is no greater. Meanwhile, Ralph was working at a translation, while I still went daily to the bookshop, though it was less enjoyable now that both Birrell and Garnett had left it. Instead our two partners—both very scholarly characters—were clever, uncharming, Communist Graham Pollard, and clever, kind but somewhat uncommunicative Jane Norton.

Ralph had more knowledge of housekeeping and cooking than I had, nor can I boast of being quick to learn. It was he who instructed Mabel, the frightened middle-aged spinster who came to 'do for us', making breakfast and even returning to cook excellent but very English meals in the evenings, so that we were able to ask our friends to dinner. That first summer we had been invited to dine with the 'Woolves', and some weeks later we asked them back, in a good deal of fear and trembling. The evening was not a great success. After dinner James, Alix and Julia joined us, and Virginia, who was not in her most genial mood, launched one of her frequent attacks on 'the younger generation', going on to say: "And I know all about you, Alix. You simply spend your whole time dancing, and sink further into imbecility every moment." It was true that Alix had fallen for the prevailing craze, but it in no way flawed her excellent brain, and when the conversation became a duel of wits between her and Virginia it was she who set the tone and plotted a course that even embraced psycho-analysis. Virginia got the worst of it, as she never would have done on her own ground; and as they left Leonard said, "Come on, Virginia, don't disgrace the older generation."

Ralph and I spent two or three weekends at Ham Spray together every month, and Ralph sometimes went there for a day or two without me. A further link was forged between Gordon Square and Ham Spray when in 1927 Lytton rented the ground-floor front of 41, as a *pied-à-terre* for his London visits, sharing our extraordinary airless dungeon of a bathroom, in which I once surprised him drying himself, pink and feminine beneath the dark beard. There was relief on all sides, I believe, to find that things were going so smoothly—Carrington saw that Lytton showed no signs of deserting her, nor Ralph of withdrawing his interest and support. Of course there were a few difficulties to surmount but much good will went to resolve them, and I am convinced that a great deal of happiness for all was salvaged by this unconventional solution of what had for a while appeared an insoluble problem. But perhaps this needs further expansion. Anyone who grew up in the Twenties will remember that it was highly unusual for a girl belonging to the professional class to live in 'open sin' with a married man.

In my opinion there is little more to be said for convention than there is for fashion. Perhaps even rather less, for though fashion may be chiefly a device to help dress-designers and clothes-shops make a living, it also provides its devotees with variety and change, titillation of their visual appetites, and a way of expressing original invention within a fixed form—just as can be done by writing a poem in the sonnet-form, a brilliant metaphor I owe to my friend Eardley Knollys.

But *social* conventions (as distinct from laws and rules of the road, for instance) have always seemed to me a means of avoiding thinking out one's own values, and clinging blindly to the security of being like other people—a process that starts among the snake-belts of prep. school or even earlier, and ends in Jennifer's Diary.

There they are, however, standing four-square like the monoliths of Stonehenge, and no-one can be unaware when they are flouting them. There is the family for one thing. Obviously my mother would have preferred us to get married after a divorce—already an accepted convention, whose only drawback was said to be that 'it prevented one going to the Royal Enclosure at Ascot'. Yet when I explained the position to her she accepted it valiantly. Parents love to be able to boast to other parents how well their children are 'doing'; I had denied her this pleasure and I was genuinely sorry. She had, I think, expected me to marry one of the eligible suitors who used to call to take me out. Oddly enough, a far more knotty problem was provided by old Nan, who was still living at Brunswick Square, though she had become even tinier with age and was sadly affected with *tic douloureux*, which caused her to rock her poor little head between her hands in agony. It was unthinkable for her to be told the true facts. What would Gentle Jesus say? So for her benefit alone a secret marriage was invented, and I was dismayed to be woken on my 'wedding morning' with tears and six tea-spoons. Fortunately my mother became extremely fond of Ralph, as he did of her.

When I try to dive into my own feelings at the time, about the ambiguity of my position, and as honestly as possible, I come up first of all with the conviction that I never for a moment thought it showed lack of love on Ralph's part. We were too happy in our mutual devotion to consider that. Nor was I much bothered by what someone has aptly called 'all that Charley's Aunt business'—confusion about names with servants, in hotels, staying with friends for the weekend and so forth. It was at worst a nuisance, and I think it splendid that so many of the young no longer bother about such things, any more than modern children do about asking the way to the W.C. in other people's houses, something that caused me tortuous embarrassment as a little girl.

No; there were two real difficulties that had to be surmounted. The first of course was Ham Spray. I loved the place; in different ways I loved both Lytton and Carrington, but I could never feel towards it and them *exactly* as Ralph did; and—more important (for naturally one of us might like treacle tart and the other detest it), it was an area which could not be spoken of between us totally without reserves. Very nearly indeed, but not totally. The trouble was that I had no actual share in Ham Spray. Much as I usually enjoyed my visits there with Ralph, I was in an ambiguous position—I was neither guest nor host—though there were many times when there was no shadow on the general happiness, there were others when I feared my presence was resented. As it was. In November 1928 Lytton took the step of writing to Ralph suggesting that he spent more time at Ham Spray without me. If Lytton supposed that Ralph wouldn't show me the letter he betrayed unusual lack of understanding of his character. Of course he did, and it was the only occasion I have seen him really furiously angry with Lytton. They talked it over, however, and things went on much as before, except that Ralph and I both stayed away from Ham Spray rather more.

I must say again that not only did I always respect Ralph's loyalty to Lytton and Carrington, but it was part of what I most loved about him: the permanence of his affections, the fact that he was so reliable, positive and constructive. (I hope that doesn't make him sound dull, for he certainly was not.) I have said elsewhere that he couldn't bear deviousness or destructiveness; as for the latter, I remember him exclaiming in horrified amazement when some young man had blacked his girl's eye, and saying that he had never felt the least impulse to hit anyone since he became an adult. This is probably also true of many of his contemporaries, such as Gerald; for 'battering' of babies, wives and lovers is, I believe, a development of more recent times—among the educated classes at least. Nor does unconventionality mean lack of manners—at any rate the important variety which depends on being sensitive to other people's wants. Ralph also had one or two conventions of his own. For instance, when he was carving a joint he refused to serve people with titles before those without, or married women before spinsters: the only criterion he acknowledged was age.

The second drawback to my ambiguous situation was that it prevented my having a child. I was quite unaware of it at the time, but I now feel sure that a mysterious illness of mine which lasted for several months at the beginning of 1929 was partly due to my suppression of my maternal instincts—and possibly also to Lytton's letter.

Yet another 'side-effect' will be noticed from the extracts from my diary: we were not always asked out together. I quite often dined or lunched with some of my men friends—such as Clive, Leo Myers, Phil Nichols, Oliver Strachey—some of whom showed that they thought of me still as a bachelor girl. But I didn't consider myself as one, and am pleased and proud to think that I lost the friendship of none of them when I convinced them of the fact.

Part Two

CHAPTER NINE

The Plateau

THE PATH TO maturity follows an eventful contour, over hills and into valleys, but there are times in most lives when it reaches a level space—a peaceful alpine meadow with flowers in the luscious grass and a chalet or two. And it may well debouch onto a plateau such as Ralph and I seemed now to have attained, for five years were to pass before any momentous change took place in our lives. A happy marriage has no history worth mentioning, or—as Alexander Herzen said of History—'no libretto'. But at about this time I fell into the habit of spasmodically scribbling notes in a journal, and I therefore propose to let extracts from these take over the thread of my story for a while.

By way of prologue, however, I shall dip a spoon into the ordinary current of the days we spent at Ham Spray. One evening after dinner, as a change from paper games or poker, Lytton read us his account of a day spent at Charleston, and afterwards someone suggested that everybody present should write down what they could remember of the day that was just ending, though our accounts were not to be shown until at least a year later. What happened to the other efforts I do not know, or indeed whether they were ever written. My own turned up recently among some papers.

One day at Ham Spray, May, 1927

From my fourposter bed in the Pink Room I heard Carrington's voice calling "Breakfast!" I had shockingly overslept, as I so often did when soothing farmyard noises took the place of the London racket and the struggle to get to the bookshop. Framed by the green and white posts and yellow curtains of my bed I saw the large square window beyond, with the branches of the pollarded aspens whipping across it diagonally, trimmed with their fluttering leaves. Every few minutes the sun came from behind a cloud, and lit them like footlights. As I slowly toppled out of bed I remembered my dream—about being in a complicated sort of train which demonstrated a new law of Nature: that it was possible to go in two different directions at the same time. My train was going both to Oxford and to Cambridge—this seemed profoundly significant. I must tell Ralph. He came in at this moment, and we talked for a little about Julia and Tommy and the prospects for their love affair, also Carrington's with Gerald; and wondered why lovers were so bad at adaptation to each other's natures, yet always expected it themselves.

Ralph said: "No-one can alter his or her character." And I: "Possibly not, but they can sometimes modify their behaviour."

I went along to the bathroom where I found Julia in a mauve silk dressing-gown. She frowned at herself in the glass: "Tut-tut, my hair—it looks just like a slum child's."

Breakfast was on the verandah, and the sun shone down brightly on the table round which sat Lytton, Alix and Tommy, discussing Virginia's new book,* especially her attitude to reality. Lytton and Alix complained that her characters weren't solid and her psychology inadequate. Tommy said, acutely I thought, that she dealt with people and with things in the same way:

"She shows her genius in her manner of describing a garden, for instance, by making you know exactly what you would feel if you were in it, with the gap over the red-hot-pokers and so on." And I added: "Yes, and it's the same with people. She doesn't delve into their motives, but shows you what it would be like to be in Mr Ramsay's company."

Julia had come down now, put up a small sunshade and was looking elegantly down her nose from under it. I thought

* *To the Lighthouse.*

about our days as children at Hindhead, and remembered the quality of our early friendship very vividly.

During the morning some of us played badminton, while Carrington was bent double putting plants in the long border, and Tommy and Lytton were deep in conversation in two deck-chairs. I wondered if Julia felt jealous; she would never hear about it later, as I would have with Ralph; Tommy is much too secretive. But now we had all collected for sherry.

Alix and Tommy love arguing, and their subject during lunch was Greed. Julia nudged my knee. "Don't you remember what I told you when we were walking under the trees yesterday?" Yes, I did. She told me how she and Tommy had quarrelled fiercely in Paris* sometimes, over food of all things.

There was a dish of spring onions on the table. Julia said suddenly: "What are those little long things some people have got?" Carrington: "Those mean they are males, dear. Ask Tommy if he'll lend you his." Julia: "Oh no, not unless I'm offered."

After lunch Lytton climbed slowly and thoughtfully upstairs to bed, while Ralph, Carrington and I started walking down to fetch Belle.† A gale was roaring softly among the topmost branches of the tall wych elms in the avenue, and we could only hear each other speak by shouting like sailors in a storm. When we reached the field Carrington ran off calling, "Belle! Belle!", jumped on her back and made off at a gallop towards the downs. Ralph and I walked after her, arm in arm, and then spread a coat on the grass and sat down among the pink and yellow spring flowers. We returned to a subject we had talked about last night in bed—modesty about facts, and how the desire to conceal facts is matched by a contrary impulse to reveal them. Lots of people are modest about facts —both Carrington and Julia for instance. Even Ralph has some little patches. "I mind people I don't like knowing

---

* They lived together there for a while before marrying.
† Carrington's white pony.

things about me," he said. I thought one should keep revelations in their proper order, never telling a person something one would keep from someone more intimate—not that one often does so except out of embarrassment. It is only a rider, I think, to my belief that it is important for feelings and behaviour to correspond. 'And what do I keep from Ralph?' I wondered. 'An infinitesimal amount, but what is it?' I began telling him about a conversation I had had with Clive concerning jealousy.

Returning we saw Lytton and Carrington on the lawn. Tea was ready. . . . Now it was over and Tommy was standing with his back to the fireplace talking to Julia and me. He couldn't fail to be aware that Lytton was putting on his outdoor shoes, in obvious hope of a walk with him. This he does in a way all his own. He puts each shoe down with great care just in front of the foot to which it belongs, and then slips it gently in, obviously enjoying the process. Tommy was manifesting his inveterate passion for being in demand by more than one person at once, and I remembered that Ralph told me how Lytton had confessed to having put a love letter under what he believed to be Tommy's door. But not till Julia had left the room did Lytton say in a peculiarly mild voice, "Do you feel like a little walk?" They set off, and as Ralph and Carrington were driving Alix home, Julia and I were left alone together, discussing whether she would look for a job or not. She was nowhere nearer a decision.

"Swallowcliffe is definitely impossible unless Tommy and I are married—but I shouldn't be surprised if we do get married." "No. Nor should I," I said somewhat untruthfully. I don't believe she is really in love with Tommy, but it might rescue her from what she fears may be an unhappy future, and so make her happier. If only Tommy weren't so neurotic and alarmingly destructive, but of course he's extremely intelligent, and this weekend he has been sane and charming.

I plunged into my book, which was *Astarte*,* and the outer

* By the Earl of Lovelace.

world grew dim beside Byron, Augusta and Lady B. I longed to go on with it after dinner. 'Oh, how I hope there's no reading aloud,' I thought, and just then Carrington said in her most coaxing tone, "Lytton, would you read to us, do you think?" Lytton screwed his face into a grimace and his mouth silently framed "No" several times. 'Hope still,' I thought. "Do." Everyone was pressing him but still he hesitated. "I can't think what to read." All was lost, he was taking down a volume of Shakespeare from the shelf. He started on a Falstaff scene in rather an unconvincing manner. I put down *Astarte* and began mending my dressing-gown. Bit by bit I found myself melting. Falstaff's charm was working on me. I laughed aloud at a joke; I was enjoying myself. Was Lytton really reading much better? And what a delightful character Pistol was. Lytton was picking scenes from here and there, and reading with gusto, his voice now deep and rich as velvet, now soaring to near treble, while all the time his long elegant left hand made pouncing movements in the air. Now Falstaff was dying, 'his nose as sharp as a pen'. The reading was over. Ralph, who had had the kitten on his lap, got up hurriedly and left the room, with a dark stain on his coat. "POOR little puss," murmured Carrington, "he didn't dare ask to be excused."

The curtains hadn't been drawn; it was pitch black outside. We drifted off to bed, but I felt wide awake and longing to talk about Byron. Ralph came in yawning and I saw he would be asleep in a moment. Aware it was cruel to hold him back from oblivion, I yet couldn't resist getting him to listen to what I was longing to tell and even to ask a few questions. "You're just like an electric hare," he said, "off with a whizz down every side-track." And then an ordinary but happy day ended in sleep.

Why did I start writing a diary? What makes any one do such a thing? The desire to pin down or preserve happiness, one might say, except that it is often in times of misery or stress that one rushes to confide in it. It is a form of talking to oneself of course—but here was I for the first time living with a loved and loving companion who liked nothing better than exchanging thoughts, for whom it was as vital a necessity as it was for me— even more so. Nor was it a propitious moment, since my days had never before been so full. Besides my working hours spent at the bookshop, and my new absorbing companionship, I now had for the first time in my life the ordinary household pre-occupations of running a flat and entertaining friends at home, instead of conducting my social life in restaurants as I had previously. Who bought the bacon, the butter, the fish? I suspect it was our faithful Mabel. I certainly have no recollection of doing it myself.

Their casual, if spontaneous, nature makes it plain that I had little time to spare for these jottings, and at times they stopped altogether; but I hope they may give some idea of the texture, as it were, of our daily existence during the next few years.

DIARY 1927-8

October 31st. London. Ralph, Carrington and I went to hear Roger [Fry] lecture on Cézanne. On the way home, Virginia and Leonard overtook us, and as we walked along Carrington invited them down to Ham Spray. Virginia: "Ah, but do you know if you *may* ask us, Carrington: hadn't you better ask the old man?" It was ungraciously, or rather maliciously said, as if to relegate Carrington to her position as Lytton's house-keeper—instead of the mistress of the house. Leonard was meanwhile complaining to me that Birrell and Garnett didn't order enough Hogarth Press books.

Lionel [Penrose]* came to dinner, running upstairs with his arms full of books and macintoshes. Throughout the meal he entertained us with medical anecdotes, tilting his chair at an alarming angle and laughing on an indrawn breath. Later he expounded a chess match between Capablanca and Halekin for our benefit. After he had gone Ralph and I agreed that he

* Later Galton Professor of Genetics, F.R.S., etc.

was one of the most lovable as well as brilliantly intelligent of our friends, and Ralph said he had felt so warmly towards him that his hand more than once moved forwards involuntarily to pat him, but he withdrew it for fear of disconcerting him. We tried to analyse what makes him so attractive, for one doesn't feel drawn to people just because they are brilliantly clever. High spirits and enjoyment, we decided, modesty, inventiveness, and a great sense of comedy. Not long ago we dined with him and Margaret, a duck being the *pièce de résistance*—in more senses than one, for as Lionel stabbed it with the carvers it shot off the plate and the table, and literally bounced on the floor. He wasn't a bit put out, burst into infectious roars of laughter, and said, "It was a present from a grateful patient!" Of course it was quite inedible.

November 2nd. To Frank and Lettice Ramsey's at Cambridge. As with many great men (and I am sure he is one) Frank is outwardly simple and unself-conscious. His tall, ungainly frame becomes somewhat thicker at the hips; his broad Slavonic face always seems ready to crack into a wide smile, and his fine, rapidly vanishing hair floats in wayward strands around his impressive cranium. He's intensely musical, and has a passion for listening to records of chamber music, especially Beethoven's last quartets. It is very difficult to imagine what sort of processes are going on in so brilliant a mind as Frank's, or even how much of the time he is pre-occupied by abstract ideas. He comes down to earth, however, with a satisfying bump, and earth is certainly the natural element of my old friend Lettice. But the effect of these two co-existent planes on which the Ramseys' lives are conducted is that there are long pauses in the conversation; nor do I think they are altogether confident about entertaining their friends.

November 7th. Read Hickey's Memoirs in the train to London. Getting home that evening after work I found Ralph sitting by the fire, and the black kitten capering about the room.

Even so short a separation leaves us with frustratingly much to tell each other.

I am infinitely grateful to Ralph for the way he has patiently worn down the invisible walls of reserve with which I have surrounded myself for so long. He believes passionately in mental intimacy between great friends and still more between lovers, and thinks the chief obstacle to it is pride. "I was once as proud as Lucifer," he said today, "and much good it did me." I don't know what can have been the source of his great gift for communication; he certainly didn't get it from his parents, nor indeed from either Lytton or Carrington—Lytton because he is shy, Carrington because of her love of privacy.

Another of Roger's lectures; there was some tension in the air as Carrington and Gerald were avoiding each other, and I was avoiding Hamish. The lecture was interesting, and started several hares which we followed up with Gerald and Alec [Penrose] on the way to Alec's room, where we sat austerely drinking water from large goblets. From painting we moved on to books, and discussed which books we read with most pleasure as distinct from thinking them the best. And why. Alec is down on Proust for 'being so preoccupied with sex', and on Cézanne because 'he distorts the human body'—his Quaker background clearly emerging.

Alec was the eldest of the four Penrose brothers—the others being the brilliant Lionel, Roland (painter, authority on Picasso, knighted for his services to art) and Bernard (always known as Beakus, who took to the sea and was later beloved of Carrington). All of them had charm. Alec had been more affected than the others by their strict Quaker upbringing; his mother must have been an extremely formidable woman, and there was a tight family network embracing several long-lived great-aunts with names like Aunt Algerina and Aunt Hannah-Maria. He had been badly disturbed by his short spell of service in the First War; though he never described his experiences to Ralph and me in detail he made no bones about the fact that he had found his courage wanting. Another source of discontent was that he had accidentally discovered that he could have inherited his grandfather's barony, had a suitable sum of money been forthcoming. "Just think! I might have been Lord Peckover of Wisbech!" he said to us once, puffing out his chest and laughing at himself at the same time.

Tall, with an unusually square head and deepset eyes rather too close together, he was not as clever as Lionel or Roland, but possessed equal charm and humour, as well as various talents such as writing unexpectedly accomplished poetry and producing plays (including Lytton's *Son of Heaven* at the Scala Theatre). He made many devoted friends at Cambridge and afterwards, but he was not a very happy man, and this—whatever the cause, Quakerism, the War or a missed title—drove him to seek help from Freudian and Jungian analysis, the Church of England and Roman Catholicism in turn. In 1927 he had been divorced from his first wife and was moving towards marriage with his second, an Old Bedales friend of mine called Frances Saxon.

November 9th. A conversation over our breakfast about sentimentality, starting from Wyndham Lewis's definition: 'Not pursuing things to their logical conclusions'. I think of it rather as some form of falsification, whose purpose might be protection against seeing into the dark recesses of one's true motives. When people are sentimental about death or disaster it's hard to resist the impression that they are at some level actually *enjoying* them, and quite often a ghoulish gleam comes into their eyes. Or just think of the crowds who rush to a street accident, like wasps to jam. Sentimentality allows them to feel how sensitive they are to human suffering. So that it might be said to come from failure of a special kind of courage—the courage to face the disagreeable elements in one's own character.

To the bookshop all day as usual, punctuated by a delightful lunch with Ralph, and being taken out for a cup of tea by Gerald. He is preoccupied by Vera Birch at present, and her influence has been to stress the romantic, quixotic side of his character, to which a slightly absurd effect is given by a thin Kensingtonian varnish brushed over the top.

Glad to get home to a hot fire and an evening alone with Ralph and the black kitten.

November 10th. Lunch with Leo [Myers] who arrived at the shop in a jaunty frame of mind. He had been drinking cocktails with Princess Bibesco, who questioned him about me. I longed to tell him—but didn't—that Lytton and Carrington had driven several miles in a taxi from Paddington behind him and the Bibesco, and watched the swanlike movement with which he bent and kissed the back of her neck.

We lunched at the Basque, off oysters, a melting chicken and pears in chocolate sauce. Our talk ranged over a great many subjects, beginning with a complete history of his *amitié amoureuse* (for it is not properly speaking a love affair) with Elizabeth Bibesco. His feelings for her are a bundle of opposites: he is fond of her, admires her generosity and impetuosity, is dreadfully exhausted by her, and will be relieved to see her go back to France. Perhaps the snobbism he admits to so freely is faintly titillated, and I'm sure it has done him good to have his over-cautious nature subjected to her recklessness and egotism. He says that in spite of all her affairs she is technically faithful to her husband. Then he told me what his friends say about me: "Oh, Frances Marshall, yes, isn't that the girl who went to live with Ralph Partridge? *What* a pity! So dreadful for her parents." They go on to imply that Ralph is a cad and I an infatuated idiot, but what really shocks them most is that we visit Ham Spray together. We ended up with Philosophy, Whitehead and mysticism. I do enjoy a talk with Leo; he is a fascinating companion.

We expected Dadie and Gerald at 41 about ten o'clock, and I had oysters for them and cold partridges in aspic. I started telling Ralph that Hamish had rung up yesterday and asked me to dine, and was about to ask his advice about how to treat rejected lovers, when I saw he was upset, and refrained.

Immediately afterwards Gerald and Dadie arrived. Gerald had just finished reading Maeterlinck's *Vie des Termites* and could talk of nothing else, imitating the dances of the Termites with the greatest animation and in a highly comical way.

Leo Myers was a very intelligent and original character; cynic, sybarite, mystic by turns, he had converted what he had intended to be a love-affair with me into a 'cool' friendship without apparent rancour. We lunched out fairly often at the most sumptuous restaurants (he adored good food and wine, but was not afraid to order tinned asparagus when fresh was in season, saying he preferred it). Our conversation was very often about 'general ideas' or philosophy, and I believe the respect and admiration I felt for him was reciprocated. We also amused each other. Towards the end of his life he became a Communist. Once when lunching at Claridges I couldn't help commenting on the contrast between our surroundings (oozing money and privilege) with the theories he was propounding. "Yes, I know," he said, "but that has absolutely no bearing on their validity." With which of course I was forced to agree.

November 11th. Exquisitely beautiful day. Ralph came early to the bookshop to fetch me out to lunch, because he felt depressed and wanted to see me. Touched by this, I did my best to cheer him up. We lunched in an Indian restaurant off delicious curries and almost too-sweet puddings. "I bring golobjumon (?) and rubberee-de-luxe," the waiter announced, appearing at a gallop from the dark recesses of the restaurant.

November 12th. Arrived at Ham Spray with the black kitten. Roger Senhouse the only visitor. Lytton seems very much in love with him, and Philip Ritchie's death* has, I think, in some way brought them together. Roger was amiable and complacent, and the effect on Lytton was to make him very gay and charming; he was peculiarly nice to me all the week-

* After a tonsilectomy.

end. Walked in the fields while Carrington galloped about
on Belle. In the evening we let off some fireworks—an
exquisite display of pink and green fountains under the
pampas grass. Began reading Hume's *History of the Tudors*,
and finished the reign of Henry VIII.

Sunday was absolutely still, warm and sunny enough for us
all to sit out on the verandah. A walk on the downs in the
morning. I got onto Belle's back, remembering in theory how
to ride, but only dimly with my body, and slipping about on
the saddle.

Lytton had a wire from Allen and Unwin today, asking
him to edit a complete edition of the Greville Diaries, and
the evening was given up to going over and checking the old
editions. A very happy weekend.

November 16th. Dined at the MacCarthys'. There were Molly,
Rachel, and Michael, just back from South Africa, tanned
brick red and talking explosively; also Gerald and us. I first
noticed tension between Ralph and Gerald when Gerald
violently attacked James and Alix for being negative and dim,
of all things. Ralph flared up in their defence, and as the three
of us took a taxi home the atmosphere was still electric.

November 18th. Lunched at Vera Birch's. John Hayward was
there; Vera seemed on her guard. Gerald came into the bookshop afterwards, clearly wanting to talk about Vera and
pump me about lunch. He said, "But don't tell Carrington
about Vera. I don't want her to know. She's no right to."
When I told Ralph this, all his bottled hostility to Gerald left
over from yesterday burst out in an instant. I realise that he
thinks I 'take sides' with Gerald in the Carrington–Gerald
imbroglio. How I *hate* the taking of sides in love affairs! I
assured him I took sides with neither, but felt sorry for both
because they make each other so unhappy, and possibly
Gerald is the unhappier of the two. Ralph is more moral than
I am about it all—I certainly don't look on their present
troubles as the fault of either. But though Ralph can easily be

irritated by Gerald, he is deeply fond of him, and sympathises with his unhappiness.

November 19th. Ham Spray, with Raymond and Roger Senhouse. Soaking rain fell all Sunday and we couldn't stir outside. Lytton and Roger were each reading a copy of my Hume, and there was none left for me; as they discussed it I felt tantalised and thwarted. Chess, paper games. At dinner an absurd conversation as to what point must be reached for a woman to be obliged to go to bed with a man, or else give him a perfect right to be furious. Ralph said a hand on the private parts; Carrington a hand on the knee; Lytton "No, no, a kiss—no—a dinner tête-à-tête!"

On Monday I travelled up with Raymond into a London dark with fog, and later lunched with him.

Dined with Clive, who was dressed in purple sponge-cloth with black frogs. Champagne, compliments and confidences, but the style was rather above my head.

November 24th. Ralph's birthday. Rachel MacCarthy to lunch with us. Cyril Connolly has been told by someone how badly he behaves about money, and indeed he used to take poor Rachel out to grand restaurants, order the most expensive dishes, and then suddenly find he had forgotten his wallet. Now he takes every opportunity of paying for Rachel in public, saying in his flat voice: "Oh no, I'll pay, or Desmond'll be complaining."

We went with Alec [Penrose] to the Ivy for dinner as a birthday treat, sole, *canard sous presse* and *crêpe suzette*. Afterwards we went back to Alec's rooms, and sat over the fire, sipping tea and talking about language and dreams.

November 26th. Only Lytton and Carrington at Ham Spray for the weekend and Lytton very busy writing. There is a new volume of Proust out—*Temps Retrouvé*. On Sunday Clive arrived, bringing pheasants, very genial, but I deduced from his manner to me that he hadn't thought our evening together was a great success. He threw out hints about journeys he planned to take to Germany and Italy with fascinating female companions, but after much mystery inadvertently let out that the German one was Raymond!

November 29th. I invited Vera Birch to lunch, and then (seized with sudden panic) I rang up and asked Gerald too, but I wished afterwards I hadn't. She might conceivably have liked to talk to me alone. She looked bloomingly lovely and young, but was not at her ease with the two of us, nor did Gerald appear to best advantage.

November 30th. Gerald came to the shop with a bouquet of dead red carnations for me, and we went across to Le Grain's coffee-shop together. He told me Vera thought yesterday's lunch was a plot, and in fact I got a letter from her the same evening to the same effect. He declares he gets on better with her every day. Ralph thinks that Gerald has specially chosen Vera to try and marry because he knows it is impossible.

Clive took me to *The Marriage of Figaro*. We got on better than last time, because he didn't feel it necessary to talk only of love affairs, but also about books, music and life in general. I was anxious to show I was enjoying myself, and so indeed I was, though our slow parade across the front of the stalls, stopping to see if there was anyone we knew or who knew us was not exactly to my taste. Afterwards we glided back to Gordon Square in a hired Daimler, for supper and talk. Clive said he thought one's most important aim should be to experience as many emotions as intensely as possible, but a person was lucky if he achieved one a month. I agreed with him in principle, but suggested that that was a small allowance. He often uttered some admirable generalisation, such as "Never ask a sacrifice of one you love," but when I wanted to pursue the subject would say something like "Now we're getting into too deep philosophical waters"—and so the conversation inevitably switched to a more personal note. He told me that at present he felt he was in a position of perfect safety, nothing could shake him. 'What amazing self-confidence,' I thought, and admitted that the same wasn't true of me; whereupon he shook his head knowingly, warning me of course of the dangers of my position. We parted on the best of terms, however.

December 5th. Quiet evening alone with Ralph, playing chess. We were in the middle of a game when Gerald dropped in on us. The mere possibility that Vera might be going to respond to his advances had produced a perverse volte-face. He "wasn't really in love with her, and wouldn't marry her except on very definite conditions, and if she was in love with him".

I am seriously thinking of giving up the bookshop, and consulted Ralph about the possibility. Among other items of gossip, Gerald told us that Clive had boasted to Vanessa of his 'certain success' with me in the future, also that Leonard and Virginia were going to try and get me as well as Frankie into the Hogarth Press.

December 21st. Yesterday, after deep thought, I screwed myself up to the point of telling Jane [Norton] that I wanted to leave the bookshop. She said: "Oh Frances, I was afraid you did. I rather thought you'd been getting the shop on your nerves lately." I tried to explain how much I longed for more leisure: but what, I wonder, will leisure be like? My hours between 9 and 6 have been accounted for during so many years now that the idea of freedom is almost alarming. Moreover I tremble at the thought of disturbing the equilibrium of the last few months, which have been as happy as any in my life.

It was the night of Maynard and Lydia's Christmas party, and I got back to 41 to find Julia and Carrington sitting over the fire discussing what they were to wear for it. When we arrived the room was still sparsely filled. Feeling like a very small boat pushing out into a large sea, I made for the nearest familiar island, which proved to be Adrian [Stephen]. He was wearing tails, and said with a white staring face: "I've just had to go home. I'd been here some time when I put my hand to my neck and found I had no tie on." Next I talked to Maynard, who was looking like a benign Pasha; Roger Fry wanted to discuss chess, and a little later a group collected round the fire—Raymond, Clive, Frankie, Peter Lucas and myself. Frankie and I plunged arm-in-arm into the supper room, and found a place next to Lydia, who with a flushed and shiny face was screeching into the ear of Mrs Courtauld. Roger Senhouse came and sat on my other side, and we drank champagne and became very jolly. Frankie told me, as a dead secret, that he had been offered a partnership in the Hogarth Press by the Woolves. He was pathetically anxious to think that he would fare better than all his predecessors, and I hadn't the heart to be as damping as I felt.

Upstairs the entertainment was about to begin. Ralph and I sat down between Sheelah Clutton-Brook and Ottoline. The performances were amusing, especially one by Duncan as Caruso, but the cold was intense, and we soon moved off to Dadie's flat at No .37, where a subsidiary party had got under way. The Bell boys,* both in dinner jackets far too large for them and both very tipsy, were laughing and shouting at each other deafeningly across the room. Rachel, who had taken part in the performance in a lovely Victorian dress, sat like a queen receiving adulation and delighted by her success. Molly was also receiving compliments. Tommy in particular was laying them on with his customary trowel: "Ah Molly, you don't know what a difference it makes just to *know* you're there in Wellington Square. Weeks may pass when we don't come and see you, but . . ." and so on. Molly cocked her head like a wise bird, but I don't think she was taken in. I had a tragi-comic exchange with Dadie about the horrors of life, and getting old (he can't be more than twenty-five) and how the Cambridge undergraduates looked on him as 'an old fogey'. During the evening a rumour was circulated, and

---

* Julian and Quentin.

afterwards confirmed that Raymond was engaged to the actress, Valerie Taylor.

If such a condition exists, as I believe it does, Stephen Tomlin was a case of dual personality. One side of his character was creatively gifted, charming and sensitive; the other was dominated by a destructive impulse (fuelled probably by deep neurotic despair) whose effect was that he couldn't see two people happy together without being impelled to intervene and take one away, leaving the other bereft. Or it would take the form of a direct bid for power over others—whether male or female, for he was bi-sexual—which he was well-equipped to exert. The sequel would be a fit of suicidal depression and guilt-feelings. The two sides of his personality were fused together as it were by an excellent brain inherited from his father the judge (Lord Tomlin), shown in his enjoyment of arguments with a distinctly legal flavour. He broke several hearts, but certainly gave more happiness than the reverse and had many loyal friends; if one could forget his darker side he was an interesting and even enchanting companion. Personally I did forget it most of the time, although on the rare occasions he switched on his charm for my benefit I found it unconvincing; but to Ralph the destructive element was anathema, and when Tommy revealed it he reacted with irritation—even dislike.

Tommy was on the short side, squarely built, with a large head set on a short neck. He had the striking profile of a Roman emperor on a coin, fair straight hair brushed back from a fine forehead, a pale face and grey eyes.

Christmas weekend. Took the evening train to Hungerford with Julia and Tommy.* I was lowered by a heavy cold; Ralph was feeling unfriendly to Tommy. The weekend began well enough, however. On Saturday James arrived, and Julia and Tommy—apparently devoted to each other— came down to breakfast just before lunch and walked about

* They were married in July.

enlaced. Marriage has altered Julia's slim and elegant outline
to that of a stately seal poised on a rock at the Zoo. She is
absorbed in household matters, furniture and cookery, stuffs
and servants; but to Carrington she is a romantic princess,
whose every remark is applauded and whose every demand
she hurries to carry out—and there are plenty of them.

On Monday night there was a heavy fall of snow, trans-
forming the garden to a pantomime scene of exquisite beauty
and leaving ditches and lanes brimful of drifts edged with
extraordinary shapes—columns, mushrooms and pagodas.
But something seemed wrong with us all. Conversation was
unreal and inconsecutive; strings of fanciful projects produced
half-hearted bursts of laughter. Or was the whole thing, I
asked myself, entirely subjective?

Next morning a brilliant sun was shining on the snow, and
a transparent blue sky without a cloud stretched from horizon
to horizon. Surely any psychological cloud should have disappeared, melted by so much beauty? Certainly a good many
did. Lytton, who had an assignation with Roger in London,
was boyishly eager to get away in spite of all difficulties, and
a procession set out to walk to Hungerford, since there was no
possibility of a car getting through the drifts. Lytton in a fur
coat and waders, Ralph in top boots, a rucksack and a crimson
hat trimmed with monkey-fur, James with his head enveloped
in a scarf—we must have looked a bizarre collection. It was
fantastically beautiful; after Inkpen the roads were full to the
top with snow; the blue sky brought out curious pink lights in
it and deep blue shadows; cottages were grotesquely hung with
post-card icicles, and the snow was marbled all over with
ripple marks of different sizes and shapes made by the wind.
At Hungerford the world suddenly became ordinary again,
people stepped into the train wearing bowler hats, and gaped
to see a troupe of performing Bulgarian peasants, headed
evidently by the Prime Minister in his fur coat. Four of us had
lunch at the Bear Hotel—Ralph, myself, Carrington and
Tommy. "We must have another round of brandy," Tommy
kept saying, and as Ralph had to pay for everything he was

rather put out by his lordly air; by the time we started home he was thoroughly on Ralph's nerves and I was comatose with whiskies and brandies. We plodded along the shining road with its sugar-icing banks, while the sky turned an exquisite clear yellow and the snow a delicate purplish pink.

December 30th. My spirits rose at the prospect of departure—but *were* we going? James, Julia and Tommy were all leaving, and Ralph said if I went he would go too, but we didn't like to leave Carrington alone and she was reluctant to make up her mind to join the rest of us. Ralph was in a state of exasperation with Carrington, and said she would bear us a grudge whatever we did. We saw the London contingent off in dazzling sunshine, but later that day snow began to fall again.

December 31st. Silence. Everything thickly buried, not a leaf stirring, and a white mist enveloping the trees, turning their silhouettes to different shades of grey. Never has snow seemed more claustrophobic and cruel, the enemy of life. Ralph plunged out towards the downs and came back for lunch glowing, excited, frosted with snow and with a dead partridge, rescued too late, which had died in his hands on the way home. Cows stumbled about glaring from red-rimmed eyes, hares loped awkwardly along, little birds pecked frenziedly at barely visible grasses. I could think of nothing but 'Shall we get away to London tomorrow?' Then came the rain and the wind, howling and buffeting the house, shaking and rattling, sending fountains squirting through the shutters.

January 3rd, 1928. Away at last! A fine morning, nearly all the snow gone, and a car from the Bear to fetch us. From the windows of our train we gazed out at acres of floods on both sides; we swam through Newbury station like a swan; the rails had disappeared under water.

January 8th. Gordon Square. Yesterday morning in the small hours a rare natural phenomenon occurred. The Thames rose suddenly to a tremendous height, burst its walls and plunged into the streets, drowning several people in their basements, surrounding the houses and tearing up some of the streets of Westminster. Aunt Ethel had her kitchen filled with black slime to the roof and all her china broken; Naomi Mitchison's two servants were silently drowned in the night at Hammersmith; and Oliver [Strachey] was woken by a policeman with a loud rat-tat and "The river's out, Sir, and will be here in a minute." Oliver ran downstairs to his basement, where he found one or two cases looking as if they contained wine. They were terribly heavy and only by dint of Herculean efforts did he manage to stagger up with them. "When I opened them," he said, laughing heartily, "what do you think I found inside? Nothing but *water!*"

Carrington and Frankie dined with us. Carrington described Lydia saying at lunch that "Geoffrey Keynes was a very good doctor for the breasts, but she had never tried him *down there.*"

January 21st. Dined at Boulestin with Phil Nichols, drinking very good champagne in celebration of his forthcoming departure to New Zealand*—though celebration hardly seemed the right word, for he described the great luxury in which he would travel, with his red morocco bags, new suits, gold cigarette cases, and how hollow it would all be with nobody to talk to about it. He said, "I want to settle down and stop being selfish. I want to have someone to enjoy things with."

January 23rd. The farewell party given by Ralph Hamlin for Phil Nichols at Claridges. All very grand. I bought yellow orchids for my white velvet dress. In the ladies' cloakroom I ran into Vera, looking lovely in a black lace shawl, and more sensitive and vulnerable than the other hard-faced females flashing their teeth at each other. We went together into the

---

* Where he was seconded by the Foreign Office.

large room set out for Hamlin's guests, and after gulping a cocktail I got into conversation with Harry Strauss* and A. P. Herbert. At dinner I sat between Harry and Robert Nichols, who is likeable if a little mad, and makes the impression of unhappily groping after something—he doesn't himself know what. I began enjoying myself, especially when confronted after dinner by Arnold Bennett's ebullient vulgarity, stammering cockney voice, and one tooth sticking out in front. "I want to dance," he said suddenly, seizing me round the waist, and away we went, talking among other things about French writers we both liked—Flaubert, Stendhal and the *Liaisons Dangereuses*. I was impressed by his insight into Robert's character.

January 28th. Ham Spray. Steady rain kept us all indoors, steadily reading. I dived into Carlyle—or rather Mrs Carlyle's letters, Froude's Explanations, Carlyle's Life. Ralph became infected, and Lytton willingly joined in to discuss various points, such as: Froude's motives, was he in love with Carlyle or Mrs Carlyle, or both, or was he merely a sensationalist? Did Carlyle go to bed with Lady Ashburton? What were Mrs Carlyle's real feelings about Lady Ashburton, etcetera. I also read some of Bertie Russell's *Outlines of Philosophy*, and we had an interesting argument about logic.

February 1st. We gave a successful dinner-party to Helen Anrep, Bunny, Lionel and Margaret. Margaret has gained confidence and launched on comic sorties with great success. When asked, "What is so-and-so like?" Helen is rather too inclined to reply: "Well, he adores *me*," but she is such a good listener and so lavish in flattery that she gives the impression of taking much more interest in other people than she really does. Julia outclasses her at that fine art, and I have often seen her content to sit a whole evening quizzing a collection of people without trying to make an impression herself. The

* Later M.P. and Lord Conesford.

The Plateau

other evening we took her and Tommy to the Chinese Restaurant, and Julia peered through her horn-rimmed spectacles with such absorbed interest at the capering tarts that they put their tongues out at her. No detail bores her.

February 4th–5th. A very happy weekend in London. On Sunday afternoon we went to the Film Society performance, sitting next to Lydia, whose small white face peered from a tight black hat, and Keith Baynes. Then on to tea with Saxon in the kitchen of his new flat. It was full of very ugly dinner-services with crests on them, while his sitting-room was cluttered with tall piles of books.

"Saxon, you must really sell some of your books," I said.

"Hm—yes—hm—perhaps. I think there are *one* or *two* I could do without—possibly. There's a treatise here on ophthalmia. I *think* I can do without that." Ralph had by now found that one of Saxon's rows of school prizes was a history of the Indian Mutiny and become immersed in it: meanwhile Saxon showed me his father's, his grandfather's and his grandmother's diaries, and several fragments of family trees. His father had kept a diary for thirty years in one enormous book with long pages, so that it was possible to compare what had happened on April 3rd for thirty successive years at a glance. This absolutely delighted Saxon and I strongly suspect he keeps one himself on the same plan.

I said, "You really must write your memoirs, Saxon."

A long pause. "Hm—yes—well I don't know—perhaps I might." But ah me! What memoirs they will be!

Three days of quiet domestic life have delighted us both, and our evenings have been devoted to talk and reading. I now have three fat volumes of Mrs Carlyle's letters from the London Library, while Ralph is still following the Indian Mutiny with a map. Happiness!

February 9th. We dined with Alec who came hot from his session with his analyst, and was in a somewhat prickly mood, and then went to the Asquith film, *Shooting Stars.*

Bunny and Ray looked in. Bunny is now a partner in the Nonesuch Press; he offers me—and I have accepted it—the job of correcting proofs for their edition of Plutarch's Lives. He says it will take me about three months and be horribly boring, especially as the same word is often spelt differently; they will pay me £75. I am delighted at this; it will just tide me over this year after I leave the bookshop. I think I must rather enjoy boring jobs—at least they don't intimidate me; and it may be a good thing to get a footing in the Nonesuch Press.

February 19th–20th. Ham Spray. A dazzling morning. We walked to the Gibbet and back, finding primroses in the copse on the way home; Carrington rode on Belle and Lytton entertained us with amusing anecdotes about Norman Douglas, to whom he has just paid a lightning visit in Paris. He was bubbling with high spirits and stories all the weekend; the fine weather made everyone serene. Returning on Monday morning, I looked out of my railway carriage window at the placid surfaces of the Kennet canal and its adjoining ponds, reflecting the sunlight so peacefully. It sometimes seems as if happiness depended on keeping a firm hold of these small daily sensations, yet sensibility is so quickly deadened to them by tiredness, gloomy weather or a monotonous job to be done. I notice that after days of starting out to work in the morning indifferent to my surroundings, hardly glancing about me, catching my bus like an automaton, I suddenly wake up or come alive and start noticing everything—colours and distances between objects, spaces between chimney-pots. And oh! what a pleasure that is.

February 21st. Ralph brought Gerald back to dinner; the two of them had been having tea with Gerald's eccentric great-aunt, Tiz. Next day she wrote Gerald a letter converting this occasion into one of her fantastic day-dreams. "Gerald and Mr Partridge came to tea the other day," she wrote, "and we had a delightful evening. We all went out to dine at the

Berkeley Grill, and Mr Partridge thought the dinner was very
good, and enjoyed his evening." Of course they hadn't been
anywhere near the Berkeley Grill. Ralph was harrowed by
Tiz's painful struggle to face old age and approaching death;
he thinks she longs to be dead, and her mind is practically gone.

February 24th. A dinner-party at the Arnold Bennetts',
looked forward to with some apprehension. Their house is
large, hideous and Victorian; its furnishings look as if they
had been chosen for their ugliness, size and pretentiousness.
The other guests were Frankie, Jack and Mary [St John]
Hutchinson and an Australian couple. Dinner was not good,
and when Bennett begged everyone to tell him what they
thought of his champagne, each in turn asked to be excused.
This would have been painful with anyone else as host, but I
felt he possessed a sort of detached interest that proofed him
against criticism. Not that he is in the least insensitive. I like
him enormously and find his extraordinary crooning, stammering voice and lively, spontaneous manner attractive; it
was to him I was attending, though I sat between Frankie
and Jack Hutchinson.

After dinner Dorothy Cheston Bennett (bad actress and
mother of Arnold's child) led all the females upstairs, where
we were supposed to indulge in 'women's talk', mental
loosening of suspender belts and chat about babies. I was
rather tickled to hear Mary Hutchinson enquire after the
Bennett baby, and stretch herself, purring, "I *do* love a fire,
don't you?" Then Dorothy Bennett told us about her famous
abdominal exercises, which are said to be her stock way of
entertaining her guests, illustrating them by lying on the floor
and wriggling her stomach in quite a spirited way.

The arrival of the men was delayed by a terrible row about
pacifism between Frankie and the Australian, but even after
they had joined us the abdomen and its 'culture' remained the
chief topic.

"N-n-nothing—about—the abdomen—can be *boring!*"
said Arnold Bennett, ending on an explosion.

March 3rd–4th. I went to the Ramseys at Cambridge, and Ralph to Ham Spray. Read *Coriolanus* all the way down in the train, in preparation for the Marlowe Society's performance. It's far from my favourite Shakespeare play, but I enjoyed reading it more than the performance—the usual affair of clanking soldiers, shouting crowds, and comic characters with permanently bent knees and cockney accents.

On Sunday, after a walk along the tow-path, we went to lunch with Frank's family—his father at the head of the table. There was a brother of Frank's called Mick,* a most curious-looking young man with a mobile white face and small red-rimmed eyes; he is said to be very clever as well as deeply religious. He seemed devoted to his little sister Margie, and I noticed him give way to an irresistible impulse and quickly and furtively stroke her cheek. Tea in Richard Braithwaite's room at King's.

March 30th. Lettice to stay the night with us and spend a quiet evening at the cinema. Something in the film brought up the subject of death and we talked about it for a long time. I tried hard to imagine my own death in different guises, either violent and sudden as in some ghastly accident, or as something possible to accept at the moment of its happening, and both for Ralph and myself. I hope to God I die before Ralph does.

March 31st. I dined at Clive's, along with Peter [F.L.] Lucas and Roger Fry. A masculine conversation about general ideas, not gossip, held the floor, and even Clive seemed to forget I was a female, which flattered me. I remembered the 'women's talk' at Arnold Bennett's dinner, and reflected that I much preferred men's.

After dinner the subject of love came up, and stayed with us for quite a time; it was interesting to hear three such different attitudes to it. First Clive, romantic, and with his eye

* Later Archbishop of Canterbury.

turned inwards. Then Peter, cynical and disillusioned, holding
that all the point of love vanished with youth. In maturity,
marriage became mere affection; affairs were sordid and dull,
and when one had gone to bed with a girl once or twice she
was a bore. Roger was realistic and optimistic: love was still
possible at sixty—a different emotion no doubt from youthful
love but just as good and, in its own way, just as exciting,
because the middle-aged were more objective than the young
and could take greater pleasure in the character of the beloved.

Raymond, Frankie and Lionel came in later. Lots more talk
and drink. I enjoyed myself enormously.

April 3rd. I walked back from work through the wet squares,
lit by pink light from the street lamps and the setting sun. We
were to give a farewell dinner to Alec and Frances Saxon*
on the eve of their departure for Spain. Of course I was
thinking of our own journey to Spain, and how it had
changed our lives, as it well might do theirs. But the evening
was not a great success. They both seemed weighed down by
the immensity of the step they were taking, and would drink
no wine because of their inoculations. Alec talked fussily
about trains and arrangements; Frances's huge eyes were full
of mournful perplexity, and I felt unreasonably annoyed with
her for not being more excited at the prospect of a Spanish
holiday. Conversation began to languish and they went off
early to bed, while we looked in on James, who was as usual
charming, amusing, *right.*

April 6th. Ralph and I spent Easter at Hilton.† A happy stay.
Francis and Vera Meynell came to lunch and were persuaded
to stay to dinner. When we sat down I suddenly noticed that
Ray had over-powdered her face and that her eyes were red.
What could have upset her? It made my inside turn over, and
for some reason I held the Meynells responsible. After dinner
Vera was looking at Bunny's books, and his bookplate.

* Later his second wife.
† Bunny and Ray Garnett's house near Huntingdon.

Bunny said, "I'm just as tired of my bookplate as most other people are of theirs." "Yes," said Vera (just as Ray came into the room, who had designed it), "but this is a good deal worse than most people's." "Oh no, I don't think so." "Oh *yes it is.*" I could have murdered Vera, though I don't quite know why Ray has such power to wring my heart.

On Saturday Frank and Lettice Ramsey came to lunch and were greeted by dumb surprise, Bunny having quite forgotten he had asked them while Ray had never been told. The question arose: were some people essentially tragic and others comic? Ray said suddenly: "I feel I'm a very tragic character, though I'm not unhappy. I feel like . . . some . . . mutilated thing."

April 11th. To see *The Cherry Orchard* acted in Russian by the Moscow Art Theatre. It was of course exasperating not to be able to understand the words, but the acting was to my eyes superb; the most exact realism is their line, achieved by a technique so perfect that it requires an effort of concentration to recognise it as such. But how greatly preferable it is to the more stylised modern forms of acting, and I like nothing better than to be so carried away that I believe I am watching Gayev himself, and not an actor who is probably wondering what he will have for dinner.

April 27th. This was my last day in the bookshop. Surely I ought to be feeling some emotion, I thought, and I don't, except for a vague suppressed excitement, as if I were leaving school for good. Perhaps I shall never again be a cog in a nine to six machine. I packed up my belongings and cleared out drawers, while Jane grew every moment visibly more uneasy and wouldn't meet my eye. This was really absurd! For want of anything better to say as we parted I asked if she would lunch with me on Monday. She murmured that that would be very nice.

We dined with Lionel and Margaret; as usual a good deal of medical conversation. On our way to the cinema in a bus

Margaret took out her optical apparatus and inspected my retina. We saw a splendid murder film. At the end of it a fat old lady sitting next to Lionel dropped her spectacles; he picked them up, saying in a small voice: "I thought it was a revolver." The old lady was shaken by painful laughter. We all went back to 41 and sat talking and drinking till late with James and Alix.

CHAPTER TEN

The Greville Memoirs

ONE UNEXPECTED EFFECT of my new freedom was that although I had much more time for writing in it, I put aside my diary for several months. It was a glorious summer, and we spent several weeks of it in Brittany with two youthful and perfectly delightful companions—Rachel and Dermod Mac-Carthy. For part of the time we stayed on the Île de Groix. I wonder what has become of it now. Fifty years ago it was an almost uninhabited, enchanted island of vast white sandy beaches, rocky inlets, and one small inn, which provided fresh fish (and a cold *langouste* for our daily picnic). The boat from Lorient came only once a week, bringing a few day visitors packed in as tightly among the mooing cows and baaing sheep as the Norman invaders are in their ships on the Bayeux tapestry. When we got home we found that Lytton had signed the contract with Macmillans to edit the first complete edition of the *Greville Memoirs* ever to be published.

September 7th, 1928. Ralph is to do all the groundwork on the new edition of the *Greville Memoirs*, supervised by Lytton, who will also write a preface. Ralph is thrilled; I can't think of any work that would suit him more, and he will do it extremely well. I am quite envious. He has now become to all intents a business man, going to the Museum every day till five; and as he lunches at present with Lytton, to discuss the innumerable points that arise and must be settled from the first page and rigorously adhered to, I don't see him from morning till evening, which is the strangest sensation after these last few months when we've been together all day.

September 21st. Ralph and I are now both working on the

Greville MSS in the British Museum. We sit side by side on a shelf just wide enough to hold a table and two chairs, in the upper part of the Documents Room, looking down upon Magna Carta. The streams of schoolchildren and others who buzz around that memorable object might be distracting, except that our work is so utterly absorbing. On our table lies the previous, incorrect and much expurgated edition of the *Memoirs* made by Henry Reeve, and the first few volumes of the diary itself, brought up from their locked safe by a museum official in the morning and taken back there at night. The mere sight of those slim quarto volumes bound in limp red leather makes one's mouth water. Inside, the paper is of fine smooth quality, closely written over in Greville's sensitive and mercifully legible hand. I see now how important it was to get every formal question settled from the very start, and never let oneself forget the decisions made. How are notes by Greville, Reeve and ourselves to be distinguished? Also passages never before published? What about abbreviations? Mis-spellings? Cross-references? And many, many more. Greville even used a cypher—generally when referring to some clandestine love affair, but it presents no difficulty. The process of collating, correcting, and adding bits left out really does need two people—one to read aloud from Reeve, the other to check. As for the material itself, I can already see what a magnetic attraction it will increasingly exert as we get to know, like or dislike the *dramatis personae*, and understand their social and political intrigues.

December 4th. This morning I have been reading in bed some diaries of Gerald's which he gave me to look at last night. They are an impassioned record of his relations with Carrington during the period between his return to England and the time when Ralph and I set up house together. He writes brilliantly, often it is painfully moving. When he is dealing with something I know about—when he makes any reference to my relations with Ralph for instance—he is sometimes wildly incorrect, at other times acute. I was distressed to read of his continual collapses sobbing on his bed, of headaches, nervous exhaustion and terrible misery. I see how difficult it must have been for Gerald and Ralph to go on being fond of each other, quite apart from concepts like 'fault' and 'blame'.

Last night Gerald and I talked long and interestingly about the past, and also about a recent incident that has greatly disturbed him, although he is aware of its comic side.

Lytton lately took it into his head to go through his cupboards and wardrobes and get rid of things he no longer liked or wore. He discarded several suits and a great many ties and handkerchiefs. Carrington, knowing that Gerald was hard up at the moment, wrote and asked him if he would like some of them, without realising (at any rate consciously) that she was presenting a red rag to a bull. Everything of Lytton's is so hallowed to her that she feels anyone ought to be delighted to be given it. The fact that Gerald *knew* she felt thus enraged him all the more. "Lytton's old clothes! How would she like it if I sent her Winnie's* disused garters?" He wrote refusing them coldly and with ironical politeness, adding a p.s. that he saw she had been giving away his presents; did this mean she was annoyed with him? The present in question was a silk handkerchief which Carrington had accidentally left behind at No. 41, and I (having no idea whose it was) had been wearing it round my neck one evening when Gerald visited us. What a concatenation of circumstances! Gerald had roused my suspicions by the unnatural voice in which he asked me: "Where did you get that nice handkerchief from, Frances?" and I, still uncertain of its provenance, merely said, "It's not mine."

This was all he was going on, but ironically enough, Carrington, who *had* given away some of his presents, was touched on a guilty spot and put up a frantic smokescreen. Yes, she had given away some of his presents, because (unlike him) she was so upset by these relics of the past that she couldn't bear to keep them.

* A friend of Gerald's who was a prostitute.

"The little hypocrite," said Gerald, "when I know that half Ham Spray is furnished with my presents." (A wild exaggeration.) But worst of all, with this letter she sent a parcel of Lytton's ties, "and such awful ones," said Gerald, "especially chosen as an ironical comment on my clothes. One was knitted from that *shiny wood-silk*," (here his voice rose to a scream), "quite *impossible to wear it*."

Two comments must be made: Carrington was like the young of today in that she had no strong feelings of property in clothes, and liked them to be freely exchanged. Gerald should have remembered that. And secondly, Gerald had a very personal, if not conventionally elegant, taste in clothes. Carrington should have remembered that.

Anyway, Gerald sent back all her presents, and existed for some days in a fine frenzy, reading his old diaries and brooding over his wrongs. He determined to make a clean cut and go back to Spain in the spring, concentrating his hurt feelings into a desire to take revenge on Carrington in his writing. He called it an "honourable revenge". I told him it was no use trying to disguise the fact that he felt wickedly inclined and would probably behave wickedly. He said that he would probably act blindly, but when he is in a wicked mood Gerald is never blind.

Then he went on to say that most people definitely take sides either with me or Carrington. Tommy thinks Carrington has been badly treated. On the other hand Eddy [Sackville-West] takes my part. A feeling of despair overwhelmed me as Gerald said this. I don't want my 'part' taken! I haven't *got* a part! I hate the stupid geometrical figures by which people try to understand the emotions of others, imposing hard straight lines—or 'sides' as they call them, onto tender curvaceous human beings who have none.

I sit in a cold room with no fire. Complete stillness and white mist preserve the trees in the square garden outside. Every minute it darkens visibly, the mist grows yellower, until now it is the colour of urine and smells as foul. Not a twig can move in the thick mixture and only very faint lights show from the houses opposite.

Last weekend at Ham Spray slipped by smoothly, with mist outside and books and fires in. Lady Strachey is ill and so is Tiz—perhaps this weather will carry off the old ladies and the King into the bargain. Yet it gave me a pang to think of the immense audience, like that in a bull-ring, watching the struggle of the King's heart to go on beating.

December 6th. Ralph didn't turn up, so I guessed he had missed his train and set out to lunch with Lionel and Margaret (married, by the way, a month ago). I dived into the fog, through which a great red sun beamed and raw red human faces rolled by. Then I saw a *Standard* placard on Southampton Row with an announcement in large red letters. 'Oh God,' I thought, 'supposing it says Dreadful Accident on the Great Western!' But of course it was only the latest bulletin about the King's health. Just then a seedy old man came staggering towards me, muttering to himself, and as he passed me I heard what he was saying: "I hope he dies. I hope he dies. Fuck him, *I* say."

December 10th. I've thought about the old man in the fog quite a bit. I believe people are far more dominated than they realise by their love of drama, and that this makes them enjoy crises and disasters. Gerald gave us an example of this last night, when he said how valuable 'pity' and 'pride' were in human relationships, because they produced 'tragic' situations for the observer. He was very amusing about Roger [Fry] and his new aesthetic words, such as 'uva', 'timbre' and so on. "But they won't adopt *my* suggestion for a new word," he said. "There ought to be a new word for Cow. One can't say Cow in literature, one has to put Cattle, and they really don't exist in England. It's most inconvenient. Now HORSE! PIG! What excellent words!"

December 13th. Weekend at Cambridge with Lettice. The town was looking icily beautiful and the Cam froze half an inch in one night. Dadie came to lunch and entertained us with stories of an undergraduate who lives in a room with the curtains permanently drawn, its walls painted black and ceiling scarlet. They lunched off vodka and oysters while a gramophone played a Victorian polka.

Back in London, carol singers are piping up, getting in their rounds I suppose in case the King dies before Christmas. Mabel's friend George, who is a printer, says the pages announcing his death are all set up. The whole of London is on tenterhooks lest he should die before Christmas and ruin the shops and theatres. Barkers is said to have bought up all the black crêpe in London.

While Ralph and I were at work on Greville the other day, I looked down towards Magna Carta and said, "There's a dreadful old woman down there making an awful fuss." "So there is," said Ralph. "It's my mother!" She had come to tell him his brother-in-law had died. He is not at all fond of her.*

For the next nine years all Ralph's working hours and most of mine were occupied in editing the Greville Memoirs, and this work must be understood as the substratum of other events whose description follows. Collating and transcribing was a considerable undertaking and a lengthy one, but after it was over there was a great deal of research to be done on the footnotes and the Index. For this we said goodbye to Magna Carta and moved over to the Reading Room. Every person and incident had to be identified, and some of the detective work involved moments of excitement or frustration such as I imagine belong to the pursuit of criminals. Each note in the eight volumes had to contain a concise biography. My own knowledge of history was quite inadequate, but I thoroughly enjoyed scouring reference books or hunting for clues in contemporary memoirs; Ralph's equipment was far better—not only did he have an

* This was the only time I saw her.

exceptionally good memory, but he also possessed the gift of thinking laterally: that is to say relating what was happening in Sicily to events in Paris at the same date. But most of our notes were vetted and added to by Lytton, whose standard of exactitude was as high as any I have met with. As for the Index, it had of course to wait for the page proofs and was therefore done after Lytton's death and at Ham Spray. We filled in and sorted hundreds of cards, the whole ending as a volume of over three hundred two-column pages. I am proud to say that I was told by a widely-read man who possessed a fine library that it was the best Index he knew.

I think nostalgically of the days and weeks we spent in that anthill of industry and research, the British Museum Reading Room, sitting among piles of books at our appointed segment of one spoke of the great wheel beneath the vast dome filled with gently revolving particles of yellowish dust. The satisfaction of being a cog in that wheel owed much to the fact that we were all absorbed in our own individual and very different tasks. Nobody paid much attention to their neighbour unless he fell asleep and snored too loudly. Notes were, I believe, sometimes passed to strangers; romances began, and Ralph declared that he once saw an old gentleman make water against the lowest shelf of folios. But prisoners though we all were in a world apart, we were somehow conscious of the passage of winter into spring and spring into summer. Ralph, who was subject to hay fever, even developed it at the appropriate season.

Illness is a dreary subject, but as an invader of normal life it cannot be ignored. Both Ralph and I were ill at times during 1928 and 1929. Ralph had several attacks of what he described as "hellish pain", terrifying to witness and agonising to endure. After various tests and X-rays, and a visit to a woman surgeon (because he argued that a male patient was probably a rarity and she would therefore take more interest) his trouble was first wrongly diagnosed as being due to an embryonic twin brother or sister afloat in his abdomen, and then rightly a good deal later as kidney stone, when it was duly dealt with. The twin theory took the fancy of the surrealist painter John Banting whom we

afterwards commissioned to paint a very large radio loud-
speaker at Ham Spray, and to his charming and characteristic
decorations he added portraits of Ralph, me, our son Burgo
(then aged about two) and a number of "tiny friends" as he
called them—Alix and James, Raymond, Julia, Rosamond
Lehmann, Eddie Gathorne-Hardy and Eddy Sackville-West.
Chuckling to himself, he depicted Ralph's twin brother inside
him—an exact replica of Ralph himself, a tiny full-grown man,
broad shoulders, jacket and trousers and all, and smoking (as
Ralph loved to do) a large cigar. Unluckily this object vanished
when I left Ham Spray and I do not know what became of it.
If anyone came across it they could well be mystified.

I have already described my own illness as 'mysterious', and
suggested that it had a psycho-somatic origin. Like all such, it
was troublesome and came and went, while I consulted different
doctors and tried a series of unsatisfactory remedies. Heartily
sick of them all, and determined to avoid doctors as much as
possible in future, I tried a treatment of my own invention,
which I truly believe played a large part in my cure. I developed
a new enthusiasm—for skating. I joined the Ice Club and
practised my addiction with persistence. I had to begin by
mastering the outside and inside edges, then threes and eights,
and finally the waltz and a more complicated dance called the
fourteen-step. What exhilaration! I loved the swish of the skates
over that grey synthetic ice, and was intoxicated by being able
to cover such a splendid distance with each stroke of my bladed
foot. There was a highly satisfying neatness and precision too
about the movements one had to learn, and I always came away
glowing after an hour or so of whirling around. When the
dance band struck up, unless I was lucky enough to have
Raymond or Arthur Waley for a partner, I used to hire the
services of one of the professionals dressed like chauffeurs in
navy blue uniform. They cost only two shillings and sixpence a
time, and their stability was wonderfully reassuring.

For a while I discarded my diary, and the only written source
I have for this time comes from letters exchanged by Ralph and
me in July 1929, when we took about ten days' separate holiday

—he with Lytton,Carrington and Sebastian Sprott in Holland, and I in East Anglia, staying with the Ramseys and Garnetts, and ending by myself in an inn at King's Lynn.

You are already rushing through the windmills and black and white cows [I wrote on June 30th], yet it was no time ago that I gave you a parting squeeze and left a wet patch on your blue collar. Bunny drove me up here in his new car, and I have been shown where they went in France. They visited the caves in the Dordogne, and after crawling down a tiny black hole, old Mr Garnett* got *stuck* if you please, between every-one else and the daylight, giving them all claustrophobia. It seems extraordinary to think of not seeing you for such a long time, my darling.

Beakus Penrose had bought a film camera, and this summer several ambitious but amateurish films were produced by Bunny or Alec, the cast of this first one, performed at Hilton, consisting of the Ramseys, Penroses, Angus Davidson and myself. I had to take the heroine's part, wearing a specially made pink print dress. I never had the smallest gift for acting, as is clear from my letter of July 1st:

I have been spending my day merrily running through hay-fields and scampering over fences, or bounding into Alec's arms—and very silly I looked too. We have seen quite a lot of Wittgenstein; he confides in Lettice that he is in love with a Viennese lady, but he feels marriage to be sacred, and can't speak of it lightly.

It was not, I think, the first time I had met the great philoso-pher, who returned to Cambridge early in 1929. He and Frank appeared to admire and respect each other greatly, and he was a frequent visitor to 4 Mortimer Road. No-one could fail to feel, when in his presence, that here was a man of formidable intel-

* Edward.

lect—even one of the few who can be classed as a 'genius'. Austerely handsome, with very deepset grey eyes, he would have been well suited by a monk's robe; his face habitually bore an expression of concentrated seriousness and pessimism; yet in mixed company his conversation was often trivial in the extreme, and larded with feeble jokes accompanied by a wintry smile. I was aware of suppressed irritability in him, and guessed that he could be roused to a quick flare of anger. He sometimes talked about academic Cambridge distinctly critically, and of the aesthetes with scorn in his voice—'these Julian Bells'— although he was himself intensely musical. Perhaps he was intolerant of everyone but philosophers, for the distinguished mathematician, Max Newman, who had several discussions with him, told me that once—when philosophy versus mathematics was at issue between them—he heard Wittgenstein muttering under his breath, "You ought to have been drowned at birth!"

With the simple jokes went a love of simple pleasures, like fairs, detective stories and the cinema, and he entered into a disastrous habit current in Cambridge at that time of mixing absolute alcohol from the labs. with different flavours to make anything from port to crême de menthe. But there was no mistaking his humanity and kindness. The well-known fact that he gave away the entire fortune he inherited from his father shows the small value he set on material things. It was as if his jokes and trivialities were his only safety-valve from the tension caused by his all-consuming dedication to abstract ideas.

While I was capering in front of the cinema-camera, and brooding over the contradictions in Wittgenstein's character, Ralph hardly seemed to be enjoying Holland, and his letters show a disgruntled mood:

It's just as flat as can be—quite impossible to be anything but phlegmatic. We talk English firmly and are understood even when we say "Bill", which we *know* is Dutch for "bottom", still "Bill" is what we stick to and eventually what we get. Then dear old "slagroom" has come back to me, do you

Frances and Clive Bell at Charleston

Ralph with E. M. Forster at Ham Spray

Roger Fry and Ralph playing chess at Fry's house

Right: Carrington at Ham Spray

Below: James and Alix Strachey
at Ham Spray

Quentin Bell and Virginia Woolf at Rodmell

Molly and Rachel MacCarthy with Ralph

Barcelona Fair: *from left:* Raymond Mortimer, Frances, Clive Bell, Ralph

Ralph and Gerald Brenan at Yegen

At Biddesden House – the last photograph of Carrington
from left: Pamela Mitford, Ralph, Carrington, David Garnett, Frances

Madame Le Roy and family with Ralph in Flanders, 1932

Ralph and Frances

Julia at Ham Spray

remember "slagroom" and "tong"?* Well, we had them both for lunch today. I hope to become more cheerful, but our tone is very low so far. [On July 3rd:] Lytton rushed into a bookshop and found it was exactly like Maggs, so grand that it was quite out of the question to buy anything except a novel by H. G. Wells. I miss you most sadly and I should be far happier if I had you with me. But things will improve I expect. At present I am snapping at everyone. [From Leyden, next day:] I have been rather maddened by the sporadic behaviour of the party—all are piano, piano, I don't know why. Perhaps we are all very old indeed, or perhaps we are growing a little Dutch. [At Amsterdam they took:] a trip in a motor-boat round the harbour, shooting under bridges and blowing our horn like a car—a Round Fart it was called, and we passed the Hotel Aarsen very properly. [And on July 7th:] Why should I not be entitled to miss you as you miss me? As a matter of fact I have been missing you very severely. On Thursday I had a satisfactory outburst and said all the hard true thoughts that had been biting their way out—'selfish egotism in others' was one—and soon got to the question, 'Why on earth did I come with you?'

Ralph and I were only separated once more that year, he going to his family house in Devonshire and I to Charleston. Clive's letter confirming my invitation is so amusing about Roger Fry that I cannot resist quoting some of it:

Remember you are not coming for 'a weekend' but for a long, a very long weekend: so don't make engagements for the following Monday or Tuesday even. Roger is our only news —he has left us today, I am not sure whether, ostensibly, to see Helen [Anrep] or a new doctor, but I presume he will see both. He has seen six new doctors since last I saw him, and the upshot of the matter is that with the help of a bread-pan,†

---

* Ralph and I had spent a long weekend in Holland in 1927. 'Slagroom' is Dutch for cream, and 'tong' for sole.
† *Sic.* Or 'bed-pan'?

some talc powder, 'no eggs' and a modicum of faith he hopes to do pretty well. The first evening he did surprise us a little by enquiring hopefully whether anyone in the room had cancer. Unluckily no-one had; but Duncan had a wart which did almost as well. The fact is he had noticed in the corner of a chemist's shop at Royat a likely-looking packet, which he bought, and which turned out to be 'Magnésium Total' with a paper inside to explain that it and it alone will cure cancer, erisypelis, Bubonic plague, yellow fever, influenza, mosquito-bites and warts. Roger says it is absolutely scientific but unluckily it tastes so bad that no-one but he can keep it down.

I duly arrived, and on August 31st I wrote to Ralph (in those happy days letters arrived even in the course of a weekend):

I am enjoying myself very much, though this is my first moment of solitude. I have avoided going on a walk with Clive and crept up to my attic to write to you. Do you see a jolt at the end of Clive's name? It's because Julian is firing off a revolver among the trees. I was met by Clive and Julian in a new Morris which Julian drives at tremendous speed and mostly on two wheels. At the house were Vanessa and Duncan (who was wildly excited about a Pig he had just won by bowling). Lydia bowled all day and spent a fortune, and when she couldn't get the Pig she horrified the village by bursting into tears. I always forget quite how charming Duncan is. Dear Angus [Davidson] was brought over from Corfe by Nancy Morris, running over a Colonel in Brighton on the way. They were most casual about it, and it only came out later that the poor old man bled freely and had to be given brandy. Last night we had an amazingly, amazingly beautiful walk to a farmhouse at the foot of the downs towards Alciston, where there was a gigantic barn and a little church-yard. Clive was at his nicest. The feud with Tilton* is kept up, why I don't know, but this morning a surprise visit from

* The Keynes's house.

Lydia found them all honey. We were sitting out in the garden, I working at my Plutarch, when in came this little figure in white trousers, a red shirt and a large straw hat trimmed with poppies—"to borrow some eggs", she said. She has asked us all over, but so has Virginia so I suppose we shall go there.

The garden here is a rampant jungle of sunflowers and holly-hocks, and the apple-trees are bowed down with scarlet apples; pears hang bobbing against one's head. Quentin came back today from sailing with Karin and Adrian. He says they have adopted a little boy and are going to make him neurotic and then psycho-analyse him.* After lunch the boys, Angus and I went down to the beach to bathe. The Bell boys are like two plump brown seals in the water, forever splashing and ducking and coming up roaring with laughter. They kept diving beneath me and hurling me into the air. Angelica is very pretty with her huge grey eyes; she has a little Jewish friend who follows her about docilely.

My little attic is exceedingly snug. Vanessa wanted me to have the room you had last time, but it smelt so dreadfully of paint that I let Angus have it. There are various queer things about this household, for instance they use very old wooden needles on the gramophone, so that everything sounds like the distant wailing of gnats—but we have just had the Mozart Clarinet Quintet, which was lovely in spite of everything.

Charleston in its heyday was an enchanted place—a place of such potent individuality that whenever I stayed there I came away grateful to it, as it were, for giving me so much pleasure, so many rich and various visual sensations, such talk, such a sense that lives were being intensely and purposefully led there (and therefore could be so led elsewhere)—for being *itself* in fact, just as one feels grateful to a very pretty girl for ravishing one's eyes. I tend to picture it at noon on a summer day, with the tall flowers motionless in the hot still air, their corollas buzzing with

---

* Typical Bloomsbury *canard*.

bees; a dragon-fly or two skimming over the duckweed-covered pond; and a small group sitting outside the drawing-room French windows in those indestructible but inelegant canvas chairs (known as 'rorkies') that everyone seemed to have inherited from an Anglo-Indian uncle—talking and laughing. The house gave the impression of having developed spontaneously, like some vigorous vegetable growth, in spite of the display of human creative energy that covered the walls of all its rooms; for Duncan and Vanessa couldn't see an empty flat space without wanting to cover it with flowers and nudes, with vases and swirls (probably surrounded by croquet hoops) all in the warm richness of their favoured colours.

But though most of my visits were in the summer, I also saw and adored it in grimmer seasons—never I think under snow, but with the tall trees standing like bare skeletons against the majestic height of the downs, and the short grey-green turf of their flanks. Not so long ago I spent a winter weekend at Charleston. How could it fail to have a ghostly air now that all the original inhabitants had died, and many of the rooms were empty and their brilliant decorations fading? All the same, as I looked out of my bedroom window—it had been Clive's—the ghost came to life again for me.

I have stayed in many houses that are beautiful or comfortable or set in marvellous surroundings, or even all three, but very few with as strong a personality as Charleston's in the Twenties and Thirties.*

In September 1929 Ralph and I took another journey to the south of Spain. It was always Ralph's favourite European country, and I had caught the infection from him. We had twice been to Catalonia and down the coast as far as Tarragona, but this was the first time we had been to the south since our crucial journey of 1925. We were to visit Gerald in his eyrie in the Alpujarra—that ridge of mountains lying between the

* I would like here to celebrate two exceptions: Tramores, belonging to Jaime and Janetta Parladé and standing between Ronda and the Costa del Sol; and the Leigh Fermors' at Kardamyli in the Peloponnese. I like to think that Ham Spray, too, once qualified.

Sierra Nevada and the sea—the village of Yegen, perched some three thousand feet above sea-level. It took us four days to get there by the shortest possible means, for of course there were then no commercial air-lines and going by sea to Gibraltar was even slower: one day was needed to get to Paris, whence we took the night train to Madrid. There was no luxurious first-class carriage this time—we had become considerably poorer, owing to the failure of some speculative shares—we sat up all night in a third-class carriage whose seats were made of shiny black horse-hair; but I was romantic enough to be kept going by the sense of adventure, the friendliness of smiling Spaniards who offered us a share of their provisions, and even by the discomfort of the buses that rattled us from Almería through so many strange and lovely places whose names bristled with the harsh 'j's and 'g's (pronounced by violently clearing the throat) that remind one of the Moorish occupation: Berja, Ugijar, Órgiva. The last part of our journey was covered on mule-back in the dusk of the fourth day, with Gerald to lead the way. I woke next morning to an astonishing vision; half the world lay spread out below me, in layer upon layer and ridge upon ridge of ochre, burnt sienna and palest green, sprinkled here and there with small villages of white houses like our own, hung outside with long strings of dark red pimentos, their flat roofs covered with maize spread out to dry, and with the mysterious black oblongs of the open terraces beneath them. They presented a composition in black, white and dark red, and nothing could have looked more Moorish.

Gerald was a considerate and amusing host, and his house was furnished simply but with exquisite taste. The lavatory was a draughty hole above a precipice, and I seem to remember that the back yard had to be cleared on the rare occasions anyone wanted to take a tub; we lived on vegetables, eggs, chick-peas and fruit, except on the days when the fish-mule came up from the valley.

But what I remember most vividly about this happy and exciting visit was the *opera buffa* which we found in progress, with Gerald in the lead and full supporting cast. Always known as Don Geraldo (pronounced 'Heraldo'), he was in the thick of a violent love-affair with a young village girl called Juliana who had come to work for him, thus arousing the displeasure of Black Maria, an older servant who looked like a sour-faced little witch at one moment and was turning cartwheels the next. There was also a rival for Juliana called Paco; and Angela and Angel, a betrothed pair. There was no mistaking the reality of Gerald's feelings, but somehow their effect was wildly comic. One day, in a frenzy of irritation with Black Maria, he threw a plate and the tortilla upon it straight out of the window into the street below. Every morning Maria brought out onto the terrace our breakfast of excellent coffee, bread and honey, which we laid on thick so as to hide the rancid taste of the tinned butter from Granada. Gerald would arrive exhausted from a night of love, emitting sighs and explosive comments, which always sent us into fits of laughter, as did the wild flapping movements aimed at killing the fleas which Juliana harboured in their dozens. She was a clean and healthy-looking girl, but I had only to ride on the same mule with her, or undress for a bathe in the same hut to be hopping-mad and flapping as much as Gerald himself. He had acquired an extraordinary little cardboard bellows filled with Keatings powder, called a 'bufador' which sent out a destructive blast when pressed.

So the weeks passed; sometimes we walked to a neighbouring village to buy from anyone who wanted to sell them the beautiful old plates and jugs, now so rare and expensive, for a few pesetas each. People ran eagerly from their cottages, offering us a lot of other things we did *not* want—such as a Moorish sword. Once we went to a *corrida* at a pretty village bull-ring, which however I soon left in tears. Gerald gave several evening parties. These began stickily: the villagers and servants sat round the walls in complete silence, but after a certain amount of *aguardiente* the thaw began, and soon there was dancing and stamping, and plenty of singing to the guitar. I remember an evening when we joined in the domestic task of taking the maize from the cobs; I cannot forget the word for this operation (*desfajar*), which had taken on an almost ritual character, nor the scene as we sat with Black Maria, Juliana and

Angela in the loft, nor the words and tune of the song they taught me to sing with them, for all Spaniards then (and many now) liked to sing as they did mechanical tasks:

> La fabrica de tabaco
> Olé! Olé! si fuera mia
> Si fuera mia la fabrica de tabaco
> Yo pusiera cañones ...*

We left with sadness, returning by Barcelona, where as arranged we met Clive, Raymond, Aldous and Maria Huxley and Charles Duthuit at the great Exhibition of that year. Here we all admired the Catalan primitives and Gaudi's architecture, but even more perhaps the fountains, for whose changing colours and shapes, said Clive, "the epithet *'féerique'* must have been expressly invented"; also some regional singing and dancing, especially when the Valencian contingent, after singing songs dating from 700 A.D., left the platform to the tune of 'Valencia', an extremely popular modern number first put over by Mistinguett at the Moulin Rouge, which—and I quote Clive again—"had become the National Anthem of the ancient province". But my favourite memento of this episode is a trick photo taken at a fair, of the heads of Ralph and myself, Clive and Raymond, peering out above the cardboard bodies of a *cuadro flamenco*. Ralph looks the most convincing; Raymond is a squat guitarist, and Clive and I female castanet dancers in flounced dresses.

We arrived home in the highest spirits and eager to get back to Greville, to be confronted with two pieces of bad news. James and Alix wanted their first-floor rooms for consulting-rooms, as Alix was now qualified to take patients of her own. I must have moaned about this to Clive, who wrote from Paris on November 3rd:

My poor dear Fanny, what an amusing melancholy letter. I

---

* "The tobacco factory—oh! if it were only mine I should fill it with cannon" But this was long before the Civil War.

never heard of skies so dull and grey to which a—what bird
is Fanny most like? Shall we say a linnet or a Kentish plover
or a Nuthatch?—could yet pipe. Whatever you do don't
leave Bloomsbury.*

It didn't take us long to find new quarters: an unfurnished
maisonette in Great James Street, in a beautiful Queen Anne
house belonging to Francis and Vera Meynell. Unfortunately
the Meynells had had the bad taste to cover the superb original
panelling in thick shiny paint of a hideous purple and emerald
green, though the sitting-room, mercifully, was a less aggressive
yellow. When our furniture, books and pictures were moved in,
and the patchwork quilt I had made myself laid on the bed, it
became more congenial. Gerald had rooms in the same street,
and we had a spare room which we rented to Bunny as a
pied-à-terre.

The other news concerned Carrington. On our first visit to
Ham Spray we found her unusually depressed, and the reason
was soon revealed. She was in utter despair because she (correct-
ly) believed herself to be pregnant. Ralph had long conversations with her and with Lytton, and came up to bed very much
worried as a result. Both he and Lytton thought that her
abhorrence of the idea had reduced her to a suicidal state, and
that something must be done. Her attitude to the situation was
brave as well as tragic, but it was unthinkable that she should go
through with it. I made myself as scarce as possible while these
critical discussions went on, and Lytton was so nice to me in the
taxi to Gordon Square that I felt my efforts to be accommodat-
ing had not been in vain. Ralph arranged everything, as well as
bearing the brunt of the expense, and Carrington's pregnancy
was safely terminated in a London nursing-home; when I
visited her there the change in her state of mind was miraculous.
Ralph's reward was her boundless gratitude, as well as 'undying
love' on the part of the author of the episode, who wrote to him
saying, "I think you have been *damned nice*."

---

* It is a fair example of Clive's epistolary style.

CHAPTER ELEVEN

Death of a Philosopher

EARLY IN 1930 I started making occasional entries in my diary
again:

January 24th, 1930. This year began in a new house, 16 Great
James Street, and I confess that I have often felt a homesick
hankering for Gordon Square. Apart from everything else,
a street is never the same as a square with its garden and huge
trees; and our rooms still retain a flavour of the Meynells.

During the last week one event has filled my life—the
death of Frank Ramsey in Guy's Hospital, after being operated
on to discover the cause of a long spell of very severe jaundice.
On Friday last week Lettice telephoned to tell me that his
condition had become critical, and asking if I would go down
and see her at Guy's that evening. I arrived after dinner, was
surprised by the beauty of the hospital buildings in the dark,
but agitated and at a loss to know how to deal with a situation
with which I was quite unfamiliar. I went up to Frank's ward,
when Lettice came out and asked me to wait. Shortly afterwards she took me into a small cubby-hole of a room, opening
off the ward only a few feet from Frank's bed. It was as hot as
a furnace, full of boxes of chocolates and photographs of
officers, and redolent of nurses and medicines. Poor Lettice
had been sitting there hour after hour, compulsively writing
postcards and crying a little now and then. Very sensibly she
at once asked me not to be sorry for her—in words at least—
as it only made her lose control. She found it easier to talk
about the medical aspect; so she told me the history of the
illness in detail, and even talked a little about what she would
do if he died. I tried to take my cue from her, and only get
her to talk of other things when it came naturally. I always

find the sights and sounds of illness terribly disturbing; Frank's bed was enclosed by screens and I could hear his laboured breathing, which I found very harrowing. I left Lettice late that night, promising to stay in London over the weekend, and went home to tell Ralph he must go alone to Ham Spray, and I would stay at my mother's house in Brunswick Square.

Next day I went to the hospital in the middle of the morning. As I entered the ward the cold and somehow menacing eyes of a doctor in a white overall looked over Frank's screen; Lettice sat in her little hot cabin, still writing postcards and crying, but she talked calmly, and told me they were giving Frank a blood-transfusion. I took her out to lunch and for a walk in the hospital grounds; her stoical attempts to control herself filled me with admiration—I felt I should have behaved much less well myself.

When I came back in the evening and went into the cubby-hole again I was surprised to see the remarkable head of Wittgenstein hoist itself over the back of a chair. Everyone reacts differently when the white face of death looks in at the window. Wittgenstein and I were brought closer together than ever before by our intense sympathy for Lettice, but our methods of expressing it were very different, though both, I think, suited her. Wittgenstein's kindness, and also his personal grief, were somehow apparent beneath a light, almost jocose tone which I myself found off-putting. Frank had had another slight operation from which he had not yet come round properly, and Lettice had had no supper, so the three of us set off to search for some, and eventually found sausage rolls and sherry in the station buffet. Then Wittgenstein went off and Lettice and I returned to our furnace. Frank was delirious, and I was moved by the extremely gentle, cultivated sound of his voice coming from behind the screen. I was painfully conscious of the struggle for life going on, and could not help unreasonably feeling that Frank was too civilised and intelligent to have a fair chance in this savage battle. The sounds of laboured breathing and hiccups were worse than before. Lettice's uncle, who is a surgeon at Guy's, came in before I left; he was a large doggy man in whom one would have confidence, but his manner was inscrutable and I couldn't gauge whether he thought Frank had a chance or not. Lettice went to her bed in the hospital and I home to mine, but not to sleep, for I couldn't stop thinking and tossing. Soon after I awoke from a fitful doze, Mother came in and told me that Frank had died at three that morning, and Lettice would like me to go to her at her uncle's. At the moment I thought little about Frank himself, but only—rather numbly—that I should in a moment be drawn into the whirlpool of poor Lettice's grief.

I found her lying red-eyed on a tousled bed looking dreadfully forlorn, and only after I had taken her hand and kissed her and we had both burst into tears did I fully realise that it was *Frank* who had died—my friend Frank, the engaging, original, brilliantly clever Frank.

In the evening she came to supper with me; exhaustion and time were telling on her and she was very miserable. She said, "I've always dramatised any unhappiness that has come my way before, but this is something so new and crushing that I've had to summon all my forces for sheer control. Dramatisation is unthinkable."

The funeral took place on Tuesday at Golders Green in a fog; the great hideous red crematorium would have been bad enough without one. I got there too early and met a jolly Dickensian party of men coming away from the last funeral with broad grins on their faces, saying "Well, at the last one I went to . . ." Frank's hearse was outside the door, but there was no-one about, until an official with incredibly neat false teeth and a cheery manner arrived and took me to the waiting-room, which was very hot and had a row of urns arranged along the chimney-piece.

"Funny, isn't it, this fog?" he said. "Not so bad in town? H'm. Funny. It's a funny thing, all the bodies have been late today and this one's early."

Then Lydia came in, followed by Maynard. She wore a

tragic expression, and I saw that for a moment she mistook
me for Lettice. Soon afterwards Lettice and the rest of the
congregation arrived and the service began. Richard
Braithwaite was shedding tears into a pocket-handkerchief,
and I was deeply moved myself to see the men carrying the
coffin past. I couldn't bear to think that Frank no longer
existed, that his massive intelligence and his charm were gone,
and his large touchingly ugly body was in that box and
would be in a few moments destroyed. There was a moment
of comic relief when the bearers struggled like piano-movers
to get the coffin onto the slab. Then Frank's brother Michael
read some of the Psalms very well, and since I had no religious
associations with them I thought of them solely as magnificent
and appropriate poetry. Nothing could be more symbolic of
death than the moment when the coffin shot through the
open door, and as it disappeared Michael's face was contorted
by grief and he practically ran out of the chapel.

Then we all trooped out, and what had been impressive
and moving became slightly ridiculous. One of Lettice's
aunts puckered up her round red face like a child and sobbed.
Alec [Penrose] arrived too late, and little Lydia, pale and wet-
eyed, exclaimed, "O-ah! I do not know what to say to
Lettus! But after a death there should be social engagements.
Do you not think so, Maynár?" In the bus home I had the
reddest-faced of Lettice's aunts just behind me, the one who
had been crying with such abandon. Now she was bubbling
over with gaiety.

I have written about this ceremony at some length because
it is the first funeral I have ever been at. I thought about the
subject all the way home. I feel sure they have a cathartic
effect on many people, but perhaps only when the feelings
involved are not very deep? I know that I want none of it for
myself or anyone I dearly love.

February 14th. We are settled in our new home, and life
resumes its ordinary course. We have a new servant, an old
Frenchwoman called Alex, who addresses us as 'Monsieur'

and 'Madame' and cooks extremely well; but our kitchen is once more in the basement, connected to our flat by a service lift on which the dishes arrive, mounting very slowly and with a great deal of creaking and squeaking. The other night when we opened it we found an empty dish! The chicken had somehow caught its foot in the ropes and fallen down the shaft. Alex was inconsolable. "Ah, que j'ai pleuré!" she told us.

We gave a little party a few days ago, which was said to be a success, though I was too preoccupied to enjoy it, and remained stone sober however much I drank. The guests were partly chosen for their youth and beauty. For some reason an epidemic of kissing broke out. Oliver kissed me, and I had a struggle to get away from Alan Clutton-Brock,* who inclines to be violent when drunk. Then Sheelah† kissed me and Ralph tried to kiss Alan, who bared his teeth and rolled his eyes like a shying horse. Finally, Oliver collapsed altogether and had to be bundled into a taxi.

Alan met Oliver later at the Cranium Club, and asked whether he had disgraced himself by kissing me. "Oh no, my dear fellow," replied Oliver: "after all, I kissed Sheelah." "Ah yes—but the licence of age, you know."

Lytton and Carrington were both upset by Frank Ramsey's death, and as they wanted to be in London for a while they suggested that I bring Lettice to Ham Spray, to convalesce as it were. Ralph stayed on at Great James Street, working at Greville, and a couple of letters mark our brief separation.

February 20th. Ham Spray. Life, if you can call it life, continues here [I wrote]. 'Elephant Flo'‡ is very sweet and obliging. Yesterday morning we walked to the top of the downs, and after lunch Lettice lay on a sofa while I read aloud to her, which seems to be what she likes best. *Memoirs of a Fox-hunting Man* does very well, I find. But she is quite

---

* Art critic of *The Times* and † Sheelah, his wife.
‡ A large, pretty and plump girl who worked at Ham Spray for a while.

knocked out, poor creature. She can't bear chamber music because Frank was so fond of it, so I went and listened to a Haydn quartet by myself. We were having a conversation about old times at 11.15 when pop—all the lights went out. I struggled to the kitchen and searched high and low for a candle but in vain, so I went up and tapped on Flo's door. She looked a picture in her long nightdress as she handed me a small stump of candle which she said was the only one in the house. And after all, the upstairs lights were on, only downstairs had gone. This morning a conversation about what is the point of existence. Puss has just come in at the window and is rubbing himself in a frenzy against my legs. There, look at that smudge—Puss did it with his whiskers. Goodbye now, my darling, I can't write in these loving pussy paroxysms. [And Ralph] My jolly evening with the John girls turned into a game of chess with Roger Fry—the only consolation being that I won, but even then I was given a bishop before I managed it. Old Alex has brisked up wonderfully and today she gave me lunch of her mustard and mackerel mélange. Will see you darling about 6.30 tomorrow.

March 8th. I've been reading *Oblomov* and it has had quite an effect on my attitude to life: I see Oblomovism as both seductive and dangerous. Determined to avoid it, I have bought a new pair of elegant red house slippers, and decided I would no longer slop about in my old striped rope-soled ones from Sagunto; also to brush my hair more often and look in the glass sometimes.

This weekend at Ham Spray, Oblomov was often with me, an invisible companion. Boris [Anrep] was the only visitor. As usual, he never stopped talking, and amazed me by the fertility of his ideas. All Sunday he was deep in discussion with Lytton. "But supposing I *do* have relations with the mayor's wife?" I heard him say—and when I went into the room he was pacing the floor like a maniac, and the sense of tension lasted for at least ten minutes while neither of them spoke. What could it all have been about? Later he told us about enormous fishes he had seen on the coasts of Brittany, some round as a ball, others rhomboid. I thought that his little, rather cruel triangular mouth in the middle of his large face must have been something like theirs, and half expected that if one were to shove a brick into it he would give one "Crack!" and spout it out as powder—just as he was telling us happened with them. On Sunday, seized with curiosity about Tennyson's life, I galloped through a rotten biography of him. Ralph and I lay in bed talking for ages about Tennyson and Boris.

March 28th. I am thirty and find grey hairs in my head, but do not greatly care.

Last week we went to a party given by Alix and Nancy Morris. About a hundred people stood close together in a stuffy basement, shouting, bellowing rather, into each other's open mouths, and sometimes twining their arms vaguely about one or two necks at once. The atmosphere was choking, the food and drink good. Almost all were homosexuals—young man after young man pushed his pretty face round the door, and a crowd of truculent Lesbians stood by the fireplace, occasionally trying their biceps or carrying each other round the room. What is the point of such functions? I ask myself. Well, I suppose the answer is obvious—'*la chasse*'. It was a pleasure to come across the faces of a few old friends, such as Oliver, Robert Medley and John Strachey.

Last weekend we went to Noel Carrington's cottage. We had the last evening to ourselves, playing chess and talking, and then going to bed in blankets only and lighting a fire in our bedroom. It was delicious lying in the rough blankets and watching the flickering flames. As I became drowsy I thought about pleasure: the biological aims of human beings are to live long and be healthy, overcome enemies and other dangers, and reproduce themselves—to which ends they have developed such pleasures as tasting food, feeling warmth, and orgasm. Natural selection ensures that those who respond to these stimuli survive best. So I thought of pleasure as a sort of biological bait; but perhaps some pleasures get detached from their objects and cultivated for their own sakes, resulting eventually in skills like cookery or architecture. Then what about the Arts? I think they may be even further refinements: music and painting from love of the human body and the human voice, as well as the fertile earth on which we depend for life.

Last night we dined with Alix and James. Our dear old rooms are now fitted up in a bleak, geometrical, modern style which makes them quite unrecognisable, and I felt little regret for them though it had been a wrench to leave them. Chess again, and exposition by Oliver of the openings.

March 29th. Invited to tea in Duncan's studio, I imagined it was to be for a business conversation about their plans for a new Omega Workshop; they have already suggested my running it for them. So I was surprised to find rows of cups and cocktail glasses. No mention of Omega, but I very much enjoyed talking to Vanessa, and later came Peter Morris, Brocas Harris, Clive and his newest girl, Joan Firminger.

Last Thursday Faith [Henderson] gave a large party. I had lunched with Raymond that same day and gone skating at the Ice Club. I forced myself to fall down once or twice to strengthen my nerve, which I suspected was weakening. No need to try when waltzing with Raymond: we came a tremendous crashing cropper.

Dinner at Rules before the party. I wore my new evening dress made to my own design out of a piece of old blue Spanish brocade bought in an antique shop at Alicante. Faith had provided lavish hospitality, including a magnificent ham. I saw Frankie and Sheelah, and at another table Carrington, Alec and Beakus, Julia and Tommy and three red-headed hollow-eyed Debenhams. "Here's Elizabeth Jenkins,"* said someone, and in came a tiny figure dressed in white muslin to the floor, with golden bobbed hair and enormous blue eyes.

* The biographer.

In the kitchen I found Adrian, looking more cadaverous than ever.

"I'm always hearing about you," he said. "Who from?" "Ah-ha." "Your patients?" "Well, ye-es." "Who?" "Several of them."

Appalled by such unprofessional conduct, I was none the less full of curiosity and pressed him to say who they were. He would only say he had two female patients who talked about me.

"One admires you from afar. Almost everyone you know is being secretly analysed, and we have meetings where everyone and everything is discussed." Good heavens!

June 3rd. Ralph and I have passed the last month as happily as any I can remember, but as often happens, the trace left behind by happiness (unlike that of *un*happiness) has little detail or definition—it is a vague golden blur. We have had Gerald staying with us for three weeks, and got a great deal of pleasure from his charm and the comedy that always surrounds him, even if it is tragi-comedy at times. He is in a state of perpetual distraction. The seven spies who write to him from Spain report that Juliana is with child and that he is the father. His agitation at this news drives him sometimes to prowl the streets at night, pick up a black girl maybe, and leave the bath full of madonna lilies and lilac; at other times he rushes onto the roof with his fieldglasses bracketed onto a distant window, through which (he declares) he can see 'A beautiful girl having a bath'. It takes Ralph's cynicism to point out that 'she' is in fact a very old gentleman. Sometimes Gerald sighs for a permanent liaison, or married life in the suburbs and a perambulator.

Then Hamish has been in London again. The news brought back the anxieties and nervous tension of the past. It was a ghost resuscitated; I saw it and was afraid. With enormous gratitude I realised the delight of the happy reciprocal love Ralph and I have enjoyed for the last four years.

June 11th. I lunched with Hamish at the Café Royal, and

though he was easy to talk to and charming, the ghost faded. I felt a strong desire to sympathise with his love for *someone else*—see him marry and be happy.

Afterwards to a private view at Coolings, to be opened by Ottoline dressed as usual most eccentrically in tawdry satin finery. When tea was served she dropped a bun and chased it avidly with claw-like hands all over the floor. Arthur Waley was there, his face bright orange from ski-ing in Norway, the Henry Lambs, the Keyneses and Faith, who was full of the news that Wollaston, a Fellow of King's, had just been shot dead by an undergraduate. She hurried to tell this stop-press news to Maynard, who had been a great friend of his and was so upset that he left immediately.

July 4th. The event of today was a Hermaphrodite Party given by Eddy Sackville-West and Nancy Morris. It didn't begin till eleven, so that the first part of a sweltering evening had to be got through first. Ralph wore a red wig and Spanish shawl over trousers, but failed to look in any way feminine. I put on my yellow silk Empire dress, a bowler hat and a tiny moustache. Most of the young men had loaded themselves with pearls, powder and paint; the atmosphere was stifling and the noise so deafening that even the music from a vast gramophone horn was inaudible. There is a vogue now for such parties as this: all the creative energy of the participants goes on their dress, and there are none of the elaborate performances of earlier parties. Personally I think this is a sad come-down, a sign of decadence. Eddie Gathorne Hardy was genial and very tipsy, though near to tears because he had been twice rebuffed by a young German who refused to dance with him.

"I've been simply *mi*serable about my costume, my dear. I've had a *good* cry about it." And then, edging me towards the German he said almost in the young man's ear: "Now *do*, my dear, just *take* him by the hand and *throw* him into my arms." I did my best, but most unfortunately the German took a fancy to me instead.

That summer we took another holiday in Spain—this time to Cadaquès, just over the Catalan border. The two girls in our party of five were Rachel MacCarthy and Janie Bussy. Molly and Desmond were in the throes of an economy campaign. Yes, Rachel could most certainly come with us, but they couldn't afford more for her expenses than fifteen pounds, including the fare. We achieved this seemingly impossible task by means of travelling third class and in a good deal of discomfort, also by staying as *pensionnaires* in a small and humble inn on the sea front. But the little white town of Cadaquès, chosen more or less at random, enchanted us by its beauty. Sea and sun-bathing filled our days very happily. Every day we walked with rucksacks containing our picnic lunches, books and writing-paper, along the shore past a bay called Port Lligat, where there was a single flat-roofed house. We were intrigued by an eccentric-looking man whom we occasionally caught sight of on its terrace. "Oh yes, a very odd man," the patron of our hotel told us, "and he paints even odder pictures. His name is Salvador Dali." No-one had heard of him then.

Janie Bussy, then in her early twenties, was the only child of Lytton's sister Dorothy (author of *Olivia*), and the French painter and friend of Matisse, Simon Bussy. Brought up among such high-powered intellectuals as Gide and Valéry, she gave the impression of keeping the balance between her good mind and strong emotions with some difficulty. She was profoundly interested in politics, always left-wing, certainly a Communist for a time, and during the Second World War she worked for the Free French and was a violent anti-collaborationist. She could be fierce and uncompromising in argument, and we sometimes felt she disapproved of us—certainly of my view that the arts should be kept as separate as possible from war and politics, and (if anything) might have a beneficial effect on those tempestuous spheres. Oh no! Cortot could never be forgiven for playing to the Germans. As for Pétain, she would gladly have had him hanged, drawn and quartered. But we were both very fond of her, and she I think of us; she had a great sense of fun and warm affections, and developed rather late in life a talent for painting that was very much her own. Janie had a slim, elegant figure and beautiful legs and hands and she moved with quick, lacertine grace. Unfortunately her face could only be described as ugly, in spite of the sparkle and wit that shone from her brown eyes. Michael MacCarthy summed this up when he said with the puzzled expression I associate with his best remarks: "She looks like a clown who has just received a bit of bad news in the wings."

A curious episode in our lives also began in the summer of 1930, and perhaps deserves inclusion here. Ralph and I had always been interested in criminology, but so far this had principally taken the form of getting volumes of the Notable Trials Series out of the London Library, or reading detective stories. (He later reviewed these for the *New Statesman* and also wrote a book on Broadmoor.) But until we got to know Hayley Morriss we had never frequented the society of anyone who had served a prison sentence of three years' hard labour.

The name 'Hayley Morriss of Pippingford Park' is now met by a blank stare—yet in the late Twenties it figured in the newspaper headlines in capital letters two inches high, and everyone was avidly reading about the shocking doings of the tycoon who kept Irish wolfhounds and a harem of pretty kennelmaids among the oriental splendours of his Sussex mansion; they also knew that one of the girls had complained to the police, and that he had served his sentence for having sexual intercourse with girls in his employment.

Pippingford Park! What a ridiculous name, invented it would seem to figure in music-hall jokes and songs, among other occasions at the party of Maynard Keynes I have described in an earlier chapter. But that was in 1926, and by 1930 the case was already almost forgotten. Almost, but not quite.

In August 1930 Ralph and I were invited to spend the weekend with Leo Myers at his house Twyford Lodge on the edge of Ashdown Forest. On the Sunday it was very hot, and a swim was suggested. "Let's go to Pippingford Park," said someone. "There's never anyone about. Hayley Morriss is still in prison I think, or else he's gone abroad." A party set off, consisting of Leo's two daughters, Rachel MacCarthy, a girl called Veronica Bigham and ourselves.

After a few miles we turned through some iron gates and entered a strange world: we had left behind the white-painted fences and clipped laurel hedges of conventional Sussex, and appeared to be driving through a tangled forest on the banks of the Amazon, whose wide stream expanded here and there into a reedy lake, while the distance echoed with the outlandish cries of invisible birds. The Myers girls led us to the lake which they said was the best for bathing, and we were just going to undress when we spotted—at the far end where a small bridge spanned the runaway—a figure leaning on the parapet and looking at us.

"It's Hayley Morriss! It must be! What shall we do?"

Ralph volunteered to go and ask the motionless figure if he was the owner of the lake, and if so whether we might have permission to bathe. He returned, saying, "It's *him* all right, and he says we may." He declared afterwards that he was amazed at the unbridled way all the females of the party scrambled into their bathing-things and rushed into the water. Such is the attraction of vice! But when he swam over and remarked politely that the water was deliciously warm, Hayley Morriss asked him suspiciously: "What's that you've got with you? A girls' school?"

The bathe over, we got dressed, but Rachel couldn't find some beads she had been wearing. They were of no value but she was fond of them and didn't want to lose them. As we were hunting about in the bracken Hayley came up and asked what we were looking for. He was a stocky man, with a flattish, rather Mongolian face and light brown, prominent eyes. He gave an impression of strength and energy, though his characteristic pose was one of rigid stillness, so as to give him a somewhat bottled look, suggesting Worcester sauce that has been too tightly corked.

The beads could not be found, but Hayley took down Rachel's address and promised to send them if they turned up.

"And now," he said briskly, "won't you all come up to the Crow's Nest for a cup of tea?" The Crow's Nest! where dogs and kennelmaids had frolicked in half-hinted-at orgies! We were expecting some sort of Medmenham Abbey as we set off through the bracken. But not a bit of it. The Big House had been destroyed by fire some years before, and the Crow's Nest in which Hayley now lived was a small grey cottage on the estate. As we approached it we passed a number of white Chinese figures of ladies, standing, leaning against each other or lying like sleeping beauties in the grass, making a strange group against a background of gooseberry bushes. There were two ugly stone dragons on either side of the front door, and the small sitting-room into which we were led was crowded with lacquer cabinets and screens bearing birds in flight. The girl who brought in the tea was not at all like a beautiful kennelmaid, and all I can remember about this first visit to Pippingford was that Rachel could no longer contain her curiosity, but leaning forward asked innocently, "Do you keep any *dogs?*"

We drove away. The sequel happened a few days later, when Molly came downstairs in her Chelsea house, saw a package on the hall table addressed to Rachel, 'short-sightedly' opened it, and found inside a string of beads and a note signed 'Hayley Morriss'. She decided that no acknowledgment must be sent, for just supposing there was a police raid on Pippingford Park and a letter with Rachel's signature was found there! At the same time it turned out that Veronica Bigham's father was Sir Trevor Bigham, Assistant Commissioner at Scotland Yard; he had been in charge of the prosecution in the Hayley Morriss case, and was not pleased at his daughter's being in any way implicated. A week or so later Leo Myers struck the same note of alarm.

"I hear you and Ralph are going to Pippingford this weekend. Well, look here. You won't have any communication with Twyford Lodge while you're there, will you, Frances?"

"No, of course not."

"I mean, you won't let Hayley Morriss ring us up, nor ring us up yourselves, and you'll be sure not to come over and see us—and *on no account whatever* bring Hayley Morriss over to Twyford. Of course I don't disapprove of him in the least," he went on. "If he hadn't been caught and done time, it wouldn't have mattered an atom." And when I feebly remonstrated at the injustice of this, "Don't you see you're being frightfully *moral*?" he asked.

"Of course I am," I replied, realising it for the first time. However priggish it may seem, Ralph and I were full of moral indignation at what we saw as an unnecessary as well as unworthy stampede among the broad-minded intellectuals. Here was a man who had done what? Gone to bed with a few pretty girls. Of which of one's friends could not the same be said? In not a single case had he been charged with rape, but because the girls were in his employ, and one under age, an unusually severe judge had given him the maximum penalty. He had served his sentence, but still was not to be treated with common decency by people of advanced views. He had become to us much as an ill-used animal is to the R.S.P.C.A. The first step had been taken when Ralph wrote and thanked him for returning Rachel's beads; the next was for him to accept an invitation to go down to Pippingford for a couple of days' pheasant shooting. No doubt curiosity played its part. But they had in fact spent the day shooting pheasants and the evening alone together eating a frugal meal and discussing the Morriss case. The wretched man was evidently desperately lonely. Well, we were in for it now; I was not surprised to hear that Ralph had asked him to lunch with us in London, and not long afterwards we spent our first weekend together at Pippingford.

There was no sign of luxury at the Crow's Nest. Hayley neither smoked nor drank, and the meals that Flora the cook set before us consisted largely of eggs, lettuces and huge glasses of milk. The first thing I heard in the mornings was a vigorous sound of gargling and brushing teeth in the bathroom next door; the next the wild shriek of the demoiselle cranes in the park. Leaping out of bed I looked out on a dreamlike scene in which there was no sign of human life—mist still hung in the woods that stretched as far as eye could see, while armies of biscuit-coloured rushes advanced from all sides into the lakes, dotted with water-birds.

Hayley was the most restless of hosts. What he liked best was to walk with us through his domain, either with a gun or just on a voyage of inspection of the creatures inhabiting his garden of Eden. Many of the birds on the lakes were exotic species, with plumed heads, or splashed and dashed with gaudy greens and reds. The deer went leaping through the bracken and heather of the neglected park, and we were often startled by a barbaric cry as some of Hayley's beautiful cranes flew up with their long legs straggling behind them. There were a great number of these birds at Pippingford; they would stalk out in stately couples from behind the trees and execute their fantastic courtship dances, soar for a moment on outstretched wings, land and bow their long necks towards each other. Once, coming back to the Crow's Nest we were confronted by a squat muff of fur on short legs. It was a wombat. And another time Hayley opened the door of a rabbit hutch and revealed the staring yellow eyes of an eagle owl. This décor he had contrived for himself evidently gave him great pleasure; for his delight in nature was strong. Intellectually he was an odd phenomenon: his mind was a good instrument—a sort of computer that worked fast and accurately on whatever material it was fed with. And though he was always thinking quick, impatient thoughts, he could hardly bear to listen to a word anyone else said and was almost physically incapable of reading.

It was the mechanical speed of his mind, he told us, which had made him rich. Soon after going out, fresh from school, as a bullion broker to Shanghai, he discovered that he could convert sums of money from one currency to another in his head faster than anyone else, and by the time he was thirty he had made a quarter of a million by so doing. Then his doctor solemnly warned him that if he went on doing mental arithmetic at top speed all day he would crack up altogether, and as his predecessor had ignored the doctor's warning and been dead in two months, Hayley took this advice seriously. He packed up at once and returned to England, an enormously rich young man, brought up a Catholic, remarkably innocent. Or so he said. But we both got the impression that he was truthful, and when we read the press reports this was confirmed.

The first thing he did was to buy Pippingford Park and stock it with cranes, Irish wolfhounds and other creatures. The next was to take up dancing, fall in love with a beautiful dance hostess at the Savoy, bring her to live with him at the Crow's Nest, and later marry her.

He confessed that Madeleine was very lovely but that she was chiefly interested in girls; she picked them up on the sea-front at Brighton, or by advertising for kennelmaids. Five or six of these girls came to live at Pippingford, ostensibly to look after the wolfhounds. There was a lot of driving in to Brighton to go dancing, and more or less everyone went to bed with everyone else. One girl took fright, ran away and informed the police, but none would testify at the trial that he had made love to her against her will. It was enough for the Law that they were in his employ, and that one girl (Madeleine's sister, and, according to Hayley, a professional prostitute) was under the age of consent. He was arrested, tried and sentenced. Madeleine remained at the Crow's Nest in charge of Jackson, the chauffeur, a trusty friend to Hayley, who was still with him when we knew him, and who met us in the same battered old Rolls which had driven so many jolly parties to Brighton. It was owing to Jackson's evidence that Hayley was able to divorce Madeleine while he was in prison, conducting his own suit, and citing as co-respondent the Scotland Yard detective who had been in charge of the case. Not that he was the only one—far from it. Once Madeleine invited the whole of Jack Hylton's band down for the night.

"I shall never forget the scene next morning," said Jackson in the witness-box, "when Mrs Morriss went tearing down to the lake to bathe, without a stitch on, and with her long hair flying out behind her, and the whole of Jack Hylton's band streaming after her." And he ended with words which created a stir in court: "Pandemonium prevailed at Pippingford."

Hayley had now served his time and regained his freedom,

and his one idea was to lead a healthy open-air life, drink milk and gargle, and avoid getting entangled with the numerous women who wrote or called, offering their services or those of their daughters. He believed, wrongly I think, that many of these were *agents provocateurs* sent by the police, but he admitted to having the same idea about our bathing party.

Apart from the interest in hearing his story and reading all the documents in the case, I must say that Hayley's company was exhausting in the extreme. Yet we felt that his persecution mania was founded on fact, and that we were in common decency obliged to give him what feeble support we could. Had he, after all, behaved very differently from Gerald in making someone he employed his mistress? Then, one hot summer day in 1931 Ralph and Janie Bussy were lunching at Boulestin's, Janie wearing a smart hat, when they caught sight of an identical hat across the room. Beneath it was a pale, piquant face, and beside it—rather redder than before—was the face of Hayley Morriss. Introductions were exchanged, and a week later the telephone rang and Hayley's voice invited us to Pippingford to meet the new Mrs Morriss. How would she have changed things, we wondered? What mark would she have made on that now familiar background?

We were met as usual by the shabby Rolls, with the faithful Jackson at the wheel, and in no time the baying of the wolf-hounds greeted our arrival at the Crow's Nest. Beside Hayley, there stepped out to meet us a short young woman, pale of face and hair, wearing slacks.

That afternoon we walked as before through the woods and beside the lake, watched the cranes' flight and visited the wombat and the eagle owl. But things had altered at Pippingford. Nothing had changed in the décor, the cranes still shrieked outside and the mist floated up from the lake, but Hayley himself was different—his bright, pale brown eyes bulged from a slightly apoplectic face, and when we sat down to dinner that night we saw the reason why. In place of scrambled eggs and a few cèpes gathered in the park and washed down with milk, there was soup, salmon and roast venison. There was a bottle of superb Château Lafite that had—alas!—been brought almost to boiling point beside the fire, and there was brandy. For breakfast next day there was a heaped mound of stag's kidneys on each plate. For lunch there was Château Yquem. Exhausted and blown-out by food, we spent the afternoon rocketing in the Rolls to Brighton and going a round of the pubs.

As we went to bed that night Ralph said: "My God, he won't last long at this rate." "Well, anyway he's not lonely and pathetic any more," I answered. "We needn't come back to Pippingford again." And we never did. As in Edward Lear's *Calico Pie*, the birds flew away 'and they never came back, they never came back'.

If this incursion into criminology suggests that we had made any change in our normal existence, it is totally misleading. Research for the notes to the Greville Memoirs was still in full swing, and my pocket diaries show that we were still seeing most of the same friends—Raymond, Frankie Birrell, the Garnetts and Penroses, Tommy and Julia, Oliver, James and Alix Strachey. There are also still many entries of 'Skating'.

Clive was often abroad or at Charleston, but we had begun a regular correspondence which he kept up almost to the day of his death, and his very amusing letters often described visitors to Charleston. Molly and Margot Asquith were two characters he was fond of writing about.

In June 1930, for instance: "Molly has been lending *Lady Chatterley's Lover* to whom do you think?—why to Lady Oxford, who was of course duly horrified: 'You must promise not to lend it to anyone else, darling, or to leave it lying about. If Puffin or Elizabeth got hold of it I don't know what I should do. But he must have been a very strong man, darling—twice in one night!'"

That September Molly was there again, discussing the breakup of Boris and Helen Anrep's marriage, when Helen went to live with Roger Fry. "How would you like it, Quentin," she said, "if Clive and Duncan were turned out of the house and Mr Sickert put in their place?" "It would be a change at any rate," said Quentin. "Which was no bad answer," Clive commented.

Of a visit to the Wharf: "As we were walking in from the garden on my last day Margot gave me a nudge—it is the only word—and articulated through her teeth, 'I wish you weren't going, Clive. I should like to talk to you about death.'"

Shortly afterwards, while staying in France, Clive was stricken with serious eye trouble. To this he refers in a letter dated October 1931, and as his letters to me contain a good many scoldings for not writing more often, I quote it with pleasure. "Do you know it was almost a year ago to the day that I came back to London blind, and you read me that admirable book about Burns? I'm quite sure I never told you how much touched I was, but I expect you knew." Indeed I very often went round to Gordon Square in the evenings and read aloud to him, as did many of his other friends. We got through several books, and I enjoyed it as much as he did. In the following January he was sent to Zürich for a very disagreeable course of treatment, which he bore with great patience and humour. It seems to have cured him. Clive was one of those people who endure major disasters with fortitude, even if they complain about small discomforts.

In the summer of 1931 Ralph's mother became seriously ill with cancer, and he and Carrington paid her a flying visit at Cofton, her house in Devon. As usual, Ralph and I wrote to each other every day.

Did you think me very grumpy this morning? [I wrote] It seemed such a horrible boat-train morning, with its grey drizzle. Find out how your mother is, bathe in the sea, give my fond love to Carrington, and love me as much as you can.

[Crossing mine, Ralph wrote:] I hope you weren't concealing pain from me when you went off—I couldn't distinguish between low spirits in general and low spirits you felt I could do something to remedy, but I can't help aching to see you again, regardless of the expression on your face, because I love you absolutely, devotedly, passionately, always.

Next day they called on Gerald and his future wife, Gamel Woolsey, in Dorset, and he wrote again:

> Back now in the old house. At East Chaldon a familiar figure was striding along the street on the look-out for us. We were shown photos of all the architecture in South Italy, and some of Gamel naked in various postures in an Italian bedroom. I declare she has female appeal, and her figure is better exposed fully to view than shrouded in lumpish mystery. After Cofton they both seemed wonderfully easy to get on with, and human. Gerald at present has a mania for house-hunting. Lytton didn't return until this morning, bringing Sebastian with him. Clive has been invited for the weekend and is coming. Carrington sends up a shriek.

Gerald had met and fallen in love with Gamel Woolsey in 1930, and before they started their life in Dorset he had brought her to visit us in London, on their way to a sanatorium in Norfolk, for she had had a return of tuberculosis brought on by emotional agitation. She was an American from the Deep South, and since coming to England she had been living in a very different world from ours—that of the Powys family. Even her clothes spoke in an unfamiliar idiom: we first saw her wearing an 'arty' purple shantung smock embroidered in coloured wools. However, its 'lumpish mystery' could not conceal her remarkable beauty; we took to her very much at first meeting, and were anxious to mitigate the shyness she obviously felt at being confronted by Gerald's friends, none of whom she knew. She was extremely intelligent and well-read, wrote accomplished poetry, and had a peculiar air of distinction about her, which became more apparent when she had developed her taste in dress under Gerald's guidance. At first she struck us as lacking in humour, but on better acquaintance she revealed a dry sense of irony, based on a fundamentally pessimistic view of the universe; and she had the indolence typical of ladies from the Southern States, who waited for a black servant to pick up their dropped handkerchief (so another American friend told me), but were brave as lionesses in times of crisis. This was true of Gamel during the Spanish Civil War. She was a highly civilised being, with no unkindness in her nature. Her indolence didn't prevent her making many devoted friends in Spain, where they spent the last part of her life, nor from having a very warm relationship with Gerald's daughter by Juliana.

That September Ralph and I took a short holiday in the South of France at Cavalaire and St Tropez, where we bathed and picnicked with Eddy Sackville-West and a friend of his. St Tropez was then at the height of its vogue, and I was fascinated by watching the smart raffish crowds looking like animated drawings by Jean Cocteau, who shrieked at one another in the bars and boîtes, dressed in striped sailor jerseys and the shortest possible shorts, and painted their toenails silver or green. I have long believed that the language of clothes is one of the means by which human beings reveal their characters, their affiliations or even moods—others being tones of voice, facial expressions and gestures. Where Gamel had meekly accepted the insignia of a limited culture, because she was fond of its devotees, the bright young people of the Riviera in the Thirties were flaunting a banner ('We are the *avant-garde*!') just as insistent as that of the processions that walk the London streets carrying placards calling for 'Death to So-and-So!' My own pleasure in other people's dress is greatest when it expresses—not too aggressively—whatever unprocessed originality there is in their natures; but I find few things more enthralling than trying to read the hieroglyphics provided by a walk through any street in any country.

Even before our French excursion Ralph and I had been caught up in a more ambitious plan, which had been zooming into the foreground and fading by turns, like music from a badly-adjusted radio. Lytton had been feeling physically low, and neither he nor Carrington had fully recovered from love affairs that had taken unhappy turns. The idea was to shut up Ham Spray and take ship to Malaga for the two or three bleakest months of the coming winter. Letters had been written to travel agents, shipping lines and hotels, and it was further suggested that while Lytton and Carrington took rooms in the best hotel in the town, Ralph and I should go too, and find ourselves a humbler and more Spanish one, suiting our tastes and finances. I'm not sure how much any of us counted on it. Lytton's subconscious awareness of his failing health may well have made him hesitate, and was also probably why he liked the idea of having Ralph's support. Carrington too has recorded her forebodings in her diary. In any case 'the two-handed engine' was 'at the door'.

CHAPTER TWELVE

Catastrophe

I HAVE HESITATED at length before deciding to write about the ghastly winter of 1931-2. Two reasons have determined my decision: firstly, if an autobiography is to have any value it must surely be an honest attempt to accept and describe the truth, and that truth must contain black as well as white; and secondly, though much has been written about that tragic episode, I do not believe there is anyone still alive who lived through it as closely as I did. I look back on those months of constant and horrible anxiety and see them like a range of mountains blackened by a forest fire, that had to be painfully surmounted. My memory is certainly incomplete, but everything that follows will be as near the truth as I can make it.

After the unusually adventurous step of going abroad alone in the late summer of 1931, Lytton complained of feeling 'seedy' in November. This was no unusual event; he had always been nervous about his health and took his lightest symptoms seriously. But this time things took a graver turn, gastric influenza was suspected, and before long the dreaded panoply of serious illness had taken possession of Ham Spray. Nurses arrived, first one, then two, finally three. The most eminent specialists came from London and diagnosed typhoid, ulcerative colitis and enteric fever by turns (but never what he was actually suffering from) while Lytton's cousin, Dr Elinor Rendel—Ellie—kept up a sort of Greek chorus of comment on their utterances. Ralph went down at once, and for a while I remained in London, anxiously reading his daily bulletins.

On December 10th he wrote:

I sit in the library on duty while the nurse takes a walk and Carrington paints a glass picture in the studio. There has been

no change in the situation. We simply have to wait now for
the result of the latest two cultures taken last night by Dr
Cassidy; until then it is regarded as one of the typhoid group
and we all have to wash our hands every time we touch
Lytton. I still don't believe it is. Cassidy is the first person to
inspire any confidence, he appeared to discuss matters quite
openly with Carrington and me—if he was lying he was
being very clever, but then he was obviously a very clever
man. I saw him alone for a moment before he left and asked
about the danger. "Whatever it may be it is dangerous," he
replied, but I have told Carrington he said it might *become*
dangerous. All yesterday she went about as if Lytton was
dying and she had killed him by going up to London last
week, so I had to tell her something quieting. Lytton asked
me this morning how long I could stay and I said I would stay
until he was better. There's a night nurse coming by the 6
o'clock tonight. Lytton still thinks we m..y 10t be taking his
illness seriously enough, and thought of a night nurse himself
this morning. Now we have Pippa wanting to come down
and hover round. The nurse we've got so far has St Vitus
Dance and is deaf as a post, but otherwise perfectly qualified.
Carrington cries every time she goes in to see him, as soon as
she gets out. She can only view it emotionally and is an equal
patient. It is with her I am trying to, deal. I talk to her hour
after hour to prevent her rushing into panics, and she flings
herself into running the house.

I shall hang on like this for the present. I hate our being
separated, but you shall come here if it goes on, by some
means or other. Our lives are all short and precarious but I
shall love you as long as I live, with all my heart.

December 11th:

The report from Cassidy came through about 11 p.m.
'Enteric definitely ruled out.' I at once rang up Ellie and
found she had been at Cassidy direct, and her version was
'Enteric *not* definitely ruled out.' She went croaking on about

the dangers of everything with Carrington in the room with me, until I could have killed her. Carrington was thrown back into the glooms by Ellie's sepulchral voice, and began imagining Cassidy had told her more than he told us, which I don't believe. I take duty while the day nurse takes a walk and Carrington paints. It is best for C. simply to run the kitchen and see Lytton for a few minutes' gossip from time to time—she's eaten up with anxiety if she thinks she has to answer his bell. Meanwhile enormous glass pictures find themselves hastily brought into the world.

On the 12th I wrote back:

I couldn't sleep last night for thinking about Lytton. If you can, do ring me up and tell me the news, because I get very anxious both about Lytton himself and about you worrying about him. But I know you are being a tremendous comfort to Carrington. Please give her my love, and fondest love to you, my darling.

Ralph to me, December 13th:

It goes on exactly the same, but the pulse is phenomenal, quite steady. That and his cheerfulness are our supports. Pippa cheers him up with her cackling laugh—he even discussed McTaggart's philosophy with her last night when his temperature was between 103 and 104. She is being very sensible and calm. I sent Carrington off to Biddesden* to tea and she stayed there till 11 p.m. Pansy and Henry [Lamb] were very pleased with their daughter Henrietta—it was nearly born in a taxi in Hyde Park at 7 in the morning. Henry was entertained by Dodo to a gala night at the Eiffel Tower, where Clive turned up, and Augustus in his cups leaned across the table and struck Clive in the face twice, which Clive took extremely well in the rest of the company's opinion. Mary Hutch, Raymond, Wogan and Rosamond [Philipps]

* Bryan and Diana Guinness's house.

and of course James keep ringing up affectionately. Lytton talks always of Malaga, so I shouldn't be surprised if we got there after all about February.

I feel back in the trenches myself, there are the same orders for the day to carry out, telephone messages from H.Q., visits from the Colonel and Staff, NCO's to question and tell to carry on doing what they do infinitely better than ever you could, and at the back of one's mind the anxiety at night, the possibility of something unexpected and certain to be unpleasant being sprung upon one. I sleep as lightly as a feather. During the dark hours I breathe with only the top half of the lungs, and when I see daylight I take a deep breath and eat a hearty breakfast. But it is entirely a defensive rôle that one is performing. Blood-transfusion is the only way I could be sent over the top in this campaign.

December 16th:

The position is now as clear as it is ever likely to be. The real danger they apprehend is perforation, and this may occur at any time, day or night. Immediate operation then becomes essential, and an injection of blood, not a transfusion, is desirable to stop the haemorrhage. I am to be ready to provide this. As far as I could judge Cassidy took a more serious view of it this time than before. Ellie rang up Pippa this morning to say there was no cause for alarm—which is the most alarming thing that's happened yet as Ellie is invariably wrong.

You will be very moved that Lytton said to me: "Why didn't you tell me you were going up. I wanted to send Frances my very fondest love." I have every confidence myself in his tough constitution, so don't you be gloomy, darling. Goodbye for the moment.

James now moved into the house more or less permanently as well as Pippa, and the Bear Hotel at Hungerford was the refuge of Oliver, Marjorie, Pernel Strachey and other visiting friends.
On December 21st I wrote to Ralph:

Well, the old Bear will open his furry arms to receive me next
Wednesday. Darling, you must *not* think that there is any
need to come and see me—please simply think that there I am
if and in case you should want a walk or talk. I was so impressed by what you said last week about determining not to
despair until one absolutely has to. Don't forget it yourself. I
think about you every minute.

I well remember my first arrival from London into a house
dominated by the possibility that Lytton was dying. Ralph met
me at Hungerford station. Always a very emotional man, easily
moved to tears, and deeply devoted to Lytton, he had been left
with his powers of resistance reduced to practically nothing by
the constant strain of trying to support Carrington in her even
more agonising state of dread. During the drive from Hungerford to Ham Spray he talked and wept without stopping, and
though I've never been prone to tears my own soon began to
flow in sympathy. I came into the 'little front sitting-room'
feeling I had already been very close to death indeed, and it was
almost a shock to find Pernel, Marjorie, Pippa and Oliver sitting
in the warm glow of lamplight with calm, even smiling faces,
doing a crossword. (Why is it that certain scenes leave their
visual imprint so very clearly on the memory?) I had not seen
Pernel since she was Principal of Peile Hall, Newnham, in the
days of the imaginary Mrs Kenyon. I had no idea what she felt
about my relationship with Ralph, and I was almost ashamed of
the reluctance of my tears to stop oozing from my eyes. So I was
grateful that she greeted me with marked kindness. Marjorie
and Oliver were by now my great friends.

I joined them at the Bear Hotel for some time, and soon got
the hang of their way of dealing with what they all obviously
felt was the end of the world, by crosswords, jokes, or screeches
of laughter when a telegram for Pernel arrived addressed
simply 'The Principal Bear'; but all these were instantly hushed
whenever the telephone rang, to report the latest temperature
figures or verdict of the newest specialist. One after another they
arrived, the great men from London, pronounced their verdicts,

uttered prognostications. The 'King's Doctor' came and there was a touch of Strachey *folie de grandeur* in the voices that passed on the news. How long did they all sit there waiting at the Bear and why? I do not think Lytton asked to see any of his family except Pippa and James, but the others liked to visit the house from time to time—in case—and it must have complicated the life of poor Carrington, who was already exhausted by unhappiness and lack of sleep, to provide for so many; for beside the Stracheys and the nurses, she, James and Ralph all wanted their supporters. Carrington's were Gerald and Tommy, James's was Alix, and I was Ralph's.

Finding the Bear expensive and far away, I took a room above the Post Office in Ham, where a very fat white lady fed me on slabs of very fat ham for breakfast which might have been cut from her own thighs. Then I walked up to Ham Spray, did some bed-making and housework, and took Ralph for a walk when circumstances allowed. Our conversations hinged on two vital points: how likely was Lytton to die, and whether Carrington would kill herself if he did? Ralph was almost certain she would try to; for one thing he had found a torn-up letter in the library waste-paper basket written at the time of an earlier crisis in Lytton's illness, and referring to the eventuality of her own death, though she ascribed it not to projected suicide but to thoughts inspired by a narrow escape when driving home from the Augustus Johns at Fryern. Ralph was determined to circumvent any plans she might have, and to exert all his intelligence and strategic powers to this end—but he knew that Carrington had the cunning born of intense despair.

Occasionally most of us took a day or two off in London. On one of my visits I dined with Alan and Sheelah Clutton-Brock. They were the first people I had seen for some time who were quite outside the aura of the sick-room, so that when Alan blurted out, "Why is everyone in such a *fearful state* about Lytton's illness?" (to be hastily hushed by Sheelah) I did stop and ask myself how the Ham Spray crisis looked to the outside world, and whether much-loved distinguished people didn't die every day? In those days bulletins were published in the daily papers mentioning the progress of well-known people's illnesses. Lytton rated this degree of importance and the press often rang up, though the nice lady at the local exchange dealt with their queries and kept them supplied with news. I look back on this time of violent emotion, and am not sure with how much detachment I am even yet able to see it, but the fact remains that Lytton's danger did excite extremely strong feeling. Since then I have met with death in many forms, near and remote, and it seems to me there *was* a vein of hysteria in the agitation that surrounded Lytton's death-bed—in Carrington's case it was because she knew she couldn't live without him; in Ralph's it was because the screw of anxiety was turned by her suspected intention to kill herself, while all Stracheys, in spite of their powerful intellects, were given to surprisingly uncontrolled outbursts. Pippa and Carrington had frequent recourse to the *sal volatile* bottle; Ralph was possessed by restlessness which he could only vent by driving in and out of Hungerford for medicines or other supplies.

I remember one of the nurses, a small pale being, saying to me suddenly: "You know, whatever the specialists say, I think he's very bad indeed. His temperature dropped terribly low in the small hours last night. That's a dangerous sign." And there was a moment when Lytton, who had surprised everyone by his stoicism as a patient, who had even made fun of his own sufferings, suddenly told Pippa he had had enough—he didn't want to go on living. This naturally upset her dreadfully; it was soon known throughout the house, and morale dropped instantly.

On Christmas Day 1931 he was given up for dead. In the evening he made an astonishing recovery from near-unconsciousness. Twice more he was given up by the doctors, and the third time he died. When did we know the end was inevitable? The day before, January 20th, Ralph wrote me a note that was delivered by Gerald at the Bear:

I thought of you all this afternoon, but I can't see you now.

D.C. won't even see Tommy, and has only changed her mind for a minute. Gerald will tell you what the situation is. Lytton is sleeping sound at present. Be nice to Gerald, he has been of great help.

It was clear from what Gerald told me that the struggle could not possibly last much longer and at 2 p.m. next day, the 21st, Lytton died.

The news was of course telephoned at once to the Bear where I was staying, but not until next morning did I get a call from Ralph saying that he must see me at once and would drive in and fetch me out to Ham Spray, the tone of his voice suggesting further unspeakable horrors. While waiting for his arrival, Gerald and I walked out along the Kennet Canal. It was a marvellous morning, still and brilliant as some winter mornings are, with a sort of finality about it like the conclusion of some complex mathematical problem. I think we both felt that the beauty and serenity of nature presented death as something peaceful, inevitable and by no means all bad—and indeed there was cause for thankfulness that Lytton's really awful sufferings were over. Then Ralph arrived, and told me the whole tragic story as he drove me back in the car. He had been confident that Carrington would be safe so long as Lytton was still alive; but in the early hours of the 21st she made her attempt. Ralph found her in the garage with the car engine running, rushed in and dragged her out, and the poor creature had the cruel fate of witnessing what she had so desperately longed to escape— Lytton's death. He took me up to Carrington's room, where she lay in her four-poster bed, very still and white, but with the hectic colour in her cheeks that comes from inhaling gas. I felt moved with more pity than I had ever felt for anyone in my life. As we kissed I felt the thick softness of her hair against my cheek. We were alone together now and I told her she must let Ralph take her abroad for a while. (Perhaps conceitedly, I didn't have a moment's fear that any temporary separation could endanger our relationship.) She answered in a faint but very calm voice that she couldn't stand being a witness of Ralph's own strong and articulate grief for Lytton, and went on, "The kindest thing you could do for me is to take him away somewhere and spare me the spectacle of it." We did in fact go and stay a few days in Wales with Wogan and Rosamond, while Tommy and Julia came to keep Carrington company; the choice of Tommy was a step in Ralph's carefully thought-out strategy—he believed that Tommy's own suicidal nature and neurotic weakness, his dependence on her and his grief for Lytton would prevent her inflicting another blow on him.

Before we left for Wales, we took a drive with Carrington, Tommy and Julia through Savernake Forest. Those tall, wintry cathedral aisles were as appropriate to mourning as the brilliant stillness on the canal had been to Lytton's death, moreover Carrington had always loved the forest. She got out of the car and took a few steps, walking like a weak invalid, but I think the familiar beauty may merely have enhanced her pain that Lytton couldn't share it with her. This outing marked the beginning of Ralph's elaborate plans to pin her to life, playing for time and devoting unflagging concern to the smallest detail that might help to prevent her finishing what she had so bravely tried to do. Yet no-one who was with her at this time could fail to be moved by the pathos of someone dragged forcibly back to face a life she had deliberately decided was unbearable. In her diary she writes of 'anger' and nothing could be more natural. I think also that she felt the restraining pressure, the anxious watchfulness she was subjected to by those who loved her, as a form of blackmail.

The only thing that gave her some comfort was that the autopsy insisted on by James showed that Lytton had died from a disease not a single one of the great men had diagnosed—incurable and inoperable cancer of the stomach.

As some erroneous comments have been made about Lytton's will, such as that he left Carrington nothing, I would like to record that he in fact left her the major part of his capital—£10,000, and all his pictures and natural history books. His other books went to his brother James and Roger Senhouse. Ralph received a legacy of £1,000. Ham Spray was already legally Ralph's, but he made it clear to Carrington that it was hers to live in, alone or sharing with us, or with anyone else she chose.

Ralph managed to extract a promise from her that she would 'try nothing' for a given period of time, which was to be neither too short, nor so long that she would disregard it—I think it was two months. She gave him her solemn promise. Of course he must try every conceivable measure, but we both knew she had never greatly respected the truth, and why should she now in her extreme anguish? One of Ralph's theories was that she must be given no time to plan ahead; there must always be something just in front of her, a visit to Fryern perhaps, or from Julia and the dependent Tommy, or that Desmond MacCarthy should come down and discuss the possibility of writing something about Lytton. Or Leonard and Virginia. Or Rosamond and Wogan. So the days passed in a state of acute anxiety. Ralph spent a large part of the time at Ham Spray; I only sometimes went down with him, though I truly believe she preferred me to be there: his anxious watch over her was more than she could bear—at the best of times she had always guarded her privacy jealously. Did she ever waver from her purpose? I don't think so. In her diary written at Fryern* she noted: "Really I have decided."

"I'm worried about her," Ralph said to me. "She's doing too much clearing and tidying, particularly of the corner of the shrubbery by the ilex" (where she had wanted Lytton's ashes to be buried, had James not decreed otherwise). Meanwhile, often in London without him, I received letters which scarcely relieved my mind:

February 10th. The truth is that it is practically impossible to discover D.C.'s intentions, but they are not entirely self-destructive outwardly. She now wants to be left alone all next week without giving any valid reason, and beyond next week she won't commit herself. She wants me to get out of

* See *Carrington, op. cit.*

the way by going abroad, but that I can't do, I tell her, until the American business* is cleared up, which will take some weeks. My only line is to temporise as much as she temporises, and refuse to look in any direction except the one she's looking. I got to Fryern late and was lucky to find some cold curry in the larder. Augustus, Dodo and Vivien were there, and tomorrow they go, or rather today, so it would have been no good for D.C. any longer at Fryern. She had painted a lot of shells on one of Dodo's cupboards. Tommy had stayed till Tuesday and Beakus drove Tommy down on Saturday and stayed till Sunday. There was no trace of any feeling in D.C.'s conversation about Beakus. Tommy and Dodo she sticks to. Julia she was rather tending to go off in this morning's talk. We drove back for tea. This morning I had to do a whole series of things in Hungerford and Newbury, and got back late for lunch. D.C. writes letters continually and sends off little presents to everyone she can think of. As I see there may be a hitch after the weekend I advise (with nothing but love and fondness in my heart for you, darling) your going to Owley, where it'll be freezing and you might skate. D.C. didn't press your coming here, and I think she had in mind a rather emotional time of it with James, and I may use leverage from your being at Owley to stay on here next week, but I shall have a talk with James first and certainly several more with D.C. every day before Monday. Tell me all your news and don't say my letters have fallen off in devotion, for you know I dote on you everlastingly.

February 11th. I've been through the bills and mended the electric bell in the dining-room. D.C. mended a screen last night and put the tiles in the library up this morning. I've changed my mind again about her—I now think she's cheerful to some extent because she has some desperate plan up her sleeve. Please don't refer to any of this when you write as she may sneak a look at your letters in my coat while I'm

* With Lytton's publisher.

sawing wood—she's so sly she'd manage anything. There is every reason to think her idea is to do something or other next week—she declares she just wants solitude but I find that unbelievable. I hardly think James will be much use because everyone but me finds her so plausible. I now think Dodo and Tommy simply believed what she wanted them to believe, and that there is no improvement whatever in her state of mind. She won't discuss any future but yours and mine, and that idea of your having a child is a suicidal compensation for her, I'm convinced—she returned to it last night and made a rosy picture of your happiness and my resemblance to Henry Lamb. The substratum of truth in what she says makes it plausible, but where does she come in? She comes in by just going out, and leaving her money to me and thinking she is procuring our happiness as she can't procure any for herself. I *must* stay on here with her if I can, and I *must* assert that you and I are not all-sufficient to each other or all is lost. I hope you see that, dearest—the truth is negligible now: it is silly to kill her by inability to tell a lie. You and I can manage all right, but she can't.

February 12th. James comes down tomorrow. Rosamond has been invited to come here for Monday night. I stay here until Tuesday at any rate. Alix has now been invited for the following weekend and this has depressed D.C. markedly. I think she intended to leave no loose ends outstanding after this weekend, which only she would imagine to be possible without making her intentions unmistakeable. Now she is faced with a future engagement she is at a loss how to proceed. I think it's possible she may pay a visit—to London perhaps to see Diana [Guinness] or Tommy—or she may stay here. If she stays I shall stay too, as she may have realised that she can never hope for a tidy situation and may decide on an untidy one. This set-back to her plans has made her gloomy and brooding—confirming my view of her previous good spirits. You see by everything I say that I take it for granted she'll have another try. All I can do is keep putting a hook in

her as fast as she unhooks herself, even then she may get
desperate and spring something sudden. It's very rare I see,
outside Elizabethan plays, for a situation to be so clearcut. If I
left a loaded revolver or an ounce of opium on the table and
went for a long walk there is little doubt what I should find
on my return—and I'm well aware that D.C. has made a will
leaving me £10,000. I *am* rather surprised though at the
number of people who can't face a situation because it would
bring on responsibility. "Let's pretend it's going to be all
right, and then we've done our best to prevent it going all
wrong," is what they say. Dodo, Tommy, James, Alix,
Gerald, the whole lot of them, can't really believe in death
until it happens. Only you believe me, and that's because you
love me perhaps, rather than because you think it inevitable
as I do. Naturally I'm not the best person to keep D.C.
company with this fixed idea—but who else to get? She
won't have Tommy down again, she says. Julia? Dodo is ill
and nursing Augustus. Sebastian busy. Where are all these
friends of hers? So that's why, dearest, I have to hang on. All
my love to you, sweetheart.

My letters to Ralph at this date merely reflect his agitation and
can have brought him little comfort, but we were not in the
habit of suppressing any of our thoughts or feelings to each
other. On February 13th I wrote:

I feel terribly worried darling by your anxieties: you must
get help in bearing them. I will do anything you think best,
but I *can't help* being fearfully anxious about you. It is
absolutely true what you say about other people avoiding all
the responsibilities, and you are right, good and kind to do
what you are doing. Don't think for one second that I mind
your being away. You *must* be with her next week if she is to
be alone. But I think her gloom is a good sign if it means even
temporarily abandoning her scheme. Do tempt her up to
London—being with friends who at least make her *pretend* to
be gay would be better. She doesn't want to go because she

feels it might shake her resolution. I think Rosamond may be some help. Why not take her into your confidence?

Ralph's next letter crossed mine:

The situation is changed. I had a long talk with D.C. last night. She has persuaded me that next week is not going to be a final week, and I am believing her to the extent of coming up to London on Tuesday. It's the only thing to do after such a conversation, as if I stayed it would show such a mistrust and desire to thwart her that she would be intractable.* I believe she'll be safe next week. The only thing is that she denied having made any plan, but in such a way that I did not really believe her. I thought that she had not worked out any details, and so felt entitled to say she had not made a plan. My darling, I love you most passionately. You will see me on Tuesday. It's melancholy work here but I'm bearing up. Keep warm and love me.

February 15th. James agrees with me that the position appears safe until next weekend at least, so I shall come up on Tuesday. Sweetie, you mustn't get over-anxious. I had to tell you what I thought, but D.C.'s disease—for it is a disease—is not necessarily fatal, and if it is not fatal it is not likely to make her a permanent invalid. I have a certain philosophy which makes the prospect anxious but not desperate: if she can't bear it she will relieve herself of a great deal of misery and she will have had only happy memories of Lyttoff† and herself. She will make my misery greater but she will herself be well out of it.

I want you to ring up Desmond and ask him if he could manage to come down on Wednesday or Thursday. I want it to be a surprise for her which she can't dodge.

It is sad all day long—I hope when I die I shan't leave such

---

* The theory that she was *never* alone till the night of her suicide is disproved by this and other letters.
† One of Carrington's pet names for Lytton.

cruel gaps in other people's lives. And now courage, my sweetie, how I love you! Don't get thin from anxiety.

Ralph stayed in London for several days in a state of convalescence: acting as warder did not come easily to him. But on February 19th he was back at his post, and writing again:

D.C. seems pretty gloomy and in rather a bad temper—she couldn't start the car so I had to come up with the wireless man. Take a cummerbund with you to Cambridge; you'll find some news at 16 when you get back on Monday—there is nothing now but unrelieved gloom to report.

During Ralph's frequent absences I continued with my usual life at Great James Street, working on various part-time jobs such as research at the British Museum, having friends to dinner, but missing Ralph continually and looking forward to his daily letters, though sometimes almost too anxious to open them. Occasionally I went away for the weekend, and it was during one of these, staying at Cambridge, that I wrote on February 21st. My host was my great friend and confidant, the writer Leo Myers.

[To Ralph I wrote then, from Cambridge:] It is odd being here entirely alone in this huge house with old Leo himself. He has been looking a little low and ashy-faced, but he is as amusing and peculiar as ever. In fact I am having a delightful time, very soothing, very comfortable. Leo is a perfect companion, though we don't see a tremendous amount of each other. Today a longish walk. The early morning is obviously Leo's worst moment, he takes a bit of thawing. Five minutes ago he said that he is continuously unhappy, anxious, bored or all at once, and life only changes according to the degree of its intolerableness. Lunch at Lettice [Ramsey]'s. What a jamboree! There was Julian [Bell] with his beard, and the children bouncing and shouting like hooligans, and Miss Muspratt, Lettice's photographic partner. I go up tomorrow early and shall hope for a letter to hear how you are. I think of you every minute, darling; don't be too depressed. I hope Carrington will come to London next week: give her my fondest love.

Meanwhile Ralph reported:

General state of D.C. is improved. She was thoroughly grumpy with me this morning for the way I blew my nose in the bathroom—an excellent sign. James and Alix arrived and she was even gay before dinner with them, but the moment we went to listen to Mozart on the wireless, at the first bar she ran out of the room, and after the quintet was over when we went to look for her she was nowhere to be found, but the front door was open: I went out and found her on top of the downs in the moonlight. She'd been as far as the Gibbet and was quite recovered when I met her. I wasn't really alarmed when I went out, but I felt peculiarly melancholy walking in the bright moonlight listening for any sound of her, with the wood-pigeons clapping out of the trees thinking I was an owl. I prefer the outside of the house to the inside—indoors the rooms look as if they'll never recover from Lytton. Today D.C. has taken Alix over to Biddesden for lunch—it seems that Tommy is there—she is going to ride with Diana first. I have had long business conversations with James, and a short walk in the sun with him before lunch.

I shall come up on Tuesday. I expect D.C. wishes to stay on here like last week, and as Dodo may come on Wednesday for a night or two I shall return on Friday presumably. No mention yet has been made of the following weekend. I feel depressed in spite of D.C. being definitely better. It is a sad prospect for us all—no getting away from that. My fondest love.

Next morning I wrote:

I have just got in and had your letter handed me by the

postman. Yesterday's dinner was not a great success. Perhaps Leo gave Peter [Lucas] nerves. He appeared to be very anxious to impress, and rattled away a series of epigrams, rather indistinct and boring, about the limitations of dons, talking in a romantic strain about London as a city of vice and adventure, full of enemies, mistresses and intellectuals. Leo's face soon turned into a series of catlike slits in an ashy grey background.

Tonight I go to Wellington Square to meet [William] Plomer and Roger le Vieux.* I don't know what that will be like.

I loved getting your sweet letter in spite of its sadness. Everything is very sad and there is no getting away from it, as you say, and the only idea seems to be to give up all idea of its being anything else. It was a soothing weekend at Cambridge, Leo was very kind, but his state of mind is terrifying.

[From Ralph, February 22nd:] I shall arrive tomorrow afternoon. You and I are to come down together on Friday if you can bear it. James comes the next weekend. The second stage with D.C. has now set in which is more irritating but less agitating than the first. She has returned from Biddesden bringing Tommy and Julia, which was more than I could bear. I had to take James and Alix in to their train at Savernake, so I let D.C. take her pets back to Biddesden, and we never spoke to each other after dinner. Quite like old times. James comes the following weekend again and I have lunch with him on Monday. If you're dining out any night you might fix me up with Molly [MacCarthy]. I'm feeling absolutely miserable but fond as can be of you.

Ralph's state of nervous strain is exceedingly obvious from this letter, and although he had no choice but to exert every effort to grapple Carrington to life, engineering event after event and marshalling all her friends to this end, the very persistence and intensity of his watchfulness must have been a

---

* Fry (as opposed to Senhouse).

torment to her. Yet, in spite of this, there were moments when she seemed to be recovering. The last weekend of February Bunny and I went down, and all of us went over and slept at Biddesden. It was during a picnic in the lovely woods surrounding the house that Carrington asked if she could borrow a shotgun, as rabbits were over-running the garden. She had very often shot pheasants and rabbits from her bedroom window, but Ralph's old gun had been given away. We all heard the request, but it was rather vaguely given, and I think everyone hoped it would be as vaguely forgotten. There is no truth, however, as I can positively state, in the story that she took the gun there and then and we all drove back with it to Ham Spray. It was very much more in character for her to come back in secret for it later, as she in fact did. Not until another week had passed did she use it, and this was on March 11th, the day before the most hopeful project was due to begin—a tour in France with her beloved Dorelia and Augustus.

Ralph was above everything a realist and he had always known, and said to me, that if she persisted in her desire to kill herself no-one could prevent her, but in the meantime he was resolved to do everything in his power to do so. I wonder now if he thought she could be happy again without Lytton? And (whether he thought so or not) I wonder if she could? We neither of us knew much about death and bereavement at that time, and now that I do know from my own experience I think his mistake was failure to realise that though, as he said, 'the disease' (of grief) 'is not necessarily fatal' it is in a sense *incurable*. It may well take a year to reach its crisis, and sometimes even two. After this, scar tissue begins to grow, but there may be terrifying relapses. But, as everyone who knows anything about her must realise, Carrington was unusually single-minded, and all her intensest emotions—the creative side of her character and her feelings for nature and poetry—were concentrated in her love for Lytton. Without him the world must have seemed meaningless to her. Moreover there was undoubtedly a suicidal substratum in her character; she was haunted by strange unmerited guilt, which expressed itself in nightmare dreams. So that it is doubtful if she would ever have been 'safe', or Ralph able to relax his guard.

When the fatal day came, Ralph and I were asleep in our flat in Great James Street, with Bunny in the room he rented from us on the floor above. The telephone rang, waking us. It was Tom Francis, the gardener who came daily from Ham; he was suffering terribly from shock, but had the presence of mind to tell us exactly what had happened: Carrington had shot herself but was still alive. Ralph rang up the Hungerford doctor asking him to go out to Ham Spray immediately; then, stopping only to collect a trained nurse, and taking Bunny with us for support, we drove at breakneck speed down the Great West Road. We were all completely silent—the thoughts of the others, I imagine, in the same strangulated condition as my own.

We found her propped on rugs on her bedroom floor; the doctor had not dared to move her, but she had touched him greatly by asking him to fortify himself with a glass of sherry. Very characteristically, she first told Ralph she longed to die, and then (seeing his agony of mind) that she would do her best to get well. She died that same afternoon.

CHAPTER THIRTEEN

Back to the First War

NEARLY EVERY SUICIDE, however logically motivated, leaves a train of guilt among those who feel they could have prevented it. I hope I have made it clear that Ralph put every ounce of willpower and strategy into his battle to save Carrington; nor was he by any means the only one who was tortured by a sense of failure. After her death, the energy he had put into the fight for her life recoiled like a spring, leaving him in a state of desperate, futile restlessness, and as close to nervous breakdown as he had ever been in his life or was ever to be again. Though I was not in much better case myself, it was my turn to adopt something of the same rôle he had been maintaining with Carrington, and I thought of nothing night and day but how I could save him from his self-torment. Yet, had I been less distraught myself, I should have known that Ralph was not a suicidal type—the life-instinct was in fact very strong in him— and that he would never inflict on me the same cruel wound he was now suffering from himself. As it was, I depended on the support of friends such as Rosamond and Wogan Philipps who drove over to see us in answer to my S.O.S., or who like Bunny and Ray asked us to stay, and so helped us tide over the soulless period that follows a death. In this case as well as lawyers and registrars there was an inquest to be faced—the verdict was 'accidental death'.

Other friends urged us to get away at once, and stay away as long as possible. One of these was Molly MacCarthy, whose letter to me is movingly sincere and characteristic of her:

Never have I known anything like this—in our lives! How strange—how *strange*. Oh alas! I have a fancy that Lytton and Carrington are looking through the windows of Ham Spray and telling you, *bidding* you and Ralph to live. Death over-came one. Death was fallen in love with by the other—for you *none of this*. Take him away, darling Frances, *right, right away at once*. There you will think of them more rightly—*more as they would have wanted it* than in the scene of this long drawn-out drama. It is too much for you. Do this darling Frances for Ralph—whether he feels *he can go or not*, you *must* take him. All my love to you, Moll.

Among a host of other letters, I would like to quote Desmond MacCarthy's to Ralph, not because it urged escape, but because of its typical wisdom and understanding:

I am naturally anxious about you, and through you about Frances. I cannot, dear Ralph, be of any help to you until you are better. I have not known the depths. But it seems to me likely that one cannot remember the dead truly—the essence of their being—until one has recovered in some measure the enjoyment of life. Their death was not *the* characteristic thing about them. It was their response to life, and it is by living oneself again that one meets them as they *were* and keeps in closest touch with them. If you can feel again delight in the thought of them, even if for a long time it is a cheating torturing delight, your life, with what you have in Frances, will be much more full of what is worth having than that of most people—you are not really an unfortunate man—far from it, although you have had to bear much worse sorrow than most. Your affectionate Desmond.

Yes, it was vital for us to get away for a while from that sense of black tragedy that hung over our heads like a thundercloud. To try, at least, for it seemed as if it might well follow us every-where. Alix and James came up with an opportune and practical suggestion. They planned to take a spring holiday motoring in the south of France, but didn't want to waste time by driving all the way there and back. Would we consider taking their car and driving as far as Avignon, where they would meet us? We would indeed; Ralph's eagerness to accept showed that a positive impulse was already at work in him; moreover it was his own idea that the best antidote to present anguish was a return to the scenes of anguish of the past—namely the battle-fields of the First World War.

Ralph had been an undergraduate at Christ Church when he joined the army in 1914, and after the usual training in England was sent out to the Western front as an infantry officer. Except for a short time in Italy he remained in France until 1918. He liked talking about it, had an excellent memory and was above all a realist; I was often amazed by the lucid detail in which he would describe his most harrowing experiences. He was not so deeply scarred by what he had gone through as were many others among my friends who took part in one of the two great wars, but although he was a brilliant soldier and his character was too forceful to be deeply dented, it was, as it were, re-orientated. I can give three examples of what I mean by this: firstly, he lost his ambition; then, like Morgan Forster and G. E. Moore, he grew to think that human relations were far the most important things in life (without however losing his passionate interest in public events); and lastly, he became a pacifist for the rest of his life.

We accepted the Stracheys' kind offer and set off less than three weeks after Carrington's death. Now I again began to keep a journal, for I felt that to concentrate on what we were seeing, and our reactions to it, might provide some sort of sorely-needed lifebelt.

March 30th, 1932. Left London at tea-time in James's car, and crept in to Owley at seven-thirty. Jill [Rendel]* was cooking an elaborate dinner with the help of a French cookery book. Dick had an apron on and was washing out the dirty utensils. Both Ralph and I were nervy and irritable, as well as some-what sodden with drugs and despair. Soon after dinner we went off to bed.

March 31st. Woke at six, a blustering morning, feeling low

* My niece.

and fearing a rough crossing. Bad beginning. Ralph very depressed; it needs very little to convince him that life is not worth living. I resolved to be more cheerful *at all costs*, and I think he must have come to some similar decision, for once out of bed we greatly reformed. Arrived at Folkestone, we entrusted the car to a sweetly smiling sailor who told us the sea was merely 'moderate'. The crossing took no time, and there coming off our boat I caught sight of Duncan, Vanessa and Angelica. Angelica shrieked "Fanny!", Duncan and Vanessa were absolutely charming. Vanessa asked us to go and see them at Cassis, pressing my arm as she did so, which touched me very much, not only because of my admiration for her but because I think of her as undemonstrative. As we walked along Duncan said that he seldom took Mothersill when going on the sea, but quite often on dry land, if he felt tired or 'a little mad' and found it 'excellent'. We saw them onto their train, followed by a porter carrying their nine very Bloomsbury-looking 'pieces'. Then we looked about for somewhere to lunch.

Leaving Boulogne in the afternoon we headed towards St Omer, through dead flat country, crowded with small red, rawly new houses on which a drizzle was beginning to fall. 'So here we are already in the War zone,' I thought numbly, and soon we were driving into the home town of Mademoiselle from Armentières of the war-time song. The dialogue between two unattractive young men in our hotel seemed appropriate.

"Tu couches avec quelqu'une ce soir?" "Mais *oui*." "Avec qui?" "Ah—moi aussi je suis jaloux."

April 1st. Grey morning, still inclined to drizzle. We drove off in the direction of Ypres, crossing the Franco-Belgian frontier through a striped barrier. While Ralph went into the customs office to fill in documents I sat in the car and was beset by little boys, who enquired "Eenglish?" and then one of them began to sing in a voice of exquisite sweetness, "It's a longa longa way to Tipperary." "Les Anglais ont beaucoup de pennies, n'est-ce pas?" said the other, and then, "Demande-lui si elle est Boche," and pointing to Ralph: "Lui soldat? Moi caporal!"

Now we set off in search of a farm called Oosthove, where Gerald and Ralph had been billeted for some time when they first went out, and where Ralph believed he might have left behind an illegitimate child. But the landscape puzzled him, and was not as he remembered it. We asked an old man the way, but he barely knew any French. We were driving through a part of Flanders where the front had been more or less 'stabilised' for a long while, and I found the sight of it strangely moving. Did it really end fourteen years ago? It looked as if it had made its momentous passage far more recently: there were no full-grown trees, only saplings, and everywhere I saw unfilled trenches and shell-holes, 'pillboxes' and barbed wire, and I could only guess how extraordinary it must all seem to Ralph. We stopped again to ask a labourer the way. "Ah! Oosthoff!" This time we were directed.

Like all the other houses, the farm had been rebuilt so as to be unrecognisable to Ralph, but in the courtyard stood a short red-cheeked woman with grey hair, who was not. When Ralph went up to her and asked if she was not Madame Le Roy an expression of jubilation succeeded the dawning wonder on her face. Exclamations of surprise, beaming smiles and violent handshakes followed; a peculiar intensity crossed her features—whether from trying to remember or from remembering too much I'm not sure, but I had seen it in the face of another old lady in an *estaminet* when we asked her if she had been there in the war. Madame Le Roy took us into her steaming kitchen, where something was sizzling on the stove. There we found a little girl and two smaller boys; the girl was about the right age to be Ralph's child and I rather thought she might have been, but he said afterwards that he couldn't believe it and any way there was nothing to be done about it. There was also a black-haired aunt with bulging black eyes, who spoke appalling Flemish-French. She grew inarticulate and excited at the mere mention of 'la guerre', and told us she had been too ill to be moved, and had to be left behind when the Germans occupied the village, but when she gabbled about the horrors she had experienced we could only gather that she had "beaucoup souffert aux reins".

Madame Le Roy brought out glasses of bitter red wine and healths were drunk. "C'était une misère," she remarked succinctly.

Ralph enquired after Berta, the girl he had had an affair with, who had asked him to give her a child; but a shutter came down over Madame Le Roy's face, and she said she had gone back to her family at Wytschaete. Before we left I asked if I could take some photographs. No sooner had I said "et les enfants", than the little boys rushed off like madmen, and I saw them frantically struggling with shoe-horns to get into hard little black boots. One tied a scarf round his neck, which dangled to his toes, the other put on a sailor hat. They were ages getting ready. We left in a chorus of farewells and good wishes; it was impossible not to be affected by such genuine human warmth.

As we drove on through Ploegstreet towards Ypres, everything we saw was bringing the war closer to me, minute by minute, making it more real and terrifying than before, while it was setting a flood of memories loose in Ralph's mind. I watched the astonishment in his face as he tried to identify different places whose configuration had once literally been a matter of life or death to him, his amazement as he looked at a gently sloping turnip field and realised that it was to gain possession of this tiny area that he and his fellows had fought so bitterly for weeks on end, and been ready to die or kill. He was gazing at such a slope, with his face a mask of incredulity, when a farm labourer came up and talked to us. Oh yes, he said, bits of equipment, bones, boots and tin hats still frequently turned up when a field was ploughed or harrowed. He pointed to a heap of relics close by. But the country people profit from this horrendous harvest, as a reward is given for any handed in to the *Mairie*.

Ypres has been almost entirely rebuilt, except for the battered ruins of the Cloth-Workers' Hall in the middle of the Grande Place, which has been left as a sort of war memorial. It must have been a beautiful if rather austere town, but patched up as it was it made me think of Greta Garbo's face after a motor accident. We had an excellent lunch before visiting the War Museum, where an ex-officer of the Belgian army showed us round his little store, gabbling away as he did so in a sing-song hotch-potch of French and English. For one franc you could look through a stereoscope and see pictures of dead men in heaps, as gruesome as you could wish for. I was reminded of similar photographs of the Boer War, possessed by my parents, and how Julia and I used to gaze ghoulishly through a little hand machine at heaps of corpses at Spion Kop, and wonder if they were real or actors. There was no question about the genuineness of those in the Ypres Museum, yet my curiosity about the war had been so violently awakened that I studied these far more convincing horrors carefully. Since becoming an adult I have been on the whole an escapist—something I am not at all proud of—yet here and now on the Western front I felt I wanted to abandon my ostrichism and look the results of modern warfare full in the face, *once and for all*. But the exhibits in the War Museum were pitiful, and we were beginning to freeze in the cold cellar where it was housed. We left it therefore, and turned north to St Julien, where Ralph wanted to see the places where he had been wounded and buried alive. A body had evidently just been dug up in a field beside our road, where two tin hats also lay—we were beginning to be hardened to this pathetic sight.

After Ralph had pored over the map and studied the lie of the land for some time he stopped the car and we got out, but although he peered about like a dog searching for a rabbit-hole, he could not make up his mind where his narrow escape from death had taken place. Had he hoped to abreact his nightmare recollections by seeing the site where they had happened? Perhaps. Instead he had to make do with describing them to me: A bursting shell had completely covered him and a few others—he made me imagine all too poignantly the weight of the loose earth on top of him, the utter darkness, the impossibility of moving in spite of his frantic desire to do so, and the impotence of hearing the faint voices of his would-be rescuers. He couldn't even call out, for every time he tried to take in a breath, earth entered his lungs instead of air. There followed acute pain in his chest and the horrible consciousness that his tongue was being forced out of his mouth. Just before he completely blacked out he heard his batman's voice say: "Wasn't the Captain around here somewhere?" And they dug him out, unconscious but alive. Soon afterwards he was wounded and sent back to base for a spell.

Through Béthune and Lens we drove, to the Vimy ridge, in a storm of rain. Here a large section of the trenches have been preserved—fossilised, one might say—by the Canadians. A guide led us down into the tunnels made by the French and Canadians forty feet beneath the chalk—a perfect rabbit warren, from which another tunnel descended steeply far out of sight to a point where the sappers had laid their mines to blow up the Germans. The trenches with their concrete sandbags and stone duckboards looked false. Far more disturbing was the surrounding confusion—somehow impossible for the mind to comprehend—of the earth's surface, broken as it was with shell-holes merging into each other, grassed over yet still containing shell-cases and old boots. And it struck me that the reason this sight was so terrible was that one of the fundamental premises on which we human beings base our lives is that the earth we stand and walk on should obey some rules. This is why we all find the idea of an earthquake so terrifying—if the very ground beneath our feet tilts, cracks and loses its solidity, why then there is no help for us. However, what I was now looking at was not the result of an earthquake, but of man's ingenuity, of 'man's inhumanity to man'. It was beyond anything I had expected, and it gave me a glimmering of what being *in* a war must be like—but a glimmering it must remain, because for all the vivid descriptions Ralph was pouring into my ears it was impossible to fill in the background to the horrible chaos; the continuous cacophony of deafening noise, the presence and smell of death, the companionship of human suffering and fear. We have talked and thought about nothing but the war all day. I would never have guessed that it could be so obsessionally absorbing.

From Vimy to Arras, where we spent the night.

April 2nd. Started late and drove steadily through pelting rain (at one moment it fell out of the sky with a sort of explosion) and blustering wind, as far as Guise, a small mild town, where we lunched alone except for some fish in a tank. A great deal of food was set before us; I began to feed the fish with crumbs of bread. One young waiter smiled apologetically, and after watching me for some time said: "Si vous leur donnez ça ils mourront!"

On again to Verdun, finding with some difficulty a little hotel, humble in appearance but in a charming position on a canal. The walls of our room were covered in enormous brown and blue pansies; the bed was painted mauve.

When we went down to dinner a wedding party was beginning to arrive in the room next door to the *salle-à-manger*. The bridegroom was tall and stalwart with a monkey face; the bride bony and plain, dressed all in white with a Juliet cap. "Est-elle jolie?" the patronne excitedly asked one of the maids, who screwed up her face. Then a jazz band arrived and struck up with overpowering noise. Everyone began dancing, but the bridal couple were evidently only allowed to dance with each other; so when a tiny little man chased the bride and seized her round the waist she got very red in the face and shrieked out, "Au secours!" A terrific smell of sweat began to percolate through from the dancing-room.

This simple scene provided a form of counter-irritant to what we had been seeing and thinking about—but it was the battlefields that filled my dreams.

April 3rd. This morning we drove to look at the battlefields north-east of Verdun: a grey, rolling, pock-marked landscape. The sense of catastrophe and gloom was more crushing here even than in Flanders, I think because so little attempt had been made at reconstruction. It was as if the heart had quite gone out of the country, and I thought with regret of the ugly little red houses of the north, which were at least a token that life had sprung up and renewed itself. In the Bois de Caures the trenches had none of them been filled in, and were full of old boots and mess-tins. The few trees still standing in the wood were gaunt skeletons riddled with bullets, and one had only to take hold of a branch and there was a rattle of shrapnel falling to the ground. Field telephones were still fixed to some. The 'Tranchée des Baionettes', where a whole regiment is supposed to 'dormir debout' with nothing but the points of its bayonets visible, had been too stagily got up, with the French passion for the macabre, to be anything but unreal, and was far from as moving as the desolate woods.

On to Metz, driving over gentle hills striped sage green and yellow; it is very much alive (especially after the graveyards we have been seeing), prosperous but rather sinister. The houses wear tin hats like the German soldiers'; we were glad to leave it and go on to Nancy. No more battlefields. We ate a magnificent meal at Nancy and then went to the cinema to see a film perfectly suited to the French palate. "Un homme dévoré par des crocodiles" said a placard outside, and so he was, screaming all the while. We were also treated to a man killed by a panther and a volcano swallowing everything as a grand finale.

April 4th. After yesterday's brief pause the rain has begun again. As it showed no signs of stopping we went out to look at the Place Stanislas and all the other architectural beauties of Nancy; they are indeed ravishing, but if only one had not to see them in this disheartening and continuous downpour! So it went on all the way to Langres.

April 5th. Woke to the sound of *rain*. It beats me how we keep going at all, but somehow or other we got to Dijon, where we lunched at the *Trois Faisans*, and it was impossible for the ice that had collected round our spirits not to melt under the influence of the divine food we had there. Left, with it still raining, to Meursault, and put up at the very beautiful Hôtel du Chevreuil.

April 6th. Hoorah, the sun is shining! We are now entirely dedicating ourselves to food, and the great event of today was our tremendous lunch at Macon. Hot *pâté en croûte*, followed by delicious sole, and when we thought we had finished six or seven magnificent puddings arrived on a trolley. Impossible to resist them all; they are the hotel's great speciality, as we should have been aware, and the inventions of the Kaiser's chef. Ralph smoked a cigar and we sat over our coffee and brandy in a state as nearly approaching content as we have yet reached, but overfed and intoxicated.

After lunch we pulled ourselves together with an immense effort and drove to Solutré. I had always been interested in what I had read about the place and its huge rock over which prehistoric man once drove his herds. It was every bit as impressive as I had hoped, and Ralph's pleasure at my excitement put him in a very sweet mood. We visited the little museum and climbed the hill, picking up fossil bones, flints and 'smagma' at every step—also incidentally walking off the effect of our Gargantuan meal.

April 7th. Tain l'Hermitage. Ralph was very sad and sleepless during the night, and I lay worrying during long anxious hours, whether I should not get him to talk about his sorrows, which he had not mentioned for some days. I broached the subject next morning, but maladroitly no doubt, only releasing an outburst, so that I felt as I stood naked in front of the wash-basin washing 'all over' in tepid water and trying to reason with him, that things had never been worse than *this*, *now*, nor would they ever be 'all right' again. The extraordinary thing is that I do not believe my efforts were so misplaced as I felt at the time: they did perhaps relieve the tension built up by silent suppression, and somehow we did find courage and calm before setting off in the car again through the Rhône valley. Now olive trees and fruit trees in flower accompanied our journey, with their exquisite mingling of grey-green and pale pink, and of fresh tender leaves with the near-black of cypresses. The day was lovely as we stopped to look at the theatre at Orange and then on to Beaumes-de-Venise, where on Helen Anrep's advice we have booked a room for a week in the hotel ensconced inside the Château.

The small village crouches under Mont Ventoux, and the Château has fine large rooms, good beds and windows opening onto a peaceful looking garden where frogs croak in a pond. Madame, a plump grey-haired woman, was rather too talkative and became more so when it transpired that we knew Roger Fry. It looks a soothing place, but with a high-brow flavour, and several artists have left their traces here. Madame looked disappointed to hear that we weren't 'artistes peintres'.

April 8th. We took the car on a last round of intensive sight-seeing before we have to hand it over. Lunched at Les Baux among its weird conglomeration of rocks, and were drawn into an antique shop by the lovely stuffs hanging outside. A walking skeleton came to serve us, but was too weak to know the prices and so fetched a little sister who was only slightly better. They said they were nursing a little nephew who was very bad with 'enterite'—I suspect they all have typhoid. Ralph very sweetly bought me a Provençal cape of pleated cotton in a delicate ferny pattern of dull purple and sage green.

April 9th. Tarascon and the Pont du Gard and then Avignon where we were due to meet Alix and James.

They arrived buttoned-up and fur-coated as if they were

off to the Arctic, and we all went to have a good dinner at Hiely's; they seem a very solid pair when confronting the world of 'abroad'. James is the dominating one of the two, and carries a neat list of places and times; Alix is a complying but wayward child—chooses pigeon though (or possibly because) it is the most expensive dish on the menu, and insists on sitting up in a café drinking grenadine when James wants to go to bed. Alix talked to me interestingly about Tommy, whom she called "a very bad case", "in a bad way", she "doesn't know what will happen to him". What she specially finds alarming is his violent objection to the slightest responsibility, or to anything being his 'fault'. He says the bad part of one's character no more belongs to oneself than to anyone else! As we sat in the café a small excited crowd began to stream past, and there among them we saw the cause of their enthusiasm—Maurice Chevalier, slouching along, straw hat on one side, cigarette, jutting jaw and all.

April 10th. We went out with the Stracheys to have some coffee and watched the natives pouring into church. Then they climbed into their car, and (with considerable agitation) drove off.

I was very sorry to see them go. They had had a good effect on Ralph's spirits and I feared they might collapse again. I asked him if he felt deserted and he said, "No," and the only effect on him was that he became increasingly considerate and loving to me. We walked into the market and bought him some blue cotton shirts, lunching afterwards out of doors in almost painfully hot sunshine.

Then we caught the bus back to Beaumes-de-Venise and were greeted by Madame with many cheerful enquiries about our "jolie excursion".

April 11th. Magnificent night's sleep for us both, but some sadness at waking. Ralph is now unfailingly angelic to me.

A violent morning shower soon cleared, leaving clean blue sky, glistening verdure and dazzling white pear-blossom. We took sandwiches and went a long walk, returning for dinner and gaining great credit from Madame and a tall stately lady with a face like a Roman Empress who has just joined us. The atmosphere of the hotel would be oppressively inquisitive and cosy, were it not that everything is a distraction, even the strange antics of the waiter, who always walks about on tip-toe, carrying the dishes in one hand and with the other on his hip, laughing quietly to himself. He wears an old-fashioned striped yellow waistcoat and has a face that might be a criminal's or a philosopher's, but is most likely a half-wit's.

April 14th. It is getting warmer every day, and yesterday we spent most of it in the garden. Unfortunately so did Madame, and a young woman—newly-wed?—who arrived with her husband last night. This evening he left for Paris, and his wife remained sad and silent until, alone with Madame (and us, deep in books) she suddenly burst out with all her woes. How "gentil" he was and "bon pour moi", how she was "très doté" in having such a good husband, but evidently he has some awful disease which can only get worse. Madame kept automatically saying, "Quel horreur!", the invariable reply to which was "On doit subir son destiné, n'est-ce pas?" Poor things—but the French are an extraordinary race.

April 15th. Hottest morning so far. We begin to burn. The post brought us a bundle of letters, including one from Gerald, which induced a spell of melancholy. Sat out and read poetry all morning. There is an asparagus field at the end of the garden, and quite a few heads are beginning to poke up; an old man and his wife came and prised up each one, very delicately, with long narrow implements. On the hillside new flowers come out every day, while grape hyacinth and rosemary, which were out when we came, are now quite faded.

April 16th. Got up early to see the first asparagus market, which began at ten. All the shoots were very thick and with barely any coloured tip to them—some had none—and their dead whiteness showed that they had been dug out of the ground before they had even peeped out of it. Sellers stood in a long row behind their baskets, and as the clock struck ten several bull-necked men, who were the buyers, began hurrying along the lines, asking prices here and there or pointing out the wretched quality of the asparagus. It was some time before a single actual deal took place. Then a dwarfish figure with a large pair of scales weighed them. Prices were evidently low, and several sellers carried their wares away in a huff. Their preference for white asparagus (as against our delicious green) and their failure to appreciate the glorious taste of blackberries, are to my mind two serious defects in French gastronomy.

Here my diary dwindles into silence, not long before the appointed time when we were to meet Alix and James and take over the car for our return journey. We dawdled for a while in the pleasant south, now so warm and pretty, visiting Moustiers and Riez, and exploring the Gorges du Verdon (a boy scout's excursion involving underground passages, dizzy climbs up metal ladders, and equipment that included an electric torch and an antidote against snake-bites). After this we turned reluctantly northwards towards home and its problems.

After taking a detour to the east of Paris we made our final excursion into the war zone, driving this time across wide, gently-rolling country, whose fresh greenery had been brought on by the spring sunshine. Here mile upon mile had been dedicated to graveyards, stretching as far as the eye could see. All place names have now vanished from my mind, indeed we crossed regions where the graveyards seemed to be substitutes for towns and villages. Each one covered a vast area and was almost at once succeeded by the next. We were seeing a very different aspect of the war from that of our outward journey; it was as if, instead of traversing a land still raw and bleeding from unhealed wounds, as we had then, we were now entering a huge well-organised hospital—sterile, impersonal and tidy—where the facts of agony and death were concealed by scrupulous neatness and flowers, and controlled by uniformed efficiency. The graveyards of northern France are (or were then) as beautifully kept as any hospital: not a weed was allowed to break the smooth surface of the shaven grass; the headstones looked as if they had a daily wash; and those bodies that were identifiable were properly and respectfully registered in a book—the old soldier in attendance being only too eager to show us the triangular Cape of Good Hope of his collection: a general perhaps, or a hero of many medals. Nor were the large sections given over to unknown soldiers, or the small black crosses marking the graves of unidentified Germans, less carefully tended. The latter were usually set a little apart, and I was irresistibly reminded of a field full of young lambs of the black-faced mountain variety, all turning their cross-shaped heads to look at one, at the same time. Often a large and hideous statue symbolising *La Patrie* or the Christian religion presided over these tragic memorials.

Now it was time to leave the war zone behind, but we could not possibly shake off the thoughts it had stimulated. These acres of graves had in a way been the most dreadful sight of our whole journey. In their bleak abstract manner they resembled an enormous addition sum, every figure in which (represented by black crosses or white—what difference did it make?) stood for a life lost—the life of a young man who might have enjoyed years of happiness, love, children. And the answer to the sum seemed to us to be *senseless destruction*.

Stunned and appalled, we headed towards the coast and England. Wilfred Owen, who wrote with full knowledge, epitomised what we had been feeling better than anyone. When he was killed in 1918 he was planning a volume which was 'to strike at the conscience of England'. Its Preface and Contents were found among his papers, and among them one reads:

> Inhumanity of war
> The unnaturalness of weapons

Willingness of the old to sacrifice the young
The insupportability of war
Horrible beastliness of war
Foolishness of war

And the last word of all is 'Disgust'.*

* *The Poems of Wilfred Owen*. Edited by Edmund Blunden, Chatto & Windus, 1931.

CHAPTER FOURTEEN

Ham Spray again

WE ARRIVED BACK in England in May and went straight to Ham Spray. In spite of the advice of some kind friends Ralph never had a moment's doubt that this was where he wanted us to live. We would give up Great James Street and take a couple of attic rooms that were going in Gordon Square, as a base for work and keeping in touch with friends—but Ham Spray would be our home. It gave us a smiling welcome. The chalky soil hardly encouraged garden flowers, but there were daffodils, pheasant's eye narcissus and polyanthus in plenty; the beech tree was bursting into leaf, and everything was pure new green from the foot of the garden steps to the top of the downs. The house shone with cleaning and polishing. Olive the maid seemed delighted to see us; I even think the cat was.

But how would Ralph take coming back? This question had been perpetually running through my head as we underwent the macabre blood-letting of our battlefield journey and afterwards.

The problems and difficulties facing me personally seemed at times insoluble and appalling. There were such practical considerations as getting on really good terms with Olive, not undertaking anything that Ralph wanted (at present, anyhow) to do himself, and taking over the housekeeping without in any way seeming to try and supplant Carrington, but without letting standards fall. Not to change anything and yet continue 'being myself' (I have never been much good at the opposite); to be sensitive to visitors' feelings. But of course by far my greatest preoccupation was with Ralph's state of mind. Since Lytton first fell ill I had thought of this with a continuous intensity which was probably unwise but also unavoidable. I got into the way of never saying or doing a thing without first thinking how it was likely to affect him, what reverberations it would set going on his feelings. Then from sheer exhaustion I would occasionally relax, sag, simply *have* to give my vigilance a rest, and very likely make some blunder. It was a tremendous strain, partly because I was aware all the time of the acuteness with which Ralph felt his misery. He was so realistic that he was unable to escape one atom of the truth, and this I admired enormously, but to see him live up to his realism under such a hideous strain was a magnificent and terrible sight, and one that had moved me almost without pause for the last six months.

I think we both now longed for a quiet uneventful life for some time to come. Ralph had come to depend on me more than ever; the streams of energy which once went into his relations with Lytton and Carrington were now deflected on to me, and sometimes it was almost more than I could bear. But luckily he was fighting hard on his own account to regain what Desmond had called 'the enjoyment of life'. He wanted to see people; we had many good friends, and they came in dozens, to stay the weekend, to meals, to play bowls, or go to our favourite bathing place in the river Kennet—Garnetts, Penroses, Brenans, Noel Carringtons, Raymond, Janie Bussy and many others. Sometimes in company Ralph developed a sort of hectic gaiety which I found unnatural; but I needn't have worried, it was a stage in the healing process.

As for me, I was leading a life with *no choices*, and there was something paradoxically both restful and strenuous about that. All I cared about was to see Ralph happy and himself again, and to achieve this had become an egotistic desire on my part.

One or two diary jottings may give some idea of this hot and beautiful summer:

August 2nd, 1932. We have had beautiful sunny gaps between showers, and in one of these we went mushrooming on the downs, taking Saxon. It's a pleasure to see him amble along, wearing his best black London suit, and then give a sudden dart and pounce. He has a surprisingly sharp eye for them. He has been charming this weekend; I never remember him gayer nor more prone to giggle. It was lovely up there among the thin waving grasses, harebells and bedstraw.

M.A.M.* has been staying here for a few days and left us this morning. Both Ralph and I took her to the station and Ralph was his most charming to her, kissing her warmly and telling her how much he had enjoyed her stay. She stood at the carriage window looking touchingly pleased and frail.

August 4th. Janie [Bussy] and Quentin [Bell] have been here two days, very perfect guests. Quentin's luggage contained nothing but a pair of dirty old overalls, in which he goes out every day and sits in the damp grass to paint.

Hot, sun-bathing weather. Janie wears shorts and lies with her lovely long legs twined like snakes, while Quentin extracts his torso from his overalls and is revealed as a pink and white cupid.

Last night I dreamed very vividly that we met Julia in Paris and she went mad on the hotel steps. Ralph was much taken with this idea. "Of course Julia *is* really mad," he said. "Why did I never see it before?" A breakfast-time discussion about the difference between madness and sanity.

August 5th. We couldn't make out whether Janie and Quentin intended leaving us today or not. It seems they stay till tomorrow. Rachel and Dermod come this evening. The atmosphere has been rather youthful and hilarious these last days. I am quite longing for a little quiet adult life, but Ralph says he finds it a distraction having people here to play bowls with, and I think it does keep his spirits up; what's more I have really enjoyed our two young visitors, who have been easy, cheerful guests.

August 14th. After so many hot days gentle rain has come and is welcome. I looked out of my bedroom window and saw the first drops falling, and smelt a delicious earthy smell which

* My mother.

gave me intense pleasure. I do relish being in the country, and I love Ham Spray very nearly as much as Ralph does—I think I shall soon be able to say 'quite as much'.

Yesterday Alix and James arrived to stay for three weeks. This is to my mind the nicest sort of visit, and they are perfectly self-supporting, so that we can leave them and go up to London with clear consciences. One thing James is going to do is inspect the books in the library and decide which he wants to take away. Lytton left the earliest ones to Roger Senhouse and all the rest to James, who has very kindly said that he won't be taking a great many at present and we can have the use of the others—including the Dictionary of National Biography, thank heavens.

Alix has just bought a new shiny motor-bike, and it arrived before she did. When she and James first appeared, Alix walked stiffly through the house with an excited yet blank expression, then out on to the lawn, where she stood gazing all round expectantly. "Where is it?" she enquired, like a child. There have since been frequent sounds of revving up in the drive, and Alix disappears at a rather stately pace, sitting very erect in her black leather coat. When Ralph went to call James to the bathroom this morning he found him lying on his back on the floor, swaddled in mufflers and bicycling hard with his legs! Surely he can't mean to have a go on Alix's new toy? I doubt whether she would let him. They are unlike anyone else in the world.

Last week we spent two grilling days in London. A delicious dinner with Phil and Phyllis Nichols* in their back garden at a table spread under the trees and lit with candles. Phyllis looked fine in a red and white striped dressing-gown—I liked her very much. But the heat was almost over-powering, un-relaxing its hold, whether we were lying naked on our bed in the attic at Gordon Square, or sitting out reading in the square gardens. Then I was half-boiled under the dryer at the hairdresser's, sticky in my thinnest dress dining at the Ivy. We

---

* Phil Nichols had married Phyllis Spender-Clay.

walked home, letting the breeze rush through our hair, but—too hot to go up to bed—we went into the Square garden and lay for a while on the hard grass, looking up at the giant black trunks and branches of the plane trees, and layer upon layer of their leaves, some caught by the street lights and shining like silver coins, some green and transparent.

We have arranged for some of the furniture from Great James Street to go to Ham Spray, in particular my solid oak table. This is to take its place in the library, and will be useful for working at the Greville Index.

August 22nd. Ralph is now mad on the idea of a swimming-pool, and all day long we have been pacing and measuring in the rain. I stood in the ha-ha with a broom on my head with a white rag tied to the top, while Ralph sighted me from the lawn through an olive-oil bottle. I suddenly wanted to laugh. Every ten minutes he says, "Well, supposing the bank is at an angle of forty-five degrees" or something of the sort. However, I got him to switch off at last and give me a driving-lesson.

August 27th. A very long walk on the downs, looking for mushrooms, took up the entire morning. It was windy and bright, the sun hot at times, the grass enormously long. Hundreds of hares jumped out of their forms and galloped away. R. walked in front with his basket and each print in the grass from his great Russian boots was a hare's form.

Yesterday at tea-time Tiber* suddenly appeared at the window stretching his yellow eyes enormously wide with greed. We saw but couldn't hear a mew. Then the whole atmosphere of Ham Spray tea surged up and brought with a stab the remembrance of Lytton waving his long white hands in exasperation, then laughing, and letting Tiber in.

I have written several letters; I drove the car into Hungerford to shop, bungling sadly at the gears (my fifth

* The cat, Tiberius, was named after Matthew Arnold's lines:
'So Tiberius might have sat, Had Tiberius been a cat.'

lesson), started to revise the library catalogue and cooked delicious mushrooms *à la crème* for our dinner.

On August 29th I went to Charleston for a few days, knowing that Ralph would have the excellent company of Alix and James. We had had Dick and Judy [Rendel] staying with us for the weekend, and the arrangement was that I should drive to Charleston with them, as it was on the way to their house, Owley. During this short separation Ralph and I wrote to each other every day.

Frances to Ralph, Charleston, August 29th and 30th.
My darling, I do not at all like this separation, and I had an owlish desire to burst into tears when I saw you looking so sweet, and left behind me on the drive. It is ten past twelve and I am just getting into bed and wondering how you are, and if you got off to sleep all right, and how the evening was spent with Alix and James.

Would you believe that after travelling an hour and a half we had only got to Kingsclere? This was because Dick, who was map-reading with tremendous pomp while Judy drove, made a great many mistakes. And he prides himself so on it. There was a great deal of useless information: "Half a mile on a road will come in from the left." (Very long pause.) "Pay no attention to it." Or, "Two miles on, at the cross roads, turn to the right." Of course by the time the cross roads were reached Judy had forgotten what he said, and turned to the left. Or again he would say, "Now, my dear, the road becomes wiggly." (Long pause.) "The road becomes wiggly now, my dear." Judy: "Yes, you've said that already, darling." They are as good as a play.

I must say Dick was very charming during tea at Charleston, and won all hearts. Clive's first words were that there was an old friend of mine here—Lettice! Otherwise there are, so far, Julian, Vanessa, Angelica and a little school friend. Julian and Lettice are off to France tomorrow, and Duncan comes back from London where Clive thinks he is "up to something". It came back to me how very beautiful this country is as we drove up to the house—a lovely evening, with a blue sky dividing up into most promising-looking little round clouds. The garden blazing and festooned with enormous flowers: the zinnias, my darling, like great mops; when I thought of ours that we have so carefully cherished it was enough to make a cat laugh—or cry. The ground was strewn with apples; Clive picked one up for us and was instantly stung by a wasp. Dick then made a tremendous impression by pulling an iodine pencil from his pocket.

* * *

[30th:] It is Tuesday morning, the sun is out, and a bell has tinkled. I shall have to get up. Clive and I are to go and see Virginia today. Till then I shall hope to find a nice book and read it by the pond. Oh dearest, what are you doing? I desperately want to know how you are and if you slept well. Did Tiber come to call you and wind round Olive's legs? What have you talked about to Alix and James? I do think they are fascinating characters. I feel a great deal more fond of them after this visit, though they are no less mysterious. I thought a great deal about them as we drove along in the car. Both Judy and Dick were enthusiastic about Alix's charm, and they had obviously enjoyed the weekend.

I hope I shall not forget all my driving before my next lesson. From being ever present in my brain, the clutch and gears have dropped to some lower level. Darling, I suppose I must get used to being away from you for a day or two, but I find it very hard to bear, and keep thinking of when I shall see you again. I do miss you badly. Vanessa bowls me over with her beauty and nobility. I never saw so many wasps. When I'm away from you I do wish I was nicer to you when you were there. I love you so desperately much.

Ralph to Frances, August 29th, Ham Spray.
My own darling. As you've only been gone three hours nothing much has had time to happen. I fetched the plums and the wine from the station and have carried all the wine

into the cellar and laid it in neat rows in dry corners. I have
not yet talked to James about the wine or any of the other
things. I did mind your going away terribly, but I try to
comfort myself by thinking it's good practice as I shall have
to accommodate myself to not seeing you for three days once
a year. You're the only person I want to see ever—this letter
had better be a testimonial: I'm more in love with you than
I have been at any time during the last nine years. You've
grown onto me, until living without you is like trying to live
a day without a leg—I can only hop from chair to chair and
wait for my leg to come back to me.

At lunch we talked about Dick and Judy. The plums are
being bottled in twelve large jars, and another twenty-four
pounds will arrive shortly; the apples will have to be picked
as the wasps are biting them savagely. Alix had a wasp in her
coffee after lunch and got it into her mouth, but ejected it
safely, except for a lasting memory of its texture on her
tongue. My fondest fondest love from your most loving R.

Ralph to Frances, August 30th.
My own darling. I'm yawning my head off before the postman comes, with the rooks cawing in the aspen and Tiber not
yet home from the hill. Everything has been so quiet since you
went away that time seems to drag. I have glued on the piece of
wood to the chair in the sitting-room and I have paid James the
enormous sum of twenty-one pounds ten shillings out of my
overdraft, so that the wine that has arrived, and has to sit for
seven years waiting, can be regarded as mine when the time
comes to drink it. I thought it was the only possible way of
regularising the situation. It was a pity that the wine should be
so young and we so old. I wish the situation was reversed. Alix
went along the Bath Road on her machine for a test, and came
back at twenty miles an hour. I've been round the garden
once or twice and kept my eye on a good many plants. A
letter from Sheelah protests that I write her 'strange letters'—
so much the better, I'll make the next one stranger yet. I wish
you were here in my arms, my sweetie. Tiber's my only

bedfellow, and not a very reliable one either. Your own devoted loving R.

Frances to Ralph, Charleston, August 31st.
My darling love. I have just got in from an afternoon of Woolfery to find your letter. It was angelic of you to write so soon, and almost more than I dared hope for. It is constantly a wonder to me that with all the misery you have to bear you manage to be so sweet to me. Your letter made me happier than for I don't know how long.

Well—the day here has been fine and sunny, with whirling clouds. The view from the bowling-green at Rodmell was ravishing—the evening sun dazzling bright coming sideways across the marsh. This morning began with a turmoil. Julian and Lettice had to be got off for France and somehow packed into the baby Austin behind Vanessa. Julian had to change his suit in the car on the road to Newhaven, and in the end it turned out they had left behind their Baedekers, several hair-brushes and a camera. I spent the morning in the garden writing and reading and talking to Clive. Wasps in hundreds gnaw the fallen apples. Wrote to Marie ordering dinner for three on Thursday. Wrote to Gerald asking him to dinner on Thursday. Didn't write to Molly but meant to. I sat reading a life of the Brontës this afternoon in Duncan's folly. Then Clive and I went to the Woolves, which I very much enjoyed. Virginia knows how to be utterly charming if she likes, and today she did. Playing bowls she is the cracked English-woman, with an old felt hat on the top of her head and long pointed canvas shoes. She started some way behind the jack, and took a little run and then hurled her bowl with wildly waving arms. Leonard's tremolo seems to me to have spread and now invaded everywhere, including his head; as you might guess, he is a devotee of counter-bias. We had some exciting games, though with quite different rules from ours. It was lovely on the bowling-green, I wished you were there. Two dogs sat about, a good deal in the way. Besides the companion dog to Clinker there is a horrible black spaniel with a head like a bloodhound, much too big for its body. Virginia told me that it had twice gone off into a dead faint on walks, through over-excitement about rabbits. She found it stretched out, gasping and blue at the lips. The Woolves drove us home. Virginia sat with me and asked me about Ham Spray and about you. I can't describe to you the *kindness* as well as fascination of everything she said—about the beauty of Ham Spray, about life in the country, about you and how she believed you could write if you wanted to. I got a feeling she was *really* fond of you. She sent you her love and asked us to come and see her whenever we were in London. I felt she meant this. She wants you of course to write something about Lytton, and she said he had told her how good Carrington's letters were, and she wanted you to think of publishing them some day. In all this there was no hint of exploitation, and the 'taste' was perfect. I felt she really wanted Ham Spray life not to be altogether lost, and for her own sake. I was bowled over by her irresistible cracked charm. Tell Alix she (Virginia) is going to be the newest motor-bicycle addict, for she says Leonard won't let her drive the car and a motor bike is just what she wants. Now I must go and polish up, for there is grouse for dinner and it is gala night.

*   *   *

I'm just getting into my narrow bed—a guttering candle on my table and the Brontë book to read myself off. Duncan is back with a long account of a film he saw in London, where Charles Laughton, Gary Cooper and Tallulah are all imprisoned in a submarine. Angelica wore a scarlet dress at dinner and looked very beautiful. The evening went quietly off. I sewed name-tabs on Duncan's silk pyjamas. Goodnight now, darling. I love you with all the love in every crack and cranny of my heart. I never loved you more and I don't feel I could ever love you less. Love to Alix and James. F.

As this was to be the last time with very few exceptions that Ralph and I were parted for more than twenty-eight years, I propose to make these four letters a sort of envoi, and also to offer them as a random sample of a relationship that continued virtually unchanged, and certainly in no way weakened, until Ralph's death in November 1960. They were very happy years, though of course they had their ups and downs; they included the birth and growth of our son Burgo, and the Second World War.* But our lives were now stabilised, and our personal history was concerned with our travels, our garden, our cats, and the music, books and pictures we enjoyed. *Above all* with our friends.

Why, I wonder, have writers paid so little honour to friendship? Sustaining, warming, refreshing and endlessly stimulating, it should surely have had almost as many poems written to it as have been dedicated to love. Yet I search anthologies and often find none.

Blood is thicker . . . well, in a sense it is true, but love of family is genetic and static in comparison: one is born possessing it, and though it may persist staunchly, and of course rates a plus sign in the vital arithmetic, its capacity for development is limited. The exciting truth about friendship is that it is founded on *choice*; its possibilities of growth and change are manifold. It fertilises the soil of one's life, sends up fresh shoots, encourages cross-pollination and the creation of new species.

Here and now I declare my infinite gratitude to my friends.

*Described in *A Pacifist's War*, The Hogarth Press. 1978.

INDEX

All Orion/Phoenix titles are available at your local bookshop or from the following address:

Littlehampton Book Services
Cash Sales Department L
14 Eldon Way, Lineside Industrial Estate
Littlehampton
West Sussex BN17 7HE
telephone 01903 721596, *facsimile* 01903 730914

Payment can either be made by credit card (Visa and Mastercard accepted) or by sending a cheque or postal order made payable to *Littlehampton Book Services.*
DO NOT SEND CASH OR CURRENCY.

Please add the following to cover postage and packing

UK and BFPO:
£1.50 for the first book, and 50p for each additional book to a maximum of £3.50

Overseas and Eire:
£2.50 for the first book plus £1.00 for the second book and 50p for each additional book ordered

----

BLOCK CAPITALS PLEASE

name of cardholder ....   *delivery address*
....   *(if different from cardholder)*
address of cardholder ....
....
....
....
postcode ....   *postcode* ....

☐ I enclose my remittance for £............................

☐ please debit my Mastercard/Visa (delete as appropriate)

card number ☐☐☐☐☐☐☐☐☐☐☐☐☐☐☐☐☐☐

expiry date ☐☐☐☐

signature ....

prices and availability are subject to change without notice

Frances Partridge was born in Bedford Square, Bloomsbury, in 1900, one of six children of an architect. She was educated at Newnham College, Cambridge, where she read English and Moral Sciences. In 1933 she married Ralph Partridge, who died in 1960. In addition to translating many books from French and Spanish and helping her husband to edit *The Greville Memoirs*, she is the author of six published volumes of diaries, *A Pacifist's War*, *Everything to Lose*, *Hanging On*, *Other People*, *Good Company* and *Life Regained*.